CONTENT TABLE

SL NO	Topic	Description	Page Number
1.	**Introduction to C Programming**	Overview of C programming and its significance.	**2-4**
2.	**Setting Up the C Environment**	Installing and configuring a C compiler and IDE.	**5-7**
3.	**Basic Structure of a C Program**	Understanding the structure of a simple C program.	**7-9**
4.	**Data Types and Variables**	Introduction to basic data types and how to declare variables.	**9-13**
5.	**Operators in C**	Explanation of arithmetic, relational, logical, and other operators.	**13-19**
6.	**Control Flow Statements**	Understanding if, else, switch, while, for, and break statements.	**19-25**
7.	**Functions in C**	Defining and using functions to modularize code.	**26-58**

8.	**Arrays in C**	Working with arrays and understanding their memory model.	**59-84**
9.	**Pointers in C**	Introduction to pointers and their usage.	**85-100**
10.	**Strings in C**	Understanding how strings are represented and manipulated.	**100-139**
11.	**Structures and Unions**	Defining and using structures and unions to group data.	**139-184**
12.	**File Handling in C**	Working with file input/output operations.	**184-195**
13.	**Dynamic Memory Allocation**	Using malloc, calloc, realloc, and free for memory management.	**196-212**
14.	**Linked Lists in C**	Implementing and manipulating singly and doubly linked lists.	**212-246**
15.	**Sorting, Hashing, and Graphs in C**	Introduction to algorithms like sorting, hashing, and graph representations.	**246-333**
16.	**C Preprocessor and Error Handling**	The C Preprocessor is a tool that processes the code before it is passed to the compiler. Error handling and debugging are crucial aspects of software development.	**333-335**
17.	**Conclusion**	Recap of C programming concepts and their real-world applications.	**336-337**

INTRODUCTION TO C PROGRAMMING

C is a high-level, general-purpose programming language that has influenced many other modern programming languages. It was developed in the early 1970s by Dennis Ritchie at AT&T Bell Labs. Known for its efficiency and flexibility, C is widely used for system software, application software, and embedded systems.

Overview of C Programming Language

C is a procedural programming language that emphasizes function-driven execution. It is widely recognized for its straightforward syntax and powerful capabilities, offering developers the ability to manipulate hardware resources efficiently. C is highly portable, which means that programs written in C can run on any machine with minimal or no modification. This flexibility, along with its simplicity, has made C a popular choice for developing operating systems, compilers, and embedded systems.

One of the core strengths of C is that it provides direct access to memory via pointers, making it highly suitable for low-level system programming. While C is more challenging to learn than many modern high-level languages, its ability to provide close control over system resources makes it indispensable for many developers.

History of C

The C programming language has its roots in the development of earlier languages such as B and BCPL. In 1972, Dennis Ritchie, working at AT&T Bell Labs, started developing C as an enhancement to the B language. Initially, C was used for system programming on the UNIX operating system, which was also being developed at the same time.

C became more widely known in the late 1970s and early 1980s when it was adopted for writing applications and operating systems. The success of the UNIX operating system, largely written in C, demonstrated the language's power and efficiency. In 1989, the American National Standards Institute (ANSI) formalized the language, creating the ANSI C standard, which remains the most widely used version of C.

Importance and Applications of C

C holds a significant position in the software development world due to its versatility, efficiency, and influence on modern programming languages. Its key applications include:

1. **System Software Development**: C is the primary language used for creating operating systems (like UNIX and Linux) and system utilities. Its close relationship with hardware makes it ideal for managing system resources like memory and processors.
2. **Embedded Systems**: Because C provides low-level access to memory and hardware, it's widely used in developing software for embedded systems, including microcontrollers and other hardware-based applications.
3. **Compilers and Interpreters**: The language has been a primary choice for writing compilers and interpreters for other programming languages. Its ability to manipulate data at a low level allows developers to write efficient software that can handle complex computations and parsing tasks.
4. **Game Development**: Many game engines, particularly older ones, are written in C. The language's efficiency allows for faster execution of complex graphics and computations.
5. **Scientific Computing**: C is also used in scientific computing for its high performance, especially in numerical computations and simulations.
6. **Database Management Systems**: Many database systems, including MySQL, PostgreSQL, and SQLite,

are written in C due to its speed and ability to handle large amounts of data effectively.

Features of C

C is known for several features that make it stand out among other programming languages:

1. **Efficiency**: C is a compiled language, which means it translates directly to machine code, making it very fast. It allows for fine-grained control over system resources, which is essential in resource-constrained environments.
2. **Portability**: One of the most important aspects of C is its portability. C programs can run on different hardware platforms with minimal modification. This characteristic is one of the reasons C became so popular in the development of operating systems and embedded systems.
3. **Structured Programming**: C supports structured programming, a programming paradigm that divides a program into functions and blocks of code. This structure promotes modularity, readability, and reusability, which is particularly useful in large projects.
4. **Low-level Memory Access**: Through the use of pointers, C allows direct manipulation of memory. This gives developers the ability to control how data is stored and accessed, leading to more efficient programs.
5. **Rich Library Support**: C comes with a rich set of standard libraries that provide pre-built functions for tasks like input/output (I/O), string manipulation, and mathematical operations.
6. **Modularity**: The ability to divide a program into smaller functions or modules is a core feature of C. This modularity makes the code more manageable and easier to debug.
7. **Recursion**: C supports recursion, which allows functions to call themselves. This is useful for solving problems like tree traversal, searching, and

sorting.

Setting Up the C Environment (e.g., GCC, Turbo C)

Before you can write and run C programs, you need to install a C compiler. The compiler converts your C code into machine-readable instructions. Popular C compilers include **GCC** (GNU Compiler Collection) and **Turbo C**.

GCC (GNU Compiler Collection)

GCC is widely used for compiling C programs. It works across multiple platforms, including Linux, macOS, and Windows (through MinGW or Cygwin).

- **For Windows**: You can install GCC via **MinGW** or **MSYS2**.
    1. Download and install **MinGW** from the official website.
    2. During installation, ensure that the mingw32-gcc-g++ package is selected.
    3. After installation, update your system's PATH variable to include the MinGW bin directory.
    4. Open a command prompt and verify the installation by typing:

```
gcc --version
```

- **For Linux**: GCC is pre-installed on many Linux distributions. If it's not, you can install it via the terminal:

```
sudo apt-get install gcc
```

- **For macOS**: You can install GCC using **Homebrew** by typing:

```
brew install gcc
```

Turbo C (Legacy Option)

Turbo C is an older IDE that was widely used in the past,

especially for beginners. It is less common nowadays due to its limitations on modern systems.

- **For Windows**: Turbo C can be downloaded and installed from various third-party sources, but it's recommended to use an emulator like **DOSBox** to run Turbo C on modern systems.

However, Turbo C is not recommended for professional development as it lacks features found in modern compilers like GCC.

SETTING UP AN INTEGRATED DEVELOPMENT ENVIRONMENT (IDE)

An **IDE** simplifies the process of writing, testing, and debugging C programs. Popular IDEs for C programming include **Code::Blocks**, **Dev-C++**, **CLion**, and **Visual Studio**.

Code::Blocks

- **Installation**:
    1. Download Code::Blocks from the official website.
    2. Choose the version with the built-in GCC compiler.
    3. Install Code::Blocks, and upon first launch, it will automatically detect and configure the installed compiler.
    4. You can now start writing your C programs.
- **Features**:
    - Code completion and syntax highlighting.
    - Debugger integration.
    - Customizable environment.
    - Multi-platform support (Windows, macOS, Linux).

Dev-C++

- **Installation**:

1. Download Dev-C++ from the official website.
2. Install the IDE, and it comes with the MinGW GCC compiler included.

- **Features**:
  - Lightweight and simple interface.
  - Works well for beginners.
  - Limited features compared to other IDEs like CLion, but effective for simple projects.

CLion (for Professionals)

- **Installation**:
  1. Download and install CLion from JetBrains' official website.
  2. CLion requires a **CMake** build system and may need additional configuration.
  3. It offers seamless integration with GCC and Clang compilers.
- **Features**:
  - Intelligent code analysis and refactoring tools.
  - Built-in debugger and profiler.
  - Excellent for large projects.

Writing the First C Program (Hello World)

Once you have set up the compiler and IDE, you're ready to write your first C program. The traditional first program is the **Hello World** program, which prints a message to the screen.

Here's the code for a simple Hello World program:

```
#include <stdio.h>

int main() {
    printf("Hello, World!\n");
    return 0;
}
```

Explanation:

- #include <stdio.h>: This line includes the standard input-output header, necessary for using functions like printf.
- int main(): The entry point of every C program. The main function is where execution begins.
- printf("Hello, World!\n");: This function prints the string "Hello, World!" to the screen. \n is used to move the cursor to a new line.
- return 0;: This indicates the successful execution of the program.

Compiling and Running C Programs

Once your program is written, the next step is to **compile** and **run** it.

In Code::Blocks:

1. After writing the program, click the **Build and Run** button or press F9.
2. The IDE will compile the code and execute it. You should see the output Hello, World! in the terminal/console window at the bottom.

Using GCC in the Terminal:

If you are using GCC from the command line:

1. Open a terminal or command prompt.
2. Navigate to the folder where your .c file is saved.
3. Compile the program using:

```
gcc -o hello hello.c
```

This tells GCC to compile hello.c and generate an executable named hello.

4. Run the compiled program:

```
./hello
```

You should see Hello, World! printed on the screen.

BASIC STRUCTURE OF A C PROGRAM

A C program follows a well-defined structure that is essential for the program to be compiled and executed successfully. Below is a breakdown of the key components that make up the structure of a basic C program:

1. Preprocessor Directives

Preprocessor directives are lines of code that are processed before the actual compilation of the C program begins. These directives are usually written at the top of the C program. The most common preprocessor directives include:

- **#include**: This directive is used to include standard or user-defined libraries into the program. It is essential for accessing built-in functions. For example:

```
• #include <stdio.h> // Standard Input/
  Output library
```

- **#define**: This directive is used to define constants or macros. For example:

```
#define PI 3.14 // Defines a constant value for PI
```

2. The main() Function

Every C program must contain a main() function. This function is the entry point of the program. When the program is executed, the code within main() is the first part of the program to be executed. The return type of the main function is typically int (integer), which indicates the status of the program execution (usually returning 0 to indicate successful execution).

Example:

```
int main() {
    // Code inside main
    return 0;
}
```

3. Statements and Expressions

- **Statements**: A statement is an individual instruction that is executed as part of the program. Statements can be of various types, including variable declarations, function calls, loops, and conditional blocks.
    - Example:

```
int a = 10; // Declaration and initialization of a
variable
printf("Hello, World!"); // Function call
```

- **Expressions**: An expression is a combination of variables, constants, operators, and function calls that produce a result. In C, expressions are used within statements to assign values, perform calculations, or compare values.
    - Example:

```
a = a + 5; // Expression that modifies the value
of a
```

4. Comments in C

Comments are used in C to explain the code and make it more understandable for humans. They are ignored by the compiler and are for documentation purposes only. There are two types of comments in C:

- **Single-line comment**: This type of comment begins

with // and continues until the end of the line.

```
// This is a single-line comment
```

- **Multi-line comment**: This type of comment starts with /* and ends with */. It can span multiple lines.

```
/* This is a multi-line comment
   that spans across multiple lines. */
```

5. Example: Simple C Program Structure

Here is an example that demonstrates the basic structure of a C program:

```
#include <stdio.h>  // Include the standard I/O library

// Function prototype
void greet();

int main() {
    // Single line comment: Starting the program
    printf("Hello, World!\n");  // Print a greeting message

    greet();  // Calling a user-defined function

    return 0;  // Return 0 to indicate successful execution
}

// Function definition
void greet() {
    printf("Welcome to C programming!\n");  // Print
another message
}
```

Explanation of the Example:

- The preprocessor directive #include <stdio.h> allows access to the printf() function, which is used to print output to the screen.

- The main() function is the entry point where the program starts execution. It contains statements like printf() to display messages.
- The program also calls a user-defined function greet(), which is declared before main() and defined after it.
- Comments are included throughout the program to explain the code, and the program terminates by returning 0, indicating successful completion.

DATA TYPES AND VARIABLES IN C

In C programming, data types define the type of data a variable can hold, such as integers, floating-point numbers, or characters. Variables are used to store data values, and each variable is associated with a data type. The C language supports both primitive data types and modifiers that extend their range and functionality.

1. Primitive Data Types in C

C provides several built-in primitive data types:

- **int**: Used to store integer values (whole numbers). The size of int depends on the system, but it is commonly 4 bytes on most platforms.

Example:

```
int num = 10; // num is an integer variable storing the
value 10
```

- **float**: Used to store single-precision floating-point numbers (decimals). A float typically occupies 4 bytes in memory.

Example:

```
float price = 99.99f; // price is a float variable storing the
value 99.99
```

- **char**: Used to store a single character. A char typically takes 1 byte of memory and stores characters in ASCII code.

Example:

```
char grade = 'A'; // grade is a char variable storing the
character A
```

- **double**: Used for double-precision floating-point numbers. A double typically occupies 8 bytes in memory and can store larger or more precise decimal values than float.

Example:

```
double pi = 3.1415926535; // pi is a double variable
storing the value of Pi
```

2. Data Type Modifiers in C

Data type modifiers are keywords used to change the size or behavior of a data type. They modify the ranges or precision of the primary data types.

- **signed**: By default, integers are signed, meaning they can store both positive and negative values. You can explicitly declare an integer as signed.

Example:

```
signed int num = -500; // signed int can store negative and
positive integers
```

- **unsigned**: The unsigned modifier allows only positive values (including zero) for integer types. It effectively doubles the upper limit of the range because it no longer reserves bits for the sign.

Example:

```
unsigned int count = 1000; // unsigned int can store only
non-negative integers
```

- **short**: The short modifier reduces the size of an integer. Typically, a short integer is 2 bytes.

Example:

```
short smallNumber = 1500; // smallNumber is a short
integer
```

- **long**: The long modifier increases the size of an integer. A long is typically 4 bytes on a 32-bit system and 8 bytes on a 64-bit system.

Example:

```
long largeNumber = 1000000000L; // largeNumber is a
long integer
```

3. Declaring and Initializing Variables

A variable in C must be declared with a specific data type before it is used in a program. You can initialize the variable at the time of declaration.

- **Declaration**: This tells the compiler the type of the variable and its name.

Example:

```
int age; // Declaring an integer variable named age
```

- **Initialization**: This assigns a value to the variable when it is declared.

Example:

```
int age = 25; // Declaring and initializing age to 25
```

You can also initialize variables later in the program:

```
int age; // Declare the variable
age = 25; // Initialize it with a value
```

4. Constants in C

Constants are values that cannot be modified during the execution of the program. C provides two ways to define constants:

- **Using #define Preprocessor Directive**: This is a preprocessor macro that defines a constant. Once defined, the constant cannot be changed throughout the program.

Example:

```
#define PI 3.14159 // Define a constant PI
```

Usage:

```
float area = PI * radius * radius; // Using the constant PI in calculations
```

- **Using const Keyword**: This defines a constant variable whose value cannot be changed after initialization.

Example:

```
const int MAX_USERS = 100; // Define a constant variable MAX_USERS
```

Usage:

```
if (currentUsers > MAX_USERS) {
    printf("Maximum users reached.");
}
```

While both #define and const can be used to define constants, the primary difference is that #define is replaced by the preprocessor before compilation, while const is checked at compile-time like regular variables.

Summary

In C, understanding data types and variables is fundamental to programming. Primitive data types such as int, float, char, and double help define the nature of the data, while data type modifiers allow for more control over the storage size and range of these types. Additionally, variables must be declared and initialized before use, and constants help ensure that certain values cannot be altered during the program's execution.

Example Code:

```
#include <stdio.h>

#define PI 3.14159 // Preprocessor constant
const int MAX_USERS = 100; // const constant

int main() {
    int num = 10; // Integer
    float price = 99.99f; // Float
    char grade = 'A'; // Char
    double pi = 3.1415926535; // Double

    unsigned int count = 1000; // Unsigned int
    short smallNumber = 1500; // Short
    long largeNumber = 1000000000L; // Long

    printf("Integer: %d\n", num);
    printf("Float: %.2f\n", price);
    printf("Char: %c\n", grade);
    printf("Double: %.10f\n", pi);
    printf("Unsigned Int: %u\n", count);
    printf("Short: %d\n", smallNumber);
    printf("Long: %ld\n", largeNumber);

    printf("Constant PI: %.5f\n", PI);
    printf("Constant MAX_USERS: %d\n", MAX_USERS);

    return 0;
}
```

OUTPUT
Integer: 10
Float: 99.99
Char: A

```
Double: 3.1415926535
Unsigned Int: 1000
Short: 1500
Long: 1000000000
Constant PI: 3.14159
Constant MAX_USERS: 100
```

OPERATORS IN C

1. Arithmetic Operators

These operators are used to perform basic arithmetic calculations.

Operator	Description	Example	Result
+	Addition	a + b	Sum of a and b
-	Subtraction	a - b	Difference of a and b
*	Multiplication	a * b	Product of a and b
/	Division	a / b	Quotient of a divided by b
%	Modulus	a % b	Remainder when a is divided by b

Example:

```
int a = 10, b = 3;
printf("Sum: %d\n", a + b);      // Output: 13
printf("Difference: %d\n", a - b); // Output: 7
printf("Product: %d\n", a * b);  // Output: 30
printf("Quotient: %d\n", a / b); // Output: 3
printf("Remainder: %d\n", a % b); // Output: 1
```

2. Relational Operators

Relational operators compare two values and return either true (1) or false (0).

Operator	Description	Example	Result
==	Equal to	a == b	Checks if a is

			equal to b
!=	Not equal to	a != b	Checks if a is not equal to b
>	Greater than	a > b	Checks if a is greater than b
<	Less than	a < b	Checks if a is less than b
>=	Greater than or equal to	a >= b	Checks if a is greater than or equal to b
<=	Less than or equal to	a <= b	Checks if a is less than or equal to b

Example:

```
int a = 5, b = 10;
printf("a > b: %d\n", a > b);    // Output: 0 (false)
printf("a < b: %d\n", a < b);    // Output: 1 (true)
printf("a == b: %d\n", a == b);  // Output: 0 (false)
```

3. Logical Operators

Logical operators are used to combine multiple conditions.

Operator	Description	Example	Result
&&	Logical AND	(a > b) && (b > c)	true if both conditions are true
`		`	Logical OR
!	Logical NOT	!(a > b)	true if the condition is false

Example:

```
int a = 5, b = 10, c = 15;
printf("(a < b) && (b < c): %d\n", (a < b) && (b < c)); //
Output: 1 (true)
printf("(a > b) || (b < c): %d\n", (a > b) || (b < c)); // Output: 1
(true)
```

4. Bitwise Operators

Bitwise operators perform operations on individual bits.

Operator	Description	Example	Result
&	Bitwise AND	a & b	Performs AND on each bit
`	`	Bitwise OR	`a
^	Bitwise XOR	a ^ b	Performs XOR on each bit
~	Bitwise NOT	~a	Inverts each bit
<<	Left Shift	a << 1	Shifts bits of a to the left
>>	Right Shift	a >> 1	Shifts bits of a to the right

Example:

```
int a = 5; // Binary: 0101
int b = 3; // Binary: 0011
printf("a & b: %d\n", a & b);    // Output: 1 (0001)
printf("a | b: %d\n", a | b);    // Output: 7 (0111)
printf("a ^ b: %d\n", a ^ b);    // Output: 6 (0110)
printf("~a: %d\n", ~a);          // Output: -6 (bitwise NOT of 5)
printf("a << 1: %d\n", a << 1);  // Output: 10 (left shift)
printf("a >> 1: %d\n", a >> 1);  // Output: 2 (right shift)
```

5. Assignment and Increment Operators

Assignment operators assign values to variables. Increment and decrement operators change values by one.

Operator	Description	Example	Equivalent
=	Assignment	a = b	a = b
+=	Add and assign	a += b	a = a + b
-=	Subtract and assign	a -= b	a = a - b
*=	Multiply and assign	a *= b	a = a * b
/=	Divide and assign	a /= b	a = a / b

++	Increment	a++	a = a + 1
--	Decrement	a--	a = a - 1

Example:

```
int a = 10, b = 5;
a += b; // a = a + b (Output: 15)
a -= b; // a = a - b (Output: 10)
a *= b; // a = a * b (Output: 50)
a /= b; // a = a / b (Output: 10)
```

6. Conditional (Ternary) Operator

The ternary operator is a shorthand for if-else statements.

Operator	Description	Example	Result
?:	Ternary operator	(a > b) ? x : y	Returns x if a > b, otherwise y

Example:

```
int a = 10, b = 20;
int max = (a > b) ? a : b; // max will be 20
```

7. Operator Precedence and Associativity

Operator precedence determines the order in which operations are evaluated in an expression. Associativity defines the direction (left-to-right or right-to-left) in which operators of the same precedence level are processed.

Common Precedence Rules:

- **Highest precedence:** (), [], ->, .
- **Arithmetic operators:** *, /, % have higher precedence than +, -
- **Relational operators**: <, >, <=, >= come before ==, !=
- **Assignment operators**: =, +=, -=, etc., have lower precedence.

Example:

```
int a = 10, b = 5, c = 2;
```

```
int result = a - b * c; // Multiplication (*) is done before
subtraction (-)
```

Here's a C program that demonstrates all the primary operators (arithmetic, relational, logical, bitwise, assignment, increment/decrement, and conditional) in one program:

```
#include <stdio.h>

int main() {
    // Variables for demonstration
    int a = 10, b = 5, c;
    int result;

    // Arithmetic Operators
    printf("Arithmetic Operators:\n");
    printf("a + b = %d\n", a + b);
    printf("a - b = %d\n", a - b);
    printf("a * b = %d\n", a * b);
    printf("a / b = %d\n", a / b);
    printf("a %% b = %d\n\n", a % b);  // Use %% to print %

    // Relational Operators
    printf("Relational Operators:\n");
    printf("a == b: %d\n", a == b);
    printf("a != b: %d\n", a != b);
    printf("a > b: %d\n", a > b);
    printf("a < b: %d\n", a < b);
    printf("a >= b: %d\n", a >= b);
    printf("a <= b: %d\n\n", a <= b);

    // Logical Operators
    printf("Logical Operators:\n");
    printf("(a > b) && (a > 0): %d\n", (a > b) && (a > 0));
    printf("(a > b) || (b > a): %d\n", (a > b) || (b > a));
    printf("!(a == b): %d\n\n", !(a == b));

    // Bitwise Operators
```

```
printf("Bitwise Operators:\n");
printf("a & b = %d\n", a & b);
printf("a | b = %d\n", a | b);
printf("a ^ b = %d\n", a ^ b);
printf("~a = %d\n", ~a);
printf("a << 1 = %d\n", a << 1);
printf("a >> 1 = %d\n\n", a >> 1);

// Assignment Operators
printf("Assignment Operators:\n");
c = a;  // Simple assignment
printf("c = a: %d\n", c);
c += b; // Add and assign
printf("c += b: %d\n", c);
c -= b; // Subtract and assign
printf("c -= b: %d\n", c);
c *= b; // Multiply and assign
printf("c *= b: %d\n", c);
c /= b; // Divide and assign
printf("c /= b: %d\n", c);
c %= b; // Modulus and assign
printf("c %%= b: %d\n\n", c);

// Increment and Decrement Operators
printf("Increment and Decrement Operators:\n");
printf("a++ = %d\n", a++); // Post-increment
printf("++a = %d\n", ++a); // Pre-increment
printf("b-- = %d\n", b--); // Post-decrement
printf("--b = %d\n\n", --b); // Pre-decrement

// Conditional (Ternary) Operator
printf("Conditional (Ternary) Operator:\n");
result = (a > b) ? a : b;
printf("Result of (a > b) ? a : b = %d\n\n", result);

// Operator Precedence Example
printf("Operator Precedence:\n");
```

```
    result = a + b * c; // Multiplication (*) has higher
precedence than addition (+)
    printf("Result of a + b * c = %d\n", result);

    return 0;
}
```

OUTPUT

```
Arithmetic Operators:
a + b = 15
a - b = 5
a * b = 50
a / b = 2
a % b = 0

Relational Operators:
a == b: 0
a != b: 1
a > b: 1
a < b: 0
a >= b: 1
a <= b: 0

Logical Operators:
(a > b) && (a > 0): 1
(a > b) || (b > a): 1
!(a == b): 1

Bitwise Operators:
a & b = 0
a | b = 15
a ^ b = 15
~a = -11
a << 1 = 20
a >> 1 = 5

Assignment Operators:
```

```
c = a: 10
c += b: 15
c -= b: 10
c *= b: 50
c /= b: 10
c %= b: 0

Increment and Decrement Operators:
a++ = 10
++a = 12
b-- = 5
--b = 3

Conditional (Ternary) Operator:
Result of (a > b) ? a : b = 12

Operator Precedence:
Result of a + b * c = 12
```

Explanation

This program demonstrates:

- **Arithmetic Operations:** Addition, subtraction, multiplication, division, and modulus.
- **Relational Operations:** Comparison between values.
- **Logical Operations:** Combining conditions with &&, ||, and !.
- **Bitwise Operations:** Performing bitwise AND, OR, XOR, complement, and shifts.
- **Assignment Operations:** Assigning values using =, +=, -=, *=, /=, and %=.
- **Increment/Decrement Operations:** Both post- and pre- increment and decrement.
- **Conditional (Ternary) Operation:** Shorthand for if-else.

- **Operator Precedence:** Showing how C evaluates expressions with different operator precedences.

CONTROL FLOW STATEMENTS

Control flow statements in C guide the sequence in which statements are executed within a program. They allow decision-making, repeating tasks, and altering the normal flow based on conditions. Here's a breakdown of the primary control flow statements in C:

---

1. If, if-else, and nested if-else

- **if statement**: Used to execute a block of code if a specified condition is true.

```
int num = 10;
if (num > 5) {
    printf("Number is greater than 5");
}
```

- **if-else statement**: Provides an alternative path if the if condition is false.

```
int num = 3;
if (num > 5) {
    printf("Number is greater than 5");
} else {
    printf("Number is less than or equal to 5");
}
```

- **Nested if-else**: Multiple if-else conditions nested to check multiple conditions sequentially.

```
int num = 0;
if (num > 0) {
    printf("Positive number");
} else if (num < 0) {
    printf("Negative number");
} else {
    printf("Zero");
}
```

---

2. Switch Case

The switch statement evaluates a variable and executes a corresponding case block based on the variable's value. It's generally used as an alternative to multiple if-else statements when comparing a single variable against several potential values.

```
char grade = 'B';
switch (grade) {
    case 'A':
        printf("Excellent");
        break;
    case 'B':
        printf("Good");
        break;
    case 'C':
        printf("Average");
        break;
    default:
        printf("Invalid grade");
}
```

In the switch block:

- break statements prevent the flow from falling through to the next case.
- default executes if none of the specified cases match.

Feature	if Statement	if-else Statement	nested if-else Statement	switch-case Statement
Purpose	Executes code if the condition is true	Executes one of two blocks based on condition	Executes multiple levels of conditions	Executes one case among multiple based on a variable's value
Syntax	if (condition) { // code }	if (condition) { // code } else { // code }	if (cond1) { // code } else if (cond2) { // code } else { // code }	switch (variable) { case value1: // code; break; ... }
Use Case	Single condition checking	Choice between two possible actions	Multiple levels of conditions to check	Multiple possible fixed values for a single variable
Ease of Readability	Simple and concise	Slightly more complex	Can be hard to read if nested deeply	Clear for cases with many discrete values
Execution Flow	Only checks the if condition	Checks if condition, then else if false	Checks each level until condition matches	Jumps to matching case block directly
Performance	Efficient for a single condition	Efficient for two branches	Becomes complex and slower with deep nesting	Fast with large numbers of discrete conditions due to direct jump to case
Condition Types	Boolean expression	Boolean expression	Boolean expressions at multiple levels	Constant expressions (integers, enums, characters)
Alternative	No alternative action if condition is false	Executes else if if condition is false	Executes next if condition if previous is false	Executes default block if no case matches
Limitations	No option if the condition is false	Limited to two outcomes	Becomes difficult to manage if nested deeply	Limited to discrete values (no ranges or expressions)

Here's a C code example that demonstrates the use of if, if-else, nested if-else, and switch statements:

```
#include <stdio.h>

int main() {
    int number;

    // Input from user
    printf("Enter a number: ");
    scanf("%d", &number);

    // Example of if statement
    if (number > 0) {
        printf("The number is positive.\n");
    }

    // Example of if-else statement
    if (number % 2 == 0) {
```

```
        printf("The number is even.\n");
    } else {
        printf("The number is odd.\n");
    }

    // Example of nested if-else statement
    if (number > 0) {
        printf("The number is positive.\n");

        if (number > 100) {
            printf("The number is greater than 100.\n");
        } else {
            printf("The number is 100 or less.\n");
        }

    } else if (number < 0) {
        printf("The number is negative.\n");
    } else {
        printf("The number is zero.\n");
    }

    // Example of switch case
    int choice;
    printf("Enter 1 for Option A, 2 for Option B, or 3
for Option C: ");
    scanf("%d", &choice);

    switch (choice) {
        case 1:
            printf("You chose Option A.\n");
            break;
        case 2:
            printf("You chose Option B.\n");
            break;
        case 3:
```

```
            printf("You chose Option C.\n");
            break;
        default:
            printf("Invalid option. Please choose 1, 2, or
3.\n");
            break;
    }

    return 0;
}
```

```
OUTPUT
Enter a number: 5
The number is positive.
The number is odd.
The number is positive.
The number is 100 or less.
Enter 1 for Option A, 2 for Option B, or 3 for Option
C: 1
You chose Option A.
```

Explanation

1. **If statement**: Checks if number is positive. If true, it prints a message.
2. **If-else statement**: Checks if number is even or odd.
3. **Nested if-else statement**: Determines if number is positive, negative, or zero. Additionally, it checks if a positive number is greater than 100.
4. **Switch case**: Uses choice to print the selected option or displays an error for invalid input.

3. Loops

Loops allow the execution of a block of code repeatedly based on a condition.

- **for loop**: Ideal when the number of iterations is known. It consists of initialization, condition checking, and increment/decrement steps in a single line.

```
for (int i = 1; i <= 5; i++) {
    printf("%d ", i); // Output: 1 2 3 4 5
}
```

- **while loop**: Continues to execute a block of code as long as a specified condition remains true.

```
int i = 1;
while (i <= 5) {
    printf("%d ", i);
    i++;
}
```

- **do-while loop**: Executes the code block at least once, as the condition is checked after the block runs.

```
int i = 1;
do {
    printf("%d ", i);
    i++;
} while (i <= 5);
```

Here's a table that compares the differences between for, while, and do-while loops in programming:

Feature	for Loop	while Loop	do-while Loop
Initialization	Typically initialized in the loop header	Typically initialized before the loop	Typically initialized before the loop
Condition Check	Condition is checked before each iteration	Condition is checked before each iteration	Condition is checked after each iteration
Execution Guarantee	Executes only if the condition is true	Executes only if the condition is true	Executes at least once, regardless of

			the condition
Syntax Structure	for (initialization; condition; increment)	while (condition)	do { ... } while (condition);
Use Case	Commonly used when the number of iterations is known	Commonly used when the number of iterations is unknown	Commonly used when the loop must run at least once
Loop Control	Initialization, condition, and increment can all be managed in the header	Only the condition is specified in the header	Only the condition is specified after the loop body
Readability	Clear and concise when iterating over a fixed range	Simpler for indefinite loops without fixed iteration count	Useful for cases where post-check looping is needed

---

4. Break and Continue Statements

- **break statement**: Used to exit a loop or switch case immediately, even if the loop condition hasn't been met.

```
for (int i = 1; i <= 10; i++) {
    if (i == 5) {
        break;
    }
    printf("%d ", i);  // Output: 1 2 3 4
}
```

- **continue statement**: Skips the rest of the loop iteration for a particular case and proceeds to the next iteration.

```
for (int i = 1; i <= 5; i++) {
    if (i == 3) {
        continue;
    }
    printf("%d ", i);  // Output: 1 2 4 5
}
```

---

5. Goto Statement

The goto statement provides an unconditional jump to

another part of the program. It should be used with caution as it can make code difficult to follow and debug.

```
int num = 1;
if (num == 1) {
    goto skip;
}
printf("This will be skipped if num is 1");
skip:
printf("Code jumped here");
```

Here, goto jumps directly to the labeled skip: line, bypassing the printf statement.

By carefully using these control flow statements, you can guide how your C programs handle different situations and conditions. Each type has its ideal usage scenarios, from looping through arrays with for loops to handling multiple conditions efficiently with switch statements.

FUNCTIONS IN C

1. Function Declaration and Definition

Functions are modular blocks of reusable code in C. They can take inputs (parameters) and produce outputs (return values). Every function has a **declaration**, a **definition**, and a way to be **called** in a program.

1.1. Function Declaration (Prototype)

A **function declaration** informs the compiler about a function's name, its return type, and its parameters. This is typically written at the beginning of the program, before the main() function, or in a header file.

Syntax:

```
return_type function_name(parameter_list);
```

- **return_type**: The type of value the function returns (e.g., int, float, void).
- **function_name**: The name of the function.
- **parameter_list**: The type and names of input variables (optional).

Example:

```
int add(int a, int b);
```

This declares a function add that takes two integers as parameters and returns an integer.

1.2. Function Definition

The **function definition** provides the actual implementation of the declared function. It specifies the logic and statements the function executes.

Syntax:

```
return_type function_name(parameter_list) {
    // Function body
    return value;  // Only if return_type is not void
}
```

Example:

```
int add(int a, int b) {
    return a + b;
}
```

- The add function computes the sum of a and b and returns the result.
- If the function does not return a value (void), the return statement is omitted.

---

2. Calling and Using Functions

To use a function, it must be **called** from another function (usually main() or another user-defined function).

Syntax for Function Call:

```
function_name(argument_list);
```

- **argument_list**: Actual values or variables that match the function's parameter list in type and order.

Example:

```
#include <stdio.h>
// Function declaration
int add(int a, int b);
int main() {
    int result = add(10, 20);  // Function call
```

```
    printf("The sum is: %d\n", result);
    return 0;
}
// Function definition
int add(int a, int b) {
    return a + b;
}
```

OUTPUT
The sum is: 30

Here's a detailed, step-by-step explanation of the code:

---

1. Preprocessor Directive

```
#include <stdio.h>
```

- **Purpose**: This includes the standard input-output library in your program.
- **Why It's Needed**: The printf function used later in the code is defined in this library.

---

2. Function Declaration

```
int add(int a, int b);
```

- **Purpose**: Declares the existence of the add function before it is used in main.
- **Details**:
    - The function add will take two integers (int) as arguments.
    - It will return an integer (int) as the result.

---

3. Main Function

```
int main() {
    int result = add(10, 20);  // Function call
    printf("The sum is: %d\n", result);
    return 0;
}
```

The main function is the entry point of the program.

a. Variable Declaration and Function Call

```
int result = add(10, 20);
```

- **Purpose**: Calls the add function with two arguments: 10 and 20.
- **What Happens**:
    1. The program jumps to the definition of the add function (see below).
    2. It calculates the sum of the two arguments.
    3. The result (30) is returned to this point and stored in the variable result.

b. Printing the Result

```
printf("The sum is: %d\n", result);
```

- **Purpose**: Outputs the sum to the console.
- **Details**:
    - %d is a format specifier used to display an integer.
    - result (value: 30) is substituted for %d, producing the output:

```
The sum is: 30
```

c. Return Statement

```
return 0;
```

- **Purpose**: Indicates that the program executed successfully.
- **Details**: 0 is typically returned to signal successful program execution.

---

4. Function Definition

```
int add(int a, int b) {
    return a + b;
}
```

- **Purpose**: Defines how the add function operates.
- **Details**:
  1. Takes two integer inputs: a and b.
  2. Adds the values of a and b (10 + 20 in this case).
  3. Returns the result (30) to the calling function.

Execution Flow

1. The program starts with the main function.
2. The add function is called with arguments 10 and 20.
3. The add function calculates the sum and returns 30.
4. The main function stores the returned value in result and prints it.
5. The program ends successfully.

Key Points:

1. **Order of Execution:** Functions execute only when called.
2. **Pass-by-Value:** In C, arguments are passed by value by default, meaning the function gets a copy of the variables, not the originals.

3. **Recursive Calls:** Functions can call themselves (recursion) if necessary.

---

3. Understanding void and Returning Values

3.1. Functions with void

The void keyword specifies that a function does not return any value.

Example:

```
void greet() {
    printf("Hello, World!\n");
}
```

Usage:

```
int main() {
    greet(); // No value is returned
    return 0;
}
```

3.2. Functions Returning Values

Functions can return values using the return keyword. The returned value must match the function's declared return type.

Example:

```
float divide(float x, float y) {
    return x / y;
}
```

Usage:

```
int main() {
    float result = divide(10.0, 2.0); // Result will be 5.0
    printf("The result is: %.2f\n", result);
    return 0;
}
```

3.3. Returning Multiple Values

Since C does not support direct multiple return values, you can use:

1. **Pointers:** Modify the caller's variables.
2. **Structures:** Return a struct containing multiple values.

Example with Pointers:

```
void swap(int *a, int *b) {
    int temp = *a;
    *a = *b;
    *b = temp;
}

int main() {
    int x = 10, y = 20;
    swap(&x, &y);
    printf("x: %d, y: %d\n", x, y); // x: 20, y: 10
    return 0;
}
```

Here's a step-by-step explanation of the code:

---

1. Include the header file

```
#include<stdio.h>
```

- The #include<stdio.h> directive imports the standard input/output library, which is required to use the printf function for output.

---

2. Define the swap function

```
void swap(int *a, int *b) {
    int temp = *a;
    *a = *b;
```

```
    *b = temp;
}
```

- **Purpose:** The swap function exchanges the values of two integers using pointers.
- **Parameters:**
    - int *a - A pointer to the first integer.
    - int *b - A pointer to the second integer.
- **Steps in the swap function:**
    1. int temp = *a;
        - The value pointed to by a (the value of the first integer) is stored in a temporary variable temp.
    2. *a = *b;
        - The value pointed to by b (the second integer) is assigned to the location pointed to by a.
    3. *b = temp;
        - The temporary value (temp, which is the original value of the first integer) is assigned to the location pointed to by b.
- This results in the values of the two integers being swapped.

---

3. Define the main function

```
int main() {
    int x = 10, y = 20;
    swap(&x, &y);
    printf("x: %d, y: %d\n", x, y); // x: 20, y: 10
    return 0;
}
```

- **Purpose:** The main function is the starting point of

the program.

Step-by-step Execution in main:

1. **Declare and Initialize Variables:**

```
int x = 10, y = 20;
```

   - x is assigned the value 10.
   - y is assigned the value 20.

2. **Call the swap function:**

```
swap(&x, &y);
```

   - The swap function is called with the addresses of x and y as arguments.
   - &x passes the address of x to the parameter a.
   - &y passes the address of y to the parameter b.
   - Inside the swap function:
     - The values of x and y are swapped:
       - The value of x becomes 20.
       - The value of y becomes 10.

3. **Print the swapped values:**

```
printf("x: %d, y: %d\n", x, y); // x: 20, y: 10
```

   - The printf function outputs the updated values of x and y to the console.
   - Output: x: 20, y: 10.

4. **Exit the program:**

```
return 0;
```

   - The program terminates successfully.

---

4. Common Practices

1. **Declare Functions Before Use:**
    - Always declare or define functions before calling them.
2. **Keep Functions Modular:**
    - Keep each function focused on a single task for readability and maintainability.
3. **Use Header Files:**
    - Place declarations in .h files for code reusability and separation.

---

5. Example Program with All Concepts

```
#include <stdio.h>

// Function declaration
void greet();
int add(int a, int b);
void swap(int *x, int *y);

int main() {
    greet();

    int sum = add(5, 7);
    printf("Sum: %d\n", sum);

    int num1 = 10, num2 = 20;
    printf("Before swap: num1 = %d, num2 = %d\n", num1,
num2);
    swap(&num1, &num2);
    printf("After swap: num1 = %d, num2 = %d\n", num1,
num2);

    return 0;
}

// Function definitions
void greet() {
    printf("Welcome to Function Concepts in C!\n");
```

```
}

int add(int a, int b) {
    return a + b;
}

void swap(int *x, int *y) {
    int temp = *x;
    *x = *y;
    *y = temp;
}
```

OUTPUT
Welcome to Function Concepts in C!
Sum: 12
Before swap: num1 = 10, num2 = 20
After swap: num1 = 20, num2 = 10

Code Explanation:

1. Preprocessor Directive

```
#include <stdio.h>
```

- The #include <stdio.h> statement includes the standard input/output library, enabling the use of functions like printf and scanf.

---

2. Function Declarations

```
void greet();
int add(int a, int b);
void swap(int *x, int *y);
```

- These are function declarations (or prototypes) that inform the compiler about the functions used later in the program:
    - greet() - A void function (does not return a value) that prints a greeting message.

- add(int a, int b) - A function that takes two integers as arguments and returns their sum.
- swap(int *x, int *y) - A void function that swaps the values of two integers using pointers.

---

3. Main Function

```
int main() {
    greet();

    int sum = add(5, 7);
    printf("Sum: %d\n", sum);

    int num1 = 10, num2 = 20;
    printf("Before swap: num1 = %d, num2 = %d\n", num1,
num2);
    swap(&num1, &num2);
    printf("After swap: num1 = %d, num2 = %d\n", num1,
num2);

    return 0;
}
```

- **Line 1 (greet();)**: Calls the greet function to display a welcome message.
- **Line 2-3 (int sum = add(5, 7); ...)**:
  - Calls the add function with arguments 5 and 7.
  - The function returns their sum, which is stored in the variable sum.
  - The value of sum is then printed.
- **Line 4-8**: Demonstrates the swapping functionality:
  - num1 and num2 are initialized to 10 and 20, respectively.
  - Their values before the swap are printed.
  - swap(&num1, &num2) is called, passing the

addresses of num1 and num2.

- The swapped values of num1 and num2 are printed after the function call.

- **Line 9 (return 0;)**: Indicates the successful execution of the program.

---

4. Function Definitions

greet Function

```
void greet() {
    printf("Welcome to Function Concepts in C!\n");
}
```

- Prints a welcome message: *"Welcome to Function Concepts in C!"*

add Function

```
int add(int a, int b) {
    return a + b;
}
```

- Takes two integer arguments (a and b).
- Returns their sum using the expression a + b.

swap Function

```
void swap(int *x, int *y) {
    int temp = *x;
    *x = *y;
    *y = temp;
}
```

- Swaps the values of two integers using pointers:
  - *x and *y represent the values stored at the memory locations pointed to by x and y.
  - A temporary variable temp is used to hold the value of *x during the swap.

Parameter Passing in C

C supports two primary methods for passing parameters to functions:

1. **Pass by Value**: A copy of the actual parameter is passed to the function. Changes made to the parameter inside the function do not affect the original variable.
2. **Pass by Reference**: Instead of passing the actual value, the memory address of the parameter is passed. This allows the function to modify the original variable.

Let's dive deeper into each concept with examples.

---

1. Pass by Value

In this method, the function creates a copy of the passed argument. Any changes made to the parameter inside the function do not affect the original value.

Example: Pass by Value

```
#include <stdio.h>

void modifyValue(int x) {
    x = x * 2; // Modifies the copy of the variable
    printf("Inside function: x = %d\n", x);
}

int main() {
    int num = 10;
    printf("Before function call: num = %d\n", num);
    modifyValue(num);
    printf("After function call: num = %d\n", num);
    return 0;
}
```

Output:

```
Before function call: num = 10
```

```
Inside function: x = 20
After function call: num = 10
```

Code Explanation:

- modifyValue receives a copy of num.
- Changing x inside modifyValue does not affect the original num.

Step-by-Step Explanation:

1. **Include Header File**:

```
#include <stdio.h>
```

   - This line includes the standard input/output library (stdio.h) to enable the use of functions like printf.

2. **Define Function modifyValue**:

```
void modifyValue(int x) {
    x = x * 2; // Modifies the copy of the variable
    printf("Inside function: x = %d\n", x);
}
```

   - A function modifyValue is defined that accepts an integer argument x.
   - Inside the function, the value of x is doubled (x = x * 2) and printed using printf.
   - Since x is a parameter, it is a copy of the value passed to the function, and modifications do not affect the original variable in main.

3. **Define the Main Function**:

```
int main() {
    int num = 10;
    printf("Before function call: num = %d\n", num);
```

```
    modifyValue(num);
    printf("After function call: num = %d\n", num);
    return 0;
}
```

- **Variable Declaration**:
    - An integer variable num is declared and initialized to 10.
- **First printf**:
    - The value of num (which is 10) is printed before calling the function.
- **Function Call**:
    - modifyValue(num) is called, passing the value of num (10) as an argument.
- **Second printf**:
    - After the function call, the value of num is printed again to demonstrate that it remains unchanged.
- **return 0;**:
    - Indicates that the program ends successfully.

4. **Execution Flow**:
    - The program starts in the main function.
    - The value of num is printed as 10.
    - The modifyValue function is called with num (value 10) as an argument:
        - Inside the function, the copy of num (parameter x) is doubled (10 → 20).
        - The doubled value (20) is printed within the function.
        - The function ends, and control returns to main.
    - Back in main, the value of num is printed again as 10, showing it was not affected by changes inside the function.

Key Concepts Demonstrated:

- **Pass-by-Value**:
    - In C, arguments to functions are passed by value by default. This means the function works on a copy of the argument, and the original variable remains unaffected.
- **Scope of Variables**:
    - x in modifyValue is local to the function and independent of num in main.
- **Flow of Execution**:
    - The sequence of function calls and how control is passed between main and modifyValue is illustrated.

---

2. Pass by Reference (Using Pointers)

In this method, the function receives the address of the parameter, allowing it to directly modify the original value.

Example: Pass by Reference

```
#include <stdio.h>

void modifyValue(int *x) {
    *x = *x * 2;  // Modifies the original variable through the
pointer
    printf("Inside function: *x = %d\n", *x);
}

int main() {
    int num = 10;
    printf("Before function call: num = %d\n", num);
    modifyValue(&num);
    printf("After function call: num = %d\n", num);
    return 0;
}
```

Output

```
Before function call: num = 10
Inside function: *x = 20
After function call: num = 20
```

Code Explanation:

- The modifyValue function receives the address of num (&num).
- Using the pointer *x, the function directly modifies the value stored at that address.

1. Preprocessor Directive

```
#include <stdio.h>
```

- This includes the standard input/output library to enable the use of functions like printf for printing to the console.

---

2. Function Declaration: modifyValue

```
void modifyValue(int *x) {
    *x = *x * 2; // Modifies the value at the memory
location pointed to by x
    printf("Inside function: *x = %d\n", *x);
}
```

- **Parameters:**
  - int *x is a pointer to an integer. This means the function receives the address of an integer, allowing it to modify the original variable.
- **Body:**
  - *x = *x * 2;
    - *x dereferences the pointer, accessing the value stored at the memory location it points to.
    - The value is doubled and reassigned

to the same memory location, thus modifying the original variable.

- printf outputs the modified value.

---

3. Main Function

```
int main() {
    int num = 10;
    printf("Before function call: num = %d\n", num);
    modifyValue(&num);
    printf("After function call: num = %d\n", num);
    return 0;
}
```

Step-by-Step Execution:

1. **Variable Declaration and Initialization:**

```
int num = 10;
```

   - num is declared as an integer and initialized to 10.

2. **Print Initial Value of num:**

```
printf("Before function call: num = %d\n", num);
```

   - Outputs: Before function call: num = 10

3. **Function Call:**

```
modifyValue(&num);
```

   - &num passes the address of num to the function. This allows modifyValue to directly modify the variable num in memory.

4. **Inside the Function:**
   - *x = *x * 2;
     - The value at the memory location pointed to by x (which is num) is

doubled. num becomes 20.

- printf("Inside function: *x = %d\n", *x);
    - Outputs: Inside function: *x = 20

5. **Back in main:**

```
printf("After function call: num = %d\n", num);
```

- Since the function modified num directly in memory, the updated value (20) is retained.
- Outputs: After function call: num = 20

---

3. Using Pointers in Functions

Pointers are essential for efficient memory management and for implementing pass-by-reference.

Example: Swapping Two Numbers Using Pointers

```
#include <stdio.h>

void swap(int *a, int *b) {
    int temp = *a;  // Dereference and store value
    *a = *b;
    *b = temp;
}

int main() {
    int x = 5, y = 10;
    printf("Before swap: x = %d, y = %d\n", x, y);
    swap(&x, &y);  // Pass the address of x and y
    printf("After swap: x = %d, y = %d\n", x, y);
    return 0;
}
```

Output:

```
Before swap: x = 5, y = 10
After swap: x = 10, y = 5
```

Code Explanation:

- The swap function uses pointers to exchange the values of x and y by modifying them at their memory addresses.

Here's a step-by-step explanation of the code:

---

1. Header File

```
#include <stdio.h>
```

- The #include <stdio.h> directive imports the standard input/output library, which allows the program to use functions like printf.

---

2. Swap Function Definition

```
void swap(int *a, int *b) {
    int temp = *a;  // Dereference and store value
    *a = *b;
    *b = temp;
}
```

Function Purpose:

- This function swaps the values of two integers using pointers.

Steps:

1. **Input Parameters:**
    - int *a and int *b are pointers to integers, meaning they store the addresses of integers passed to this function.
2. **Temporary Variable:**
    - int temp = *a; creates a temporary variable temp to store the value at the memory location pointed to by a.
3. **Swapping Values:**

- *a = *b; assigns the value at the memory location pointed to by b to the location pointed to by a.
- *b = temp; assigns the value stored in temp (initially from *a) to the location pointed to by b.

---

3. Main Function

```
int main() {
    int x = 5, y = 10;
    printf("Before swap: x = %d, y = %d\n", x, y);
    swap(&x, &y); // Pass the address of x and y
    printf("After swap: x = %d, y = %d\n", x, y);
    return 0;
}
```

Steps:

1. **Variable Declaration:**
   - Two integer variables x and y are declared and initialized with values 5 and 10, respectively.
2. **Print Initial Values:**
   - printf("Before swap: x = %d, y = %d\n", x, y); displays the initial values of x and y as Before swap: x = 5, y = 10.
3. **Call Swap Function:**
   - swap(&x, &y); passes the **addresses** of x and y to the swap function.
     - The & operator is used to get the address of the variables x and y.
4. **Print Final Values:**
   - After the function call, printf("After swap: x = %d, y = %d\n", x, y); displays the updated values of x and y, now swapped as After swap: x = 10, y = 5.
5. **Return Statement:**
   - return 0; indicates the program terminated

successfully.

---

4. Scope and Lifetime of Variables

Scope:

- **Local Variables**: Declared inside a function; accessible only within that function.
- **Global Variables**: Declared outside all functions; accessible throughout the program.

Lifetime:

- **Automatic (Local)**: Created when the function is called; destroyed when the function exits.
- **Static**: Retains its value between function calls.
- **Dynamic**: Managed manually using malloc and free.

Example: Scope and Lifetime

```
#include <stdio.h>

void testScope() {
    static int staticVar = 0;  // Retains value between calls
    int localVar = 0;          // Reinitialized on every call
    staticVar++;
    localVar++;
    printf("Static Variable: %d, Local Variable: %d\n",
staticVar, localVar);
}

int main() {
    for (int i = 0; i < 3; i++) {
        testScope();
    }
    return 0;
}
```

Output:

```
Static Variable: 1, Local Variable: 1
Static Variable: 2, Local Variable: 1
Static Variable: 3, Local Variable: 1
```

Code Explanation:

- staticVar retains its value across function calls.
- localVar is reinitialized to 0 each time testScope is called.

Here's a step-by-step explanation of the provided code:

Code Structure

1. **Include Header File**:

```
#include <stdio.h>
```

   - The stdio.h header file is included for input-output operations like printf().

2. **Function Definition (testScope)**:

```
void testScope() {
    static int staticVar = 0;  // Retains value between calls
    int localVar = 0;          // Reinitialized on every call
    staticVar++;
    localVar++;
    printf("Static Variable: %d, Local Variable: %d\n", staticVar, localVar);
}
```

   - A function named testScope() is defined, demonstrating the behavior of **static** and **local variables**:
     - **static int staticVar = 0;**:
       - This variable retains its value between function calls.

        - It is initialized only once (on the first function call) and retains its updated value for subsequent calls.
    - **int localVar = 0;**:
        - This is a standard local variable.
        - It is reinitialized to 0 every time the function is called.
  - The function increments both variables and prints their values.

3. **Main Function**:

```
int main() {
    for (int i = 0; i < 3; i++) {
        testScope();
    }
    return 0;
}
```

  - In the main() function:
    - A for loop runs 3 times.
    - During each iteration, the testScope() function is called.

Execution Flow

1st Iteration (i = 0):

- **Static Variable** (staticVar):
    - Initialized to 0 (only once).
    - Incremented: staticVar = 0 + 1 = 1.
- **Local Variable** (localVar):
    - Initialized to 0 (reinitialized for each call).
    - Incremented: localVar = 0 + 1 = 1.
- Output:

```
Static Variable: 1, Local Variable: 1
```

2nd Iteration (i = 1):

- **Static Variable** (staticVar):
  - Retains its previous value: 1.
  - Incremented: staticVar = 1 + 1 = 2.
- **Local Variable** (localVar):
  - Reinitialized to 0.
  - Incremented: localVar = 0 + 1 = 1.
- Output:

```
Static Variable: 2, Local Variable: 1
```

3rd Iteration (i = 2):

- **Static Variable** (staticVar):
  - Retains its previous value: 2.
  - Incremented: staticVar = 2 + 1 = 3.
- **Local Variable** (localVar):
  - Reinitialized to 0.
  - Incremented: localVar = 0 + 1 = 1.
- Output:

```
Static Variable: 3, Local Variable: 1
```

Key Concepts Demonstrated

1. **Static Variable**:
   - Preserves its value across function calls.
   - Initialized only once.
2. **Local Variable**:
   - Reinitialized every time the function is called.
3. **Function Behavior**:
   - Understanding the scope and lifecycle of variables.
4. **for Loop Execution**:

- Demonstrates calling the function multiple times to observe variable behavior.

This code helps distinguish between static and non-static local variables in C.

Key Takeaways

- **Pass by Value** is safe and does not modify the original variable, but it can be less efficient for large data.
- **Pass by Reference** is efficient and allows modification of the original data, but it requires careful handling to avoid unintended side effects.
- Understanding **scope** and **lifetime** is crucial for effective memory management in C.

Recursion in C

Recursion is a technique in programming where a function calls itself to solve smaller instances of a problem until it reaches a base case. This approach is particularly useful for problems that can be divided into similar sub-problems, such as factorial computation, Fibonacci series, and tree traversals.

Basics of Recursion

Key Components of Recursion:

1. **Base Case:**
   - This is the condition where the recursion terminates. Without a base case, recursion will lead to infinite function calls and eventually a stack overflow.
2. **Recursive Case:**
   - The function calls itself with modified arguments that move towards the base case.

Structure of a Recursive Function

```
void recursiveFunction() {
    if (baseCaseCondition) {
```

```
        // Base case logic
    } else {
        // Recursive call with adjusted parameters
        recursiveFunction();
    }
}
```

Examples of Recursive Functions

1. Factorial of a Number

The factorial of nnn (denoted n!n!n!) is the product of all positive integers less than or equal to nnn. It can be defined as:

n!=n×(n−1)!

Where 0!=1

Code Example:

```
#include <stdio.h>

int factorial(int n) {
    if (n == 0 || n == 1) { // Base case
        return 1;
    } else { // Recursive case
        return n * factorial(n - 1);
    }
}

int main() {
    int num = 5;
    printf("Factorial of %d is %d\n", num, factorial(num));
    return 0;
}
```

Output:

```
Factorial of 5 is 120
```

Code Explanation:

This program calculates the factorial of a given number using a **recursive function** in C. Let's break it down step by step:

---

1. Include the Required Library

```
#include <stdio.h>
```

- The #include <stdio.h> directive includes the Standard Input/Output library, which is needed for functions like printf() to display output on the screen.

---

2. Define the Recursive Function

```
int factorial(int n) {
    if (n == 0 || n == 1) { // Base case
        return 1;
    } else { // Recursive case
        return n * factorial(n - 1);
    }
}
```

- **Function Name:** factorial
- **Parameter:** n (the number whose factorial is to be calculated)
- **Return Type:** int (the result of the factorial calculation)

Logic:

1. **Base Case:**
    - If n is 0 or 1, the function directly returns 1 because the factorial of 0 and 1 is defined as 1. This stops further recursion.
2. **Recursive Case:**
    - If n is greater than 1, the function calls itself with a smaller argument (n - 1).
    - Example: For n = 5, it will compute 5 *

factorial(4), 4 * factorial(3), and so on.

---

3. The main() Function

```
int main() {
    int num = 5;
    printf("Factorial of %d is %d\n", num, factorial(num));
    return 0;
}
```

1. **Variable Declaration:**
   - int num = 5; declares a variable num and assigns it the value 5.
2. **Function Call and Output:**
   - factorial(num) computes the factorial of 5 using the recursive function.
   - printf() displays the result in the format Factorial of 5 is 120.
3. **Return Statement:**
   - return 0; indicates the successful completion of the program.

---

4. Execution Flow

For num = 5, the recursive calls work as follows:

1. factorial(5) = 5 * factorial(4)
2. factorial(4) = 4 * factorial(3)
3. factorial(3) = 3 * factorial(2)
4. factorial(2) = 2 * factorial(1)
5. factorial(1) = 1 (Base case reached)

The results are then multiplied in reverse order:

1. factorial(2) = 2 * 1 = 2
2. factorial(3) = 3 * 2 = 6
3. factorial(4) = 4 * 6 = 24
4. factorial(5) = 5 * 24 = 120

2. Fibonacci Series

The Fibonacci sequence is a series where each term is the sum of the two preceding ones:

F(n)=F(n−1)+F(n−2)

Where:

F(0)=0andF(1)=1

Code Example:

```
#include <stdio.h>

int fibonacci(int n) {
    if (n == 0) return 0; // Base case
    if (n == 1) return 1; // Base case
    return fibonacci(n - 1) + fibonacci(n - 2); // Recursive
case
}

int main() {
    int n = 10;
    printf("Fibonacci series up to %d terms:\n", n);
    for (int i = 0; i < n; i++) {
        printf("%d ", fibonacci(i));
    }
    return 0;
}
```

Output:

```
Fibonacci series up to 10 terms:
0 1 1 2 3 5 8 13 21 34
```

Code Explanation:

Here's a step-by-step explanation of the code:

---

1. Header file inclusion

```
#include <stdio.h>
```

- The #include <stdio.h> directive includes the standard input/output library, which is required to use functions like printf().

---

2. Fibonacci function definition

```
int fibonacci(int n) {
    if (n == 0) return 0; // Base case
    if (n == 1) return 1; // Base case
    return fibonacci(n - 1) + fibonacci(n - 2); // Recursive
case
}
```

This function calculates the Fibonacci number at position n using recursion:

1. **Base cases**:
    - If n is 0, return 0.
    - If n is 1, return 1. These are the starting points of the Fibonacci sequence.
2. **Recursive case**:
    - For any n greater than 1, the function calls itself twice:
        - Once with n - 1 (to compute the previous term).
        - Once with n - 2 (to compute the term before the previous term).
    - The two results are added together to give the Fibonacci number at position n.

---

3. Main function definition

```
int main() {
    int n = 10;
```

- The program starts execution from main().

- The variable n is set to 10, indicating that the first 10 terms of the Fibonacci sequence will be generated.

---

4. Print a header

```
printf("Fibonacci series up to %d terms:\n", n);
```

- A message is displayed to inform the user about the number of terms in the Fibonacci sequence that will be printed.

---

5. Generate and print Fibonacci terms

```
for (int i = 0; i < n; i++) {
        printf("%d ", fibonacci(i));
    }
```

A for loop iterates from 0 to n - 1 (i.e., 10 terms).

- For each iteration:
    - The fibonacci(i) function is called to compute the i-th term in the Fibonacci sequence.
    - The computed term is printed to the console using printf("%d ").

---

6. Program end

```
    return 0;
}
```

The program terminates by returning 0, indicating successful execution.

Execution Flow

1. The program calculates Fibonacci numbers recursively.
2. For n = 10, the sequence generated is:

```
0, 1, 1, 2, 3, 5, 8, 13, 21, 34
```

Each term is computed by summing the two preceding terms.

Pros and Cons of Recursion

Advantages:

1. **Elegant and Readable Code:**
    - Recursive functions are often easier to read and write for problems with a natural recursive structure (e.g., factorial, Fibonacci, tree traversals).
2. **Reduces Code Complexity:**
    - Avoids the need for explicit loops and additional data structures in some cases.
3. **Better for Divide-and-Conquer Algorithms:**
    - Algorithms like quicksort, mergesort, and backtracking are easier to implement using recursion.

Disadvantages:

1. **Higher Memory Usage:**
    - Each recursive call consumes stack space. Deep recursion may lead to stack overflow.
2. **Performance Overhead:**
    - Recursive functions have additional overhead due to repeated function calls and return operations.
3. **Harder to Debug:**
    - Tracing recursive calls can be challenging, especially in deeply nested calls.

Comparison of Recursion vs. Iteration

Feature	Recursion	Iteration
Code Simplicity	Simpler for problems like Fibonacci or factorial	May require more lines of code
Memory Usage	Uses more	Uses less memory

	memory (call stack)	
Performance	Can be slower due to overhead	Generally faster
Termination	Requires a base case	Relies on condition checks

Optimizing Recursion: Tail Recursion

A **tail-recursive function** is one where the recursive call is the last operation in the function. Tail recursion can be optimized by the compiler to use less stack space.

Example: Factorial Using Tail Recursion

```
#include <stdio.h>

int factorialTailRecursive(int n, int accumulator) {
    if (n == 0 || n == 1) return accumulator; // Base case
    return factorialTailRecursive(n - 1, n * accumulator); //
Tail recursion
}

int main() {
    int num = 5;
    printf("Factorial of %d is %d\n", num,
factorialTailRecursive(num, 1));
    return 0;
}
```

OUTPUT
Factorial of 5 is 120

Code Explanation

Here's a detailed explanation of the code, step by step:

Code Breakdown

Function: factorialTailRecursive

```
int factorialTailRecursive(int n, int accumulator) {
```

```
    if (n == 0 || n == 1) return accumulator; // Base case
    return factorialTailRecursive(n - 1, n * accumulator); //
Tail recursion
}
```

This is a **tail-recursive** implementation of calculating the factorial of a number. Let's break it down:

1. **Function Parameters:**
   - n: The number whose factorial is to be calculated.
   - accumulator: A helper variable used to store the intermediate result as the recursion progresses. It starts with 1 in the initial call.
2. **Base Case:**

```
if (n == 0 || n == 1) return accumulator;
```

If n is 0 or 1, the factorial is simply 1. The function returns the value of accumulator at this point, as it holds the calculated factorial.

3. **Recursive Case:**

```
return factorialTailRecursive(n - 1, n * accumulator);
```

- This updates accumulator by multiplying it with n, effectively accumulating the product for the factorial.
- The function then calls itself with:
  - n - 1: Decrementing the current number.
  - n * accumulator: The updated result.

This ensures that the factorial computation continues until n reaches the base case.

Function: main

```
int main() {
    int num = 5;
```

```
    printf("Factorial of %d is %d\n", num,
factorialTailRecursive(num, 1));
    return 0;
}
```

1. **Declare a variable num:**

```
int num = 5;
```

Here, the variable num is assigned the value 5, representing the number whose factorial will be calculated.

2. **Call factorialTailRecursive:**

```
printf("Factorial of %d is %d\n", num,
factorialTailRecursive(num, 1));
```

   - The function factorialTailRecursive is called with:
     - n = 5 (the number to calculate the factorial for).
     - accumulator = 1 (the initial value for the accumulator).

3. **Print the result:**
   - The returned value (factorial of 5) is printed in the format:

```
Factorial of 5 is 120
```

4. **End of Program:**

```
return 0;
```

The main function ends successfully.

Step-by-Step Execution:

1. **Initial Call:**

```
factorialTailRecursive(5, 1);
```

- n = 5, accumulator = 1.

2. **First Recursive Call:**

```
factorialTailRecursive(4, 5 * 1);
```

- n = 4, accumulator = 5.

3. **Second Recursive Call:**

```
factorialTailRecursive(3, 4 * 5);
```

- n = 3, accumulator = 20.

4. **Third Recursive Call:**

```
factorialTailRecursive(2, 3 * 20);
```

- n = 2, accumulator = 60.

5. **Fourth Recursive Call:**

```
factorialTailRecursive(1, 2 * 60);
```

- n = 1, accumulator = 120.

6. **Base Case Reached:**

```
return accumulator; // Returns 120
```

- The recursion stops, and the final result 120 is returned up the call stack.

7. **Output:**

```
Factorial of 5 is 120
```

Key Concepts:

1. **Tail Recursion:**
   - The function's recursive call is the last operation performed in the function.

  - This allows the compiler to optimize the recursion (tail call optimization).
2. **Accumulator:**
    - Helps carry the intermediate results to avoid creating new stack frames for each step.

This makes the tail-recursive approach more memory-efficient compared to standard recursion.

Recursion is a powerful tool when used appropriately. However, for large input sizes, iterative solutions or optimized recursion (like memoization or dynamic programming) may be more efficient.

ARRAYS IN C

1. Declaring and Initializing Arrays

In C, an array is a collection of elements of the same data type stored in contiguous memory locations. The syntax for declaring an array is as follows:

```
data_type array_name[array_size];
```

- **data_type**: Specifies the type of data the array will hold (e.g., int, float).
- **array_name**: The name of the array.
- **array_size**: The number of elements the array will hold.

Example: Declaring and Initializing a Single-Dimensional Array

```
#include <stdio.h>

int main() {
    int arr[5]; // Declaration of an integer array of size 5

    // Initializing the array
    arr[0] = 10;
    arr[1] = 20;
    arr[2] = 30;
    arr[3] = 40;
    arr[4] = 50;

    // Printing the array elements
    for(int i = 0; i < 5; i++) {
        printf("Element at index %d: %d\n", i, arr[i]);
```

```
    }

    return 0;
}
```

Output:

```
Element at index 0: 10
Element at index 1: 20
Element at index 2: 30
Element at index 3: 40
Element at index 4: 50
```

Code Explanation:

Here's a step-by-step explanation of the code:

---

1. Include Header File

```
#include <stdio.h>
```

- This line includes the standard input-output header file (stdio.h), which contains functions like printf for displaying output on the console.

---

2. Main Function Declaration

```
int main() {
```

- The main function is the entry point of the program. Execution begins here.

---

3. Declare an Integer Array

```
int arr[5];
```

- An integer array named arr of size 5 is declared. It can store 5 integer values.

---

4. Initialize the Array

```
arr[0] = 10;
arr[1] = 20;
arr[2] = 30;
arr[3] = 40;
arr[4] = 50;
```

- Each index of the array (arr[0] to arr[4]) is explicitly assigned a value.
  - arr[0] = 10 → First element of the array is set to 10.
  - arr[1] = 20 → Second element is set to 20.
  - This pattern continues until arr[4] = 50.

---

5. Loop Through the Array

```
for(int i = 0; i < 5; i++) {
```

- A for loop is used to iterate over the array. The loop runs 5 times:
  - i starts from 0.
  - The condition i < 5 ensures the loop runs only for valid indices (0 to 4).
  - i++ increments the value of i after each iteration.

---

6. Print Each Array Element

```
printf("Element at index %d: %d\n", i, arr[i]);
```

- During each iteration, this statement prints:
  - The current index (i).
  - The value of the array element at that index (arr[i]).

Example output for each iteration:

- Element at index 0: 10

- Element at index 1: 20
- Element at index 2: 30
- Element at index 3: 40
- Element at index 4: 50

---

7. End of Program

```
return 0;
```

- The program returns 0, signaling successful execution.

Overall Workflow

1. An integer array of size 5 is declared and initialized.
2. A for loop iterates through each element of the array.
3. The elements are printed with their corresponding indices.
4. Program execution ends.

You can also initialize an array at the time of declaration:

int arr[] = {10, 20, 30, 40, 50};

Length of an Array

In C, an array is a collection of elements of the same data type stored in contiguous memory locations. Determining the length of an array in C depends on whether the array is a **statically declared array** or a **dynamically allocated array**.

---

1. Statically Declared Arrays

These are arrays whose size is determined at compile time.

Example:

```
#include <stdio.h>

int main() {
    int arr[] = {1, 2, 3, 4, 5};
```

```
    // Calculate the length of the array
    int length = sizeof(arr) / sizeof(arr[0]);

    printf("Length of the array: %d\n", length);
    return 0;
}
```

Code Explanation:

1. **sizeof(arr)**: Gives the total memory occupied by the array in bytes.
   - For example, if arr has 5 integers and each integer is 4 bytes (on most platforms), sizeof(arr) will return 20 bytes.
2. **sizeof(arr[0])**: Gives the memory occupied by the first element of the array, which is the size of one integer (4 bytes in this case).
3. **sizeof(arr) / sizeof(arr[0])**: Divides the total size of the array by the size of one element, yielding the number of elements in the array.

Here's a step-by-step explanation of the code:

```
#include <stdio.h>
```

1. **Include Standard Input/Output Library**:
   - This line includes the stdio.h header file, which is necessary for using standard input and output functions like printf.

```
int main() {
```

2. **Define the main Function**:
   - This is the entry point of the program. Execution starts from this function.

```
int arr[] = {1, 2, 3, 4, 5};
```

3. **Declare and Initialize an Array**:
   - arr[] is an integer array that contains 5 elements: {1, 2, 3, 4, 5}.
   - The size of the array is implicitly determined to be 5 based on the number of elements provided.

```
int length = sizeof(arr) / sizeof(arr[0]);
```

Calculate the Length of the Array:

- **sizeof(arr)**:
  - This calculates the total size of the array in bytes. For example, if each int is 4 bytes, the total size of arr is 5 * 4 = 20 bytes.
- **sizeof(arr[0])**:
  - This calculates the size of the first element of the array (or any single element). If arr[0] is an integer, its size is 4 bytes.
- **sizeof(arr) / sizeof(arr[0])**:
  - Dividing the total size of the array by the size of one element gives the total number of elements in the array.
  - In this case: 204=5\frac{20}{4} = 5420 =5.

The result is stored in the variable length.

```
printf("Length of the array: %d\n", length);
```

5. **Print the Length of the Array**:
   - printf outputs the calculated length value to the console.
   - %d is the format specifier for integers.

```
return 0;
```

6. **End of Program**:
   - The main function returns 0, indicating that the program executed successfully.

Program Output

When the program runs, it calculates the number of elements in the array arr and prints the following to the console:

```
Length of the array: 5
```

Key Points:

- This method only works for arrays declared within the same function.
- Once an array is passed to a function, it decays into a pointer, and sizeof will no longer provide the total size.

---

2. Dynamically Allocated Arrays

When arrays are created using dynamic memory allocation (e.g., malloc), their size must be managed explicitly.

Example:

```
#include <stdio.h>
#include <stdlib.h>

int main() {
    int n = 5; // Size of the array
    int *arr = (int *)malloc(n * sizeof(int)); // Dynamically
allocated array

    // Fill the array
    for (int i = 0; i < n; i++) {
        arr[i] = i + 1;
    }

    // Length of the array is stored explicitly
```

```
    printf("Length of the array: %d\n", n);

    // Free the allocated memory
    free(arr);
    return 0;
}
```

Code Explanation:

- Dynamically allocated arrays don't retain their size in memory.
- You must manually keep track of the size when allocating or using the array.

The provided C program demonstrates the use of **dynamic memory allocation** to create and manage an array. Let's break it down step by step:

---

1. Header Files

```
#include <stdio.h>
#include <stdlib.h>
```

- **#include <stdio.h>**: Includes the standard input/output library, which provides functions like printf for displaying output.
- **#include <stdlib.h>**: Includes the standard library, which provides functions like malloc for memory allocation and free for deallocating memory.

---

2. Declare and Initialize Variables

```
int n = 5; // Size of the array
```

- n is an integer variable representing the size of the array (5 elements).

---

3. Dynamic Memory Allocation

```
int *arr = (int *)malloc(n * sizeof(int));
```

- malloc(n * sizeof(int)):
    - Allocates memory for n integers dynamically.
    - sizeof(int) determines the size (in bytes) of an integer on the system.
    - For example, if sizeof(int) is 4 bytes, malloc(5 * 4) allocates 20 bytes.
- (int *): Casts the returned pointer (of type void *) to an int *, making it a pointer to integers.
- arr: Stores the address of the allocated memory block.

---

4. Fill the Array with Values

```
for (int i = 0; i < n; i++) {
    arr[i] = i + 1;
}
```

- A for loop iterates from 0 to n-1 (5 iterations for i = 0, 1, 2, 3, 4).
- Inside the loop:
    - arr[i]: Accesses the ith element of the dynamically allocated array.
    - i + 1: Assigns consecutive integers (1, 2, 3, 4, 5) to the array.

---

5. Print the Length of the Array

```
printf("Length of the array: %d\n", n);
```

- Prints the value of n, which represents the length of the array (5).

---

6. Free Allocated Memory

free(arr);

- free(arr): Deallocates the memory allocated to arr to prevent memory leaks. After this, the memory block is no longer valid for use.

---

7. Return from main

return 0;

- Indicates successful termination of the program.

Program Output

Length of the array: 5

Key Points

1. **Dynamic Memory Allocation**:
   - Memory for the array is allocated during runtime using malloc.
   - Size is not fixed during compilation.
2. **Manual Memory Management**:
   - Memory allocated by malloc must be explicitly freed using free.
3. **Pointer Arithmetic**:
   - Array indexing (arr[i]) works with pointers, allowing access to specific memory locations.

This program is a basic example of dynamically managing memory in C.

---

3. Arrays Passed to Functions

When an array is passed to a function, it decays into a pointer, losing size information.

Example:

```
#include <stdio.h>

void printArraySize(int arr[], int size) {
```

```
    printf("Size of the array: %d\n", size);
}

int main() {
    int arr[] = {1, 2, 3, 4, 5};
    int size = sizeof(arr) / sizeof(arr[0]); // Calculate size
before passing
    printArraySize(arr, size);
    return 0;
}
```

Key Points:

- Pass the array size explicitly to functions.
- Inside the function, sizeof(arr) will give the size of the pointer (not the array).

Summary

1. For **static arrays**, use sizeof(arr) / sizeof(arr[0]).
2. For **dynamic arrays**, keep track of the size during allocation.
3. Always pass the size explicitly when working with arrays in functions.

2. Single-Dimensional Arrays

A **single-dimensional array** is essentially a list of elements of the same type. Each element can be accessed using an index.

Example: Accessing and Manipulating Elements in a 1D Array

```
#include <stdio.h>

int main() {
    int arr[5] = {1, 2, 3, 4, 5}; // Single-dimensional array

    // Accessing elements
```

```
    printf("First element: %d\n", arr[0]);
    printf("Last element: %d\n", arr[4]);

    // Changing an element
    arr[2] = 100;
    printf("Updated third element: %d\n", arr[2]);

    return 0;
}
```

Output:

```
First element: 1
Last element: 5
Updated third element: 100
```

3. Multi-Dimensional Arrays (2D, 3D)

3.1 Two-Dimensional Arrays (2D)

A **two-dimensional array** is like a table with rows and columns. It is defined by two indices: one for the row and one for the column.

```
#include <stdio.h>

int main() {
    int arr[2][3] = { {1, 2, 3}, {4, 5, 6} }; // 2D array with 2
rows and 3 columns

    // Accessing elements
    printf("Element at [0][0]: %d\n", arr[0][0]);
    printf("Element at [1][2]: %d\n", arr[1][2]);

    return 0;
}
```

Output:

```
Element at [0][0]: 1
Element at [1][2]: 6
```

Code Explanation:

This C code demonstrates how to declare and access elements of a 2D array. Let's break it down step by step:

1. Array Declaration:

```
int arr[2][3] = { {1, 2, 3}, {4, 5, 6} };
```

- int arr[2][3]: This declares a 2D array with 2 rows and 3 columns, meaning the array will have a total of 6 elements.
  - 2 represents the number of rows.
  - 3 represents the number of columns.
- The array is initialized with two sets of values:
  - The first row ({1, 2, 3}) contains the elements 1, 2, and 3.
  - The second row ({4, 5, 6}) contains the elements 4, 5, and 6.

The resulting array looks like this:

```
arr[0][0] = 1, arr[0][1] = 2, arr[0][2] = 3
arr[1][0] = 4, arr[1][1] = 5, arr[1][2] = 6
```

2. Accessing Elements:

```
printf("Element at [0][0]: %d\n", arr[0][0]);
printf("Element at [1][2]: %d\n", arr[1][2]);
```

These two lines use the printf function to print specific elements of the array.

- arr[0][0]: This accesses the element at the first row (index 0) and the first column (index 0). In the array, this element is 1. The first printf will output:

```
Element at [0][0]: 1
```

- arr[1][2]: This accesses the element at the second row

(index 1) and the third column (index 2). In the array, this element is 6. The second printf will output:

```
Element at [1][2]: 6
```

3. Return Statement:

```
return 0;
```

- This line signifies the end of the main function and returns 0 to the operating system, indicating that the program has completed successfully.

Final Output:

When you run the program, the output will be:

```
Element at [0][0]: 1
Element at [1][2]: 6
```

3.2 Three-Dimensional Arrays (3D)

A **three-dimensional array** is like a cube where you access elements using three indices.

```
#include <stdio.h>

int main() {
    int arr[2][2][3] = {
        { {1, 2, 3}, {4, 5, 6} },
        { {7, 8, 9}, {10, 11, 12} }
    }; // 3D array with 2 blocks, 2 rows, and 3 columns

    // Accessing elements
    printf("Element at [0][1][2]: %d\n", arr[0][1][2]);
    printf("Element at [1][0][0]: %d\n", arr[1][0][0]);

    return 0;
}
```

Output:

```
Element at [0][1][2]: 6
Element at [1][0][0]: 7
```

Code Explanation:

Here is a step-by-step explanation of the provided C code:

1. Header File

```
#include <stdio.h>
```

This includes the standard input/output library (stdio.h), which allows you to use functions like printf() to print output to the console.

2. Main Function

```
int main() {
```

The program execution starts from the main function. The return type int indicates that the function will return an integer value (typically 0 to indicate successful execution).

3. 3D Array Declaration

```
int arr[2][2][3] = {
    { {1, 2, 3}, {4, 5, 6} },
    { {7, 8, 9}, {10, 11, 12} }
};
```

- arr is a 3-dimensional array with the size [2][2][3]. This means:
    - **2 blocks** (first dimension),
    - Each block has **2 rows** (second dimension),
    - Each row contains **3 columns** (third dimension).
- The array is initialized with values:
    - The first block:
        - First row: {1, 2, 3}
        - Second row: {4, 5, 6}

- The second block:
    - First row: {7, 8, 9}
    - Second row: {10, 11, 12}

The array can be visualized as follows:

```
Block 0:
  Row 0: 1  2  3
  Row 1: 4  5  6

Block 1:
  Row 0: 7  8  9
  Row 1: 10 11 12
```

4. Accessing Elements

```
printf("Element at [0][1][2]: %d\n", arr[0][1][2]);
printf("Element at [1][0][0]: %d\n", arr[1][0][0]);
```

- **First printf statement:**
    - arr[0][1][2] accesses the element at:
        - **Block 0, Row 1, Column 2.**
        - From the array, this corresponds to 6, so the output will be:

```
Element at [0][1][2]: 6
```

- **Second printf statement:**
    - arr[1][0][0] accesses the element at:
        - **Block 1, Row 0, Column 0.**
        - From the array, this corresponds to 7, so the output will be:

```
Element at [1][0][0]: 7
```

5. Return Statement

```
return 0;
```

The main function returns 0, which indicates successful

execution of the program.

Summary of Output

- The program will output:

```
Element at [0][1][2]: 6
Element at [1][0][0]: 7
```

This demonstrates how to initialize and access elements in a 3D array in C.

4. Array Manipulation

You can perform various operations on arrays, such as finding the maximum or minimum, summing the elements, or searching for a specific value.

Example: Finding the Maximum Element in a 1D Array

```
#include <stdio.h>

int main() {
    int arr[5] = {2, 8, 3, 6, 1};
    int max = arr[0];

    for(int i = 1; i < 5; i++) {
        if(arr[i] > max) {
            max = arr[i];
        }
    }

    printf("Maximum element: %d\n", max);
    return 0;
}
```

Output:

```
Maximum element: 8
```

Code Explanation:

This C code is designed to find the maximum element in an

array. Let's go through the code step by step:

Step 1: Initialize the array and max variable

```
int arr[5] = {2, 8, 3, 6, 1};
int max = arr[0];
```

- **int arr[5] = {2, 8, 3, 6, 1};**: This declares and initializes an array arr of size 5 with the values {2, 8, 3, 6, 1}.
- **int max = arr[0];**: This initializes the variable max with the value of the first element of the array, which is arr[0] = 2.

Step 2: Loop through the array

```
for(int i = 1; i < 5; i++) {
```

- The for loop starts with i = 1 (the second element of the array) and runs until i = 4 (the fifth element of the array). It compares each element with the current maximum value (max).

Step 3: Compare each element with max

```
if(arr[i] > max) {
    max = arr[i];
}
```

- **if(arr[i] > max)**: In each iteration, the program checks if the current element arr[i] is greater than the current maximum (max).
    - If this condition is true, it updates max to be the current element (max = arr[i]).

Step 4: Print the maximum value

```
printf("Maximum element: %d\n", max);
```

- After the loop completes, the program prints the maximum value found in the array using printf(). It outputs the value of max, which holds the largest element found after the loop.

Step 5: Return from main()

```
return 0;
```

- The program ends and returns 0, indicating successful execution.

Example Walkthrough

For the array {2, 8, 3, 6, 1}, here's how the loop works:

- Initially, max = 2.
- First iteration (i = 1, element arr[1] = 8): Since 8 > 2, max becomes 8.
- Second iteration (i = 2, element arr[2] = 3): 3 is not greater than 8, so max remains 8.
- Third iteration (i = 3, element arr[3] = 6): 6 is not greater than 8, so max remains 8.
- Fourth iteration (i = 4, element arr[4] = 1): 1 is not greater than 8, so max remains 8.

Finally, max holds the value 8, which is printed as the maximum element.

5. Passing Arrays to Functions

Arrays can be passed to functions in C by passing the array's reference (pointer to the first element).

Example: Passing a Single-Dimensional Array to a Function

```
#include <stdio.h>

void printArray(int arr[], int size) {
    for(int i = 0; i < size; i++) {
        printf("%d ", arr[i]);
    }
    printf("\n");
```

```
}

int main() {
    int arr[5] = {1, 2, 3, 4, 5};
    printArray(arr, 5);
    return 0;
}
```

Output:

```
1 2 3 4 5
```

Code Explanation:

Here's a step-by-step explanation of the code:

```
#include <stdio.h>
```

- This line includes the standard input-output library (stdio.h), which provides the functionality to use input/output functions like printf.

```
void printArray(int arr[], int size) {
```

- This is the declaration of the function printArray. It takes two parameters:
    - arr[]: an integer array (we will be passing the array to this function).
    - size: an integer representing the size of the array (how many elements are in the array).

```
for(int i = 0; i < size; i++) {
```

- This is a for loop that starts with i = 0. The loop will run as long as i is less than size. On each iteration, i will increment by 1.
- It allows us to loop through all the elements of the array one by one.

```
printf("%d ", arr[i]);
```

This line prints the element of the array at the index i using printf. %d is a format specifier that prints the integer value of the element.

- The space after %d ensures that the numbers are printed with a space between them.

```
    }
    printf("\n");
```

- After the loop finishes, printf("\n"); prints a newline to move the cursor to the next line. This separates the printed array from any subsequent output.

}

- This closes the body of the printArray function.

```
int main() {
```

- The main function is the entry point of the program. The program starts executing here.

```
    int arr[5] = {1, 2, 3, 4, 5};
```

- This line defines an integer array arr of size 5 and initializes it with the values {1, 2, 3, 4, 5}.

```
printArray(arr, 5);
```

- This calls the printArray function, passing the array arr and the size of the array (5) as arguments.
- The function will print the elements of the array.

```
    return 0;
}
```

- This indicates that the program has executed successfully. The value 0 is returned to the operating system to signal successful completion.
- This closes the main function.

Example: Passing a 2D Array to a Function

```
#include <stdio.h>

void print2DArray(int arr[2][3]) {
    for(int i = 0; i < 2; i++) {
        for(int j = 0; j < 3; j++) {
            printf("%d ", arr[i][j]);
        }
        printf("\n");
    }
}

int main() {
    int arr[2][3] = { {1, 2, 3}, {4, 5, 6} };
    print2DArray(arr);
    return 0;
}
```

Output:

```
1 2 3
4 5 6
```

Code Explanation

Here's a step-by-step explanation of the code:

1. Header File Inclusion:

```
#include <stdio.h>
```

- This line includes the standard input/output library

(stdio.h) to allow the program to use functions like printf, which is used to print output to the console.

2. Function Definition:

```
void print2DArray(int arr[2][3]) {
```

- This line defines a function print2DArray that takes a 2D array of integers (arr) with 2 rows and 3 columns as an argument. The dimensions of the array are specified in the parameter arr[2][3]. The function has no return value, as indicated by void.

3. Nested Loops to Print the Array:

```
    for(int i = 0; i < 2; i++) {
        for(int j = 0; j < 3; j++) {
            printf("%d ", arr[i][j]);
        }
        printf("\n");
    }
```

- These are two nested for loops. The outer loop (with the variable i) iterates over the rows of the 2D array, and the inner loop (with the variable j) iterates over the columns of each row.

Outer loop:
The loop runs from i = 0 to i = 1, so it will execute twice (once for each row).

Inner loop:
The inner loop runs from j = 0 to j = 2, so it will execute three times (once for each column in a row).

Printing elements:
Inside the inner loop, the printf function prints each element of the 2D array (arr[i][j]). After printing all the elements in a row, the printf("\n"); in the outer loop prints a newline character to move to the next line, starting the next row of the array on a new line.

4. Main Function:

```
int main() {
```

- The main function is the entry point of the program. The program starts executing here.

5. Array Declaration:

```
int arr[2][3] = { {1, 2, 3}, {4, 5, 6} };
```

This line declares and initializes a 2D array arr with 2 rows and 3 columns. The array is explicitly initialized with values:

  - Row 1: {1, 2, 3}
  - Row 2: {4, 5, 6}

6. Function Call:

```
print2DArray(arr);
```

- This line calls the print2DArray function and passes the arr array to it. This will trigger the function to print the elements of the 2D array.

7. Return Statement:

```
    return 0;
}
```

The return 0; statement ends the main function and returns a value of 0 to the operating system, indicating that the program has executed successfully.

What happens when you run this code?

- The program defines a 2D array arr with values:

```
1 2 3
4 5 6
```

- The function print2DArray is called, which uses

nested loops to print each element of the 2D array, row by row.

- The output will be:

```
1 2 3
4 5 6
```

6. Common Array Problems

Here are a few examples of common array problems you might encounter:

6.1 Reversing an Array

```
#include <stdio.h>

void reverseArray(int arr[], int size) {
    int start = 0, end = size - 1;
    while(start < end) {
        int temp = arr[start];
        arr[start] = arr[end];
        arr[end] = temp;
        start++;
        end--;
    }
}

int main() {
    int arr[5] = {1, 2, 3, 4, 5};
    reverseArray(arr, 5);

    for(int i = 0; i < 5; i++) {
        printf("%d ", arr[i]);
    }

    return 0;
}
```

Output:

```
5 4 3 2 1
```

Code Explanation

Here's a step-by-step explanation of the code you provided:

1. Header File Inclusion:

```
#include <stdio.h>
```

This line includes the standard input-output library, stdio.h, which allows the program to use functions like printf to print output to the console.

2. Function to Reverse Array:

```
void reverseArray(int arr[], int size) {
    int start = 0, end = size - 1;
    while(start < end) {
        int temp = arr[start];
        arr[start] = arr[end];
        arr[end] = temp;
        start++;
        end--;
    }
}
```

- **reverseArray Function**:
  - **Input Parameters**: This function takes an array arr[] and its size as arguments. The goal is to reverse the elements in the array.
  - **Local Variables**:
    - start is initialized to 0, which points to the first element of the array.
    - end is initialized to size - 1, which points to the last element of the array.
  - **While Loop**:
    - The loop runs as long as start < end (i.e., until the two pointers meet or cross).

- **Swapping Elements**: Inside the loop, the elements at arr[start] and arr[end] are swapped:
  - The value at arr[start] is temporarily stored in temp.
  - The value at arr[end] is assigned to arr[start].
  - The value in temp (which was the original value at arr[start]) is assigned to arr[end].
- **Pointer Update**: After swapping, start is incremented (to move to the next element from the beginning), and end is decremented (to move to the previous element from the end).

- The loop continues until the two pointers meet, at which point the array is completely reversed.

3. Main Function:

```
int main() {
    int arr[5] = {1, 2, 3, 4, 5};
    reverseArray(arr, 5);

    for(int i = 0; i < 5; i++) {
        printf("%d ", arr[i]);
    }

    return 0;
}
```

- **Declaring an Array**:
  - int arr[5] = {1, 2, 3, 4, 5};: This line creates an array arr of size 5 and initializes it with values {1, 2, 3, 4, 5}.
- **Calling the reverseArray Function**:
  - The reverseArray(arr, 5) function call is used to reverse the contents of the array arr of size

5.

- **Printing the Reversed Array**:
    - The for loop iterates over the elements of the reversed array.
    - printf("%d ", arr[i]);: For each element arr[i], it prints the value followed by a space.
    - After the array is reversed, the for loop prints the new order of elements.

4. Return Statement:

```
return 0;
```

- The main function returns 0, which indicates that the program has executed successfully.

Example of the Execution Flow:

1. Initially, the array arr is {1, 2, 3, 4, 5}.
2. After calling reverseArray(arr, 5), the array becomes {5, 4, 3, 2, 1}.
3. The for loop prints the reversed array: 5 4 3 2 1.

6.2 Finding the Second Largest Element

```
#include <stdio.h>

int findSecondLargest(int arr[], int size) {
    int largest = arr[0], secondLargest = arr[0];
    for(int i = 1; i < size; i++) {
        if(arr[i] > largest) {
            secondLargest = largest;
            largest = arr[i];
        } else if(arr[i] > secondLargest && arr[i] != largest) {
            secondLargest = arr[i];
        }
    }
    return secondLargest;
}
```

```
int main() {
    int arr[5] = {2, 8, 5, 1, 6};
    printf("Second largest element: %d\n",
findSecondLargest(arr, 5));
    return 0;
}
```

Output:

```
Second largest element: 6
```

Let's go through the C code step by step:

1. Function Definition: findSecondLargest

```
int findSecondLargest(int arr[], int size) {
    int largest = arr[0], secondLargest = arr[0];
    for(int i = 1; i < size; i++) {
        if(arr[i] > largest) {
            secondLargest = largest;
            largest = arr[i];
        } else if(arr[i] > secondLargest && arr[i] != largest) {
            secondLargest = arr[i];
        }
    }
    return secondLargest;
}
```

This function is designed to find the second largest element in an array of integers.

- **Parameters:**
    - arr[]: The input array of integers.
    - size: The size of the array (i.e., the number of elements in the array).
- **Local variables:**
    - largest: Initially set to the first element of the array (arr[0]), it will hold the largest value

encountered during the iteration.

- secondLargest: Initially also set to the first element of the array, it will hold the second largest value encountered.

- **The loop (for loop):**
  - Starts iterating from index 1 (because index 0 is already considered as the starting point for both largest and secondLargest).
  - **First if condition:**

```
if(arr[i] > largest)
```

- If the current element arr[i] is greater than the largest, it means we've found a new largest number.
- We then update secondLargest to be the previous largest, and set largest to the current element arr[i].

- **else if condition:**

```
else if(arr[i] > secondLargest && arr[i] != largest)
```

- If the current element arr[i] is greater than the current secondLargest and not equal to largest, then we update secondLargest to the current element arr[i]. This ensures that we skip over duplicates of the largest number.

- **Returning the result:**
  - After completing the loop, the function returns the secondLargest value, which holds the second largest element in the array.

2. Main Function:

```
int main() {
    int arr[5] = {2, 8, 5, 1, 6};
```

```
    printf("Second largest element: %d\n",
findSecondLargest(arr, 5));
    return 0;
}
```

- **Declaring and initializing the array:**
  - arr[5] = {2, 8, 5, 1, 6} initializes an array with 5 elements: 2, 8, 5, 1, and 6.
- **Calling findSecondLargest:**
  - findSecondLargest(arr, 5) is called with the array arr and its size 5.
  - The function will find the second largest element in the array and return it.
- **Printing the result:**
  - The result returned by findSecondLargest is printed using printf. The %d format specifier is used to print an integer.
- **Return Statement:**
  - return 0; indicates that the program has finished executing successfully.

3. Execution Walkthrough:

Given the array arr = {2, 8, 5, 1, 6}, here's how the function works:

1. Initial values:
   - largest = 2, secondLargest = 2
2. First iteration (i = 1, arr[1] = 8):
   - arr[1] = 8 is greater than largest (2), so:
     - secondLargest = largest = 2
     - largest = arr[1] = 8
3. Second iteration (i = 2, arr[2] = 5):
   - arr[2] = 5 is less than largest (8), but greater than secondLargest (2), so:
     - secondLargest = arr[2] = 5
4. Third iteration (i = 3, arr[3] = 1):
   - arr[3] = 1 is neither greater than largest nor

secondLargest, so no change.

5. Fourth iteration (i = 4, arr[4] = 6):
    - arr[4] = 6 is less than largest (8), but greater than secondLargest (5), so:
        - secondLargest = arr[4] = 6
6. Final result:
    - After the loop ends, secondLargest = 6.

POINTER IN C

Pointers are one of the most powerful and flexible features in programming, especially in languages like C, C++, and others that support low-level memory manipulation. Understanding pointers is crucial for efficient coding, dynamic memory management, and working with data structures like linked lists, trees, and graphs.

What is a Pointer?

A **pointer** is a variable that stores the **memory address** of another variable. Instead of storing a value directly, a pointer "points to" the location in memory where the value is stored.

Key Terminologies:

- **Address**: The unique location of a variable in memory.
- **Dereferencing**: Accessing the value stored at the memory address held by a pointer.
- **Null Pointer**: A pointer that does not point to any valid memory address (value is NULL or nullptr in C++).

Why Use Pointers?

1. **Dynamic Memory Management**:
    - Allocate and deallocate memory during runtime (e.g., using malloc in C or new in C++).
2. **Efficient Passing of Arguments**:
    - Pass large structures or objects by reference, reducing memory overhead.
3. **Flexibility**:

- Create complex data structures like linked lists, trees, and graphs.

4. **Low-Level Programming**:
    - Directly manipulate memory and hardware registers, critical in systems programming.

Declaring and Initializing a Pointer

```
int x = 10;     // Variable of type int
int *p;        // Declaration of a pointer to an int
p = &x;         // Pointer p stores the address of x
```

Here:

- int *p; declares a pointer p that can point to an integer.
- &x gives the memory address of x.
- p = &x; assigns the address of x to p.

Accessing Values Through Pointers

To access the value of the variable x using pointer p, you use the **dereference operator (*)**:

```
printf("%d\n", *p); // Outputs: 10
```

Here, *p means "value at the memory address stored in p."

Pointer Arithmetic

Pointers can perform arithmetic operations to navigate through contiguous memory blocks, especially useful in arrays. **Pointer Arithmetic** in C/C++ allows you to perform arithmetic operations directly on pointers to navigate through memory locations. This is particularly useful when dealing with arrays or dynamic memory allocation.

Example:

```
#include<stdio.h>
int main() {
```

```
int arr[3] = {10, 20, 30};
int *p = arr;    // Points to the first element of the array

printf("for *p: %d\n", *p);      // Outputs: 10
printf("for *(p+1): %d\n", *(p + 1)); // Outputs: 20
printf("for *(p+2): %d\n", *(p + 2)); // Outputs: 30
}
```

Code Explanation:

This C code demonstrates pointer arithmetic with arrays. Here's a step-by-step explanation:

1. **Array Declaration and Initialization**

```
int arr[3] = {10, 20, 30};
```

- An integer array arr of size 3 is declared and initialized with the values {10, 20, 30}.
- The array elements are stored in contiguous memory locations. Let's assume the base address of arr is 0x1000, and since each integer takes 4 bytes (on most systems), the memory layout will be:

```
Address  Value
0x1000   10 (arr[0])
0x1004   20 (arr[1])
0x1008   30 (arr[2])
```

2. **Pointer Initialization**

```
int *p = arr;
```

- A pointer p is declared and initialized to point to the first element of the array arr.
- p = arr is equivalent to p = &arr[0] because the name of an array represents the address of its first element.

3. **Pointer Dereferencing and Arithmetic**
    - Pointer arithmetic and dereferencing are used to access array elements. Here's what happens for each printf statement:

First printf:

```
printf("for *p: %d\n", *p);
```

- *p dereferences the pointer p, retrieving the value stored at the address it points to.
- Initially, p points to arr[0], which is 10.
- **Output:** for *p: 10

Second printf:

```
printf("for *(p+1): %d\n", *(p + 1));
```

- p + 1 moves the pointer p to the next integer in the array. This happens because pointer arithmetic considers the size of the data type being pointed to. For int, p + 1 increments the address by 4 bytes (from 0x1000 to 0x1004).
- *(p + 1) dereferences the pointer at the new address, retrieving the value 20.
- **Output:** for *(p+1): 20

Third printf:

```
printf("for *(p+2): %d\n", *(p + 2));
```

- p + 2 moves the pointer p to the second next integer in the array (from 0x1000 to 0x1008).
- *(p + 2) dereferences the pointer at this address, retrieving the value 30.
- **Output:** for *(p+2): 30

Key Points

- **Pointer Arithmetic:** When you add an integer n to a pointer p, the resulting pointer points to the memory location n * sizeof(data type) bytes ahead of the original location.
- **Array-Pointer Relationship:** In C, the name of an array is essentially a constant pointer to its first element.
- **Dereferencing:** The * operator accesses the value stored at the address a pointer is pointing to.
- Adding 1 to a pointer moves it to the next memory block of its type.
- For int, which typically occupies 4 bytes, p + 1 moves the pointer by 4 bytes.

Program Output

```
for *p: 10
for *(p+1): 20
for *(p+2): 30
```

Here's an in-depth explanation:

---

1. Pointers and Memory Addresses

A pointer is a variable that stores the address of another variable. For example:

```
int a = 10;
int *ptr = &a; // ptr now stores the address of a
```

If &a is 0x100, the value of ptr becomes 0x100. The type of the pointer (int *) determines the size of the memory chunk it refers to.

---

2. Pointer Arithmetic Operations

Pointer arithmetic is valid only for pointers that point to elements of the same array or a contiguous block of memory.

a. Increment (++)

When a pointer is incremented, it moves to the next memory location based on the size of the type it points to.

Example:

```
int arr[5] = {1, 2, 3, 4, 5};
int *ptr = arr;  // Points to the first element (arr[0])
ptr++;           // Now points to arr[1]

printf("%d\n", *ptr); // Output: 2
```

Here, if ptr was initially 0x100 (assuming int is 4 bytes), after incrementing, ptr becomes 0x104.

b. Decrement (--)

Decrementing a pointer moves it backward in memory:

ptr--; // Moves the pointer to the previous element

c. Addition (+)

Adding an integer to a pointer moves it forward by that many elements:

```
int *ptr = arr;
ptr = ptr + 2; // Points to arr[2]
```

d. Subtraction (-)

Subtracting an integer moves the pointer backward:

```
int *ptr = arr + 3;
ptr = ptr - 1; // Points to arr[2]
```

e. Pointer Difference

You can subtract two pointers to find the number of elements between them:

```
int *ptr1 = &arr[3];
int *ptr2 = &arr[1];
int diff = ptr1 - ptr2; // diff = 2
```

3. Rules and Constraints

1. **Type Safety**: Pointer arithmetic depends on the type of the pointer. The compiler uses the size of the type to calculate the new address.
    - For int *, each increment moves sizeof(int) bytes.
    - For char *, each increment moves sizeof(char) bytes (usually 1 byte).
2. **Pointer Arithmetic on Arrays**:
    - Arrays are contiguous memory blocks, so pointer arithmetic works seamlessly.
    - The name of the array itself acts as a pointer to its first element.
3. **Invalid Operations**:
    - Adding two pointers is not allowed.
    - Multiplying or dividing pointers is also invalid.
    - Performing arithmetic on void * requires casting because void does not have a size.

---

4. Practical Uses

a. Iterating Through Arrays

Pointer arithmetic can replace array indexing:

```
int arr[] = {10, 20, 30, 40};
int *ptr = arr;

for (int i = 0; i < 4; i++) {
    printf("%d ", *(ptr + i)); // Output: 10 20 30 40
}
```

b. Accessing 2D Arrays

Pointer arithmetic is particularly useful for accessing elements in multi-dimensional arrays:

```
int matrix[3][3] = {
    {1, 2, 3},
```

```
    {4, 5, 6},
    {7, 8, 9}
};

int *ptr = &matrix[0][0];
printf("%d\n", *(ptr + 4)); // Output: 5 (row 1, column 1)
```

c. Dynamic Memory Allocation

When working with dynamically allocated memory (e.g., malloc), pointer arithmetic helps traverse the memory:

```
int *arr = (int *)malloc(5 * sizeof(int));
for (int i = 0; i < 5; i++) {
    *(arr + i) = i * 10; // Assign values
}
free(arr);
```

---

5. Example

```
#include <stdio.h>

int main() {
    int arr[5] = {1, 2, 3, 4, 5};
    int *ptr1 = arr;
    int *ptr2 = &arr[4];

    printf("Difference: %ld\n", ptr2 - ptr1); // Output: 4
(elements between them)

    for (int *p = ptr1; p <= ptr2; p++) {
        printf("%d ", *p);
    }

    return 0;
}
```

This C program demonstrates pointer arithmetic and the relationship between pointers and arrays. Let's break it down step by step:

Step 1: Declare and Initialize an Array

```
int arr[5] = {1, 2, 3, 4, 5};
```

- A fixed-size integer array arr of size 5 is declared and initialized with values {1, 2, 3, 4, 5}.
- Internally, arr is a contiguous block of memory where each element is stored sequentially.

Step 2: Declare and Initialize Pointers

```
int *ptr1 = arr;
int *ptr2 = &arr[4];
```

- ptr1 is assigned the address of the first element of arr (equivalent to &arr[0]).
- ptr2 is assigned the address of the last element of arr (index 4, accessed via &arr[4]).

Step 3: Calculate and Print the Pointer Difference

```
printf("Difference: %ld\n", ptr2 - ptr1);
```

- **Pointer Arithmetic**:
  - Subtracting one pointer from another gives the number of elements between them, not the byte difference.
  - Here, ptr2 - ptr1 calculates the number of elements between ptr1 (pointing to arr[0]) and ptr2 (pointing to arr[4]).
  - Since the pointers point to the same array:
    - ptr2 - ptr1 = 4 - 0 = 4.

Step 4: Iterate Through the Array Using a Pointer

```
for (int *p = ptr1; p <= ptr2; p++) {
    printf("%d ", *p);
}
```

- A for loop uses a pointer p to iterate through the array

from ptr1 to ptr2.

- Initialization: p = ptr1 (start at the first element).
- Condition: p <= ptr2 (loop until the pointer reaches the last element).
- Increment: p++ (move to the next element in memory).

- **Dereferencing the Pointer**:
  - Inside the loop, *p accesses the value stored at the address p.
  - This outputs each element of the array sequentially:
    - 1 2 3 4 5.

Step 5: Program Output

When executed, the program produces:

Difference: 4

1 2 3 4 5

- **Explanation of Output**:
  - Difference: 4 is from the pointer difference calculation.
  - 1 2 3 4 5 is the result of the for loop iterating through the array using pointers.

Key Concepts Demonstrated

1. **Pointer Arithmetic**:
   - Subtracting pointers gives the number of elements between them.
   - Incrementing a pointer moves it to the next element in memory, based on the size of the data type.
2. **Array and Pointer Relationship**:
   - The name of an array (arr) represents the address of the first element.
   - Elements of the array can be accessed using pointer arithmetic or indexing.

3. **Pointer Dereferencing**:
   - Using *ptr accesses the value stored at the memory location the pointer points to.

---

6. Key Takeaways

- Pointer arithmetic is a low-level, efficient way to traverse arrays or manage memory.
- Always ensure pointers stay within valid bounds to avoid undefined behavior.
- Familiarity with pointer arithmetic is essential for system-level programming and optimizing code in C/C++.

Null Pointers

A **null pointer** is initialized to ensure that it points to "nothing" until explicitly assigned a valid address. It avoids dangling references.

```
int *p = NULL;  //
if (p == NULL) {
    printf("Pointer is not pointing to any memory address.
\n");
}
```

Pointers and Dynamic Memory Allocation

Pointers are essential for dynamic memory allocation. For example:

Using malloc in C:

```
int *p = (int *)malloc(sizeof(int)); // Allocates memory for
one integer
*p = 25;                // Assign value to the allocated
memory
printf("%d\n", *p);           // Outputs: 25
```

```
free(p);                    // Frees the allocated memory
```

Double Pointers

A **double pointer** is a pointer that stores the address of another pointer.

```
int x = 10;
int *p = &x;      // Pointer to an int
int **pp = &p;    // Pointer to a pointer

printf("%d\n", **pp); // Outputs: 10
```

Step-by-Step Explanation:

1. **Declare an integer variable x:**

```
int x = 10;
```

- A variable x of type int is declared and initialized with the value 10.
- Memory is allocated for x, and it holds the value 10.

Memory representation:

```
Address  Variable  Value
0x100      x       10
```

2. **Declare a pointer p and initialize it with the address of x:**

```
int *p = &x;
```

- p is a pointer to an int (denoted by int *), which means p will store the address of an integer variable.
- p is assigned the address of x using the &x operator.

Memory representation:

```
Address  Variable  Value
0x200     p      0x100 (Address of `x`)
```

3. **Declare a pointer-to-pointer pp and initialize it with the address of p:**

```
int **pp = &p;
```

- pp is a pointer to a pointer to an int (denoted by int **), which means pp will store the address of a pointer that, in turn, points to an integer.
- pp is assigned the address of p using the &p operator.

Memory representation:

```
Address  Variable  Value
0x300     pp     0x200 (Address of `p`)
```

4. **Dereferencing pp to access the value of x:**

```
printf("%d\n", **pp);
```

- **pp involves two levels of dereferencing:
  1. *pp: Dereferences pp to get the value stored at the address pp points to. In this case, pp points to p, so *pp gives the value of p (which is 0x100).
  2. **pp: Dereferences the pointer value obtained from *pp. Since *pp is the address of x, **pp gives the value stored at x (which is 10).

Execution:

```
**pp -> *(*pp) -> *(p) -> x -> 10
```

Final Output:

The printf statement prints 10 to the console.

Diagram for Better Understanding:

```
x:  [10]    (value 10 is stored in memory)
p:  [0x100] (stores the address of x)
pp: [0x200] (stores the address of p)
```

Dereferencing flow:

```
**pp -> *(*pp) -> *(p) -> x -> 10
```

Use Case:

- Double pointers are widely used in dynamic allocation of multi-dimensional arrays.

Common Pitfalls with Pointers

1. **Dereferencing a Null Pointer**:
   - Leads to undefined behavior or program crashes.
2. **Memory Leaks**:
   - Failing to deallocate memory allocated dynamically (free or delete).
3. **Dangling Pointers**:
   - Pointers that reference deallocated memory.
4. **Pointer Mismanagement**:
   - Incorrect use of pointer arithmetic or casting.

Pointers and Arrays

Pointers and arrays are closely related. The name of an array acts as a pointer to its first element.

```
int arr[3] = {1, 2, 3};
int *p = arr;  // Points to the first element of the array

printf("%d\n", *p);      // Outputs: 1
printf("%d\n", *(p + 1)); // Outputs: 2
```

1. Array Initialization

```
int arr[3] = {1, 2, 3};
```

- arr is declared as an array of size 3 and initialized with the values {1, 2, 3}.
- Internally, the array is laid out in contiguous memory locations like this:

```
Memory Address    Value
0x1000          1 // arr[0]
0x1004          2 // arr[1]
0x1008          3 // arr[2]
```

(Assuming each int is 4 bytes; the exact memory address will vary.)

- The array name arr is equivalent to the address of the first element (&arr[0]).

---

2. Pointer Assignment

```
int *p = arr;
```

- A pointer p of type int * is declared.
- p is assigned the value arr, which points to the first element of the array (&arr[0]).
    - Now, p contains the address of the first element:

```
p = 0x1000 // Points to the value 1
```

---

3. Dereferencing the Pointer

```
printf("%d\n", *p);
```

- *p dereferences the pointer p, meaning it accesses the value stored at the memory address p points to.
- Currently, p points to the first element of the array

(arr[0]), which is 1.

---

4. Pointer Arithmetic

```
printf("%d\n", *(p + 1));
```

- p + 1 performs pointer arithmetic. Since p is of type int * and each int occupies 4 bytes (assumed), adding 1 to p moves the pointer to the next integer in memory.
  - New memory address:

```
p + 1 = 0x1004  // Points to arr[1]
```

- *(p + 1) dereferences the pointer p + 1, accessing the value at the address 0x1004, which is 2.

Pointers and Functions

Pointers can be used to:

1. **Pass by Reference**:
   - Modify the original value of a variable within a function.
2. **Function Pointers**:
   - Store the address of a function to call dynamically.

Example of Passing by Reference:

```
void updateValue(int *p) {
    *p = 20;  // Changes the original value
}

int main() {
    int x = 10;
    updateValue(&x);
    printf("%d\n", x);  // Outputs: 20
}
```

Step-by-Step Explanation:

1. **Declare the function updateValue:**

```
void updateValue(int *p) {
    *p = 20; // Changes the original value
}
```

- updateValue is a function that takes a pointer to an integer (int *p) as an argument.
- Inside the function:
  - The expression *p = 20 dereferences the pointer p to directly modify the value of the variable it points to.

---

2. **Inside the main function:**

```
int x = 10;
```

- An integer variable x is declared and initialized with the value 10.

```
updateValue(&x);
```

- The address of x is passed to the function updateValue using the address-of operator (&).
- &x provides the memory address of x, enabling the function to modify x directly.

---

3. **Execution of the updateValue function:**
   - Inside updateValue, the pointer p now holds the address of x.

```
*p = 20;
```

- The pointer p is dereferenced (*p) to access the memory location of x.
- The value at this memory location is set to

20.

- This effectively changes the value of x from 10 to 20.

---

4. **Print the value of x:**

```
printf("%d\n", x);
```

- After returning from the updateValue function, x has been modified to 20.
- The printf statement outputs the value of x, which is now 20.

Summary of Execution Flow:

1. int x = 10;
   - x is initialized to 10.
2. updateValue(&x);
   - The address of x is passed to the function, allowing updateValue to modify x directly.
3. Inside updateValue:
   - The value of x is updated to 20 via the pointer p.
4. printf("%d\n", x);
   - Prints the updated value of x, which is 20.

Conclusion

Pointers are a cornerstone of advanced programming concepts, enabling efficient memory management, dynamic behavior, and complex data structure creation. While they offer tremendous power, they demand careful handling to avoid common pitfalls like memory leaks and dangling references. Mastery of pointers is essential for system-level programming and understanding how memory works in detail.

STRINGS IN C

What Are Strings in C?

In C, a **string** is a sequence of characters stored in contiguous memory locations and terminated by a special null character '\0'. Unlike many modern programming languages, C does not have a dedicated data type for strings; instead, they are implemented using arrays of characters.

Key Points About Strings in C:

1. **Strings are arrays of characters**: Memory is allocated as a block of contiguous locations.
2. **Null Terminator (` '\0')**: Essential to mark the end of a string. Without it, C cannot determine the string's length or manipulate it properly.
3. **Strings are mutable in arrays but immutable in literals**: Strings declared as literals cannot be altered.

Example: Anatomy of a String

```
char name[6] = "Alice";
// Internally stored as: {'A', 'l', 'i', 'c', 'e', '\0'}
```

String Handling in C

C's <string.h> library provides a set of **string-handling functions** to simplify operations such as copying, concatenation, comparison, and searching. These functions rely heavily on pointers, making string manipulation in C both flexible and complex.

Overview of Common String Functions

Function	Description	Example

strlen()	Finds the length of a string (excluding '\0').	strlen("Hello") returns 5.
strcpy()	Copies one string to another.	strcpy(dest, src)
strcat()	Concatenates two strings.	strcat(dest, src)
strcmp()	Compares two strings lexicographically.	strcmp("abc", "xyz") returns < 0.
strchr()	Finds the first occurrence of a character.	strchr("hello", 'e') returns pointer.
strstr()	Finds the first occurrence of a substring.	strstr("hello", "lo") returns pointer.

These functions allow users to handle strings with minimal boilerplate code. Let's delve deeper into specific tasks.

Declaring and Initializing Strings

C allows strings to be initialized in various ways. Here, we'll cover the primary methods along with their constraints and typical usage.

1. Character Arrays

A common way to declare strings is to use character arrays. Here, the size of the array must be sufficient to store the string and the null terminator:

```
char name[6] = "Alice"; // Correct, size includes '\0'
char invalid[5] = "Alice"; // Incorrect, not enough space
```

The array allows modification of the string:

```
name[0] = 'B';
printf("%s", name); // Outputs: "Blice"
```

2. String Literals

A pointer to a string literal allocates read-only memory:

```
char *greeting = "Hello";
```

Attempting to modify the literal results in undefined behavior:

```
greeting[0] = 'M'; // Error: Read-only memory access
```

3. Dynamic Memory Allocation

For strings whose size is determined at runtime, dynamic memory is used:

```
#include <stdlib.h>
char *dynamicStr = (char *)malloc(50 * sizeof(char));
strcpy(dynamicStr, "Dynamic memory allocation");
free(dynamicStr); // Free memory after use
```

String Manipulation Functions

Here's an in-depth look at commonly used string-handling functions, along with examples to clarify their behavior.

1. Copying Strings

- strcpy(dest, src) copies the source string to the destination. The destination must have enough space to hold the source string and its null terminator.

Example:

```
#include <string.h>
char src[] = "Hello, World!";
char dest[20];
strcpy(dest, src);
printf("%s", dest); // Outputs: "Hello, World!"
```

Potential Pitfall: If the destination is smaller than the source, it leads to **buffer overflows**.

- Use strncpy(dest, src, n) to limit copying to n characters.

Example:

```
char dest[10];
strncpy(dest, "Overflow here!", 9);
dest[9] = '\0'; // Ensure null termination
```

2. Concatenation

- strcat(dest, src) appends src to dest. Ensure dest has enough space.

Example:

```
char str1[20] = "Hello, ";
char str2[] = "World!";
strcat(str1, str2);
printf("%s", str1); // Outputs: "Hello, World!"
```

- strncat(dest, src, n) limits the number of characters appended.

3. String Length

- strlen(str) returns the length of the string excluding '\0'.

Example:

```
char str[] = "C programming";
printf("Length: %lu", strlen(str)); // Outputs: 13
```

4. String Comparison

- strcmp(str1, str2) compares strings lexicographically. Returns:
    - < 0 if str1 < str2
    - 0 if str1 == str2
    - > 0 if str1 > str2

Example:

```
if (strcmp("apple", "banana") < 0) {
    printf("apple comes before banana");
}
```

5. Searching

- strchr(str, c) locates the first occurrence of c in str.

Example:

```
char *result = strchr("hello", 'e');
if (result) {
    printf("Found 'e' at position: %ld", result - "hello"); //
Outputs: 1
}
```

- strstr(str, substr) locates the first occurrence of a substring.

Example:

```
char *result = strstr("Programming in C", "gram");
if (result) {
    printf("Substring found at position: %ld", result -
"Programming in C"); // Outputs: 3
}
```

Working with Character Arrays

Direct Initialization

Arrays can be initialized using either string literals or individual characters:

```
char word1[] = "Code"; // Automatically adds '\0'
char word2[5] = {'C', 'o', 'd', 'e', '\0'};
```

Manipulation

Character arrays offer granular control:

```
char arr[10] = "Example";
arr[0] = 'e'; // Change 'E' to 'e'
printf("%s", arr); // Outputs: "example"
```

Boundary Management

C does not perform bounds checking, so accessing or writing beyond array limits leads to undefined behavior:

```
char str[5] = "Test";
str[5] = '!'; // Undefined behavior, memory corruption
```

Best Practices and Common Pitfalls

1. **Always Null-Terminate**: When manually constructing strings, ensure they end with '\0'.
2. **Avoid Buffer Overflows**: Always allocate sufficient memory for operations.
3. **Use Safe Functions**: Prefer strncpy and strncat over their unsafe counterparts.

Conclusion

C strings provide unparalleled control over memory but require disciplined handling to avoid errors. Mastering their nuances—from initialization to manipulation—empowers developers to write efficient, robust programs. With this knowledge, you're equipped to tackle real-world string challenges in C programming.

Advanced Exploration: Strings in C

---

1. Memory Allocation Challenges in Strings

Dynamic memory allocation is a powerful tool in C, allowing programmers to allocate memory for strings at runtime. However, improper handling of allocated memory can lead to errors such as **memory leaks** and **dangling pointers**. Let's explore these challenges.

Dynamic Memory Allocation

Dynamic memory functions (malloc, calloc, realloc, and free) allow flexible allocation:

```
char *dynamicStr = (char *)malloc(50 * sizeof(char));
if (dynamicStr == NULL) {
    printf("Memory allocation failed");
```

```
    return 1; // Exit the program
}
strcpy(dynamicStr, "Dynamic memory allocation");
printf("%s", dynamicStr);
free(dynamicStr); // Free the memory
```

Here's a step-by-step explanation of the given code:

---

1. Dynamic Memory Allocation

char *dynamicStr = (char *)malloc(50 * sizeof(char));

- **Purpose**: This line allocates memory dynamically for a char array to hold up to 50 characters.
- **Key Functions and Syntax**:
    - malloc(50 * sizeof(char)):
        - Allocates memory for 50 bytes (sizeof(char) is typically 1 byte).
        - The memory is uninitialized.
    - (char *):
        - Typecasts the pointer returned by malloc to a char * type.
- **Result**: dynamicStr now points to the allocated memory block in the heap.

---

2. Memory Allocation Check

```
if (dynamicStr == NULL) {
    printf("Memory allocation failed");
    return 1;
}
```

- **Purpose**: Checks if malloc was successful.
- **Explanation**:
    - malloc returns NULL if it fails to allocate memory (e.g., due to insufficient heap space).
    - If dynamicStr is NULL, an error message is printed, and the program exits with a return

value of 1 (indicating an error).

---

3. Copying a String

strcpy(dynamicStr, "Dynamic memory allocation");

- **Purpose**: Copies the string "Dynamic memory allocation" into the allocated memory.
- **Key Function**:
  - strcpy(destination, source):
    - Copies the source string (including the null terminator \0) to destination.
    - Assumes the destination has enough allocated space.
- **Note**: The string being copied is shorter than 50 characters, so it fits safely in the allocated memory.

---

4. Printing the String

printf("%s", dynamicStr);

- **Purpose**: Prints the string stored at dynamicStr to the standard output.
- **Key Function**:
  - %s: Format specifier to print a null-terminated string.

---

5. Freeing Allocated Memory

free(dynamicStr);

- **Purpose**: Deallocates the memory allocated by malloc to avoid memory leaks.
- **Key Function**:
  - free(pointer):
    - Releases the memory block pointed to by pointer.
    - After freeing, the pointer becomes invalid and should not be

dereferenced.

Summary of Execution:

1. **Memory Allocation**: Allocates memory for 50 characters.
2. **Error Check**: Ensures allocation was successful.
3. **String Copy**: Copies the string into the allocated memory.
4. **Print**: Outputs the string.
5. **Deallocation**: Frees the memory to prevent resource wastage.

Common Challenges

1. **Forgetting to Free Memory**

c

Copy code

```
char *leakStr = (char *)malloc(100);
strcpy(leakStr, "Forgot to free memory");
// No free() call here leads to a memory leak
```

2. **Reallocating Memory Without Freeing**

```
char *str = (char *)malloc(20);
str = (char *)realloc(str, 50); // Previous 20 bytes are leaked if not freed
```

The provided code snippet involves dynamic memory allocation and reallocation using the malloc and realloc functions in C. Let's analyze it step by step:

Step-by-Step Explanation

1. Initial Allocation with malloc:

```
char *str = (char *)malloc(20);
```

- **What Happens:**
    - malloc(20) allocates 20 bytes of memory on the heap.
    - It returns a pointer to the starting address of

the allocated memory block.

- The cast (char *) ensures that the pointer type matches the variable str (a char *).

- **State:**
  - str now points to a block of 20 bytes in the heap.
  - This memory block is ready to be used for storing data.

2. Reallocation with realloc:

str = (char *)realloc(str, 50);

- **What Happens:**
  - realloc tries to resize the memory block pointed to by str from 20 bytes to 50 bytes.
  - Depending on memory availability:
    - **If enough contiguous space is available:** The block is resized in place, and str continues pointing to the same address.
    - **If not:** A new 50-byte block is allocated elsewhere, the data from the old block (first 20 bytes) is copied to the new block, and the old block is **freed automatically**.
  - str is updated to point to the new memory block.
- **Potential Issue:**
  - If realloc fails (e.g., insufficient memory), it returns NULL, and the original memory block (20 bytes) remains allocated but inaccessible because str is overwritten with NULL.

3. Memory Leak Risk:

- The statement **"Previous 20 bytes are leaked if not freed"** is **incorrect** if you're directly passing str to realloc. Here's why:
  - When you pass the pointer str to realloc, the

original memory (20 bytes) is automatically freed if a new block is allocated.

- **When Does a Leak Occur?**
    - If you overwrite str before checking the return value of realloc, like this:

str = (char *)realloc(str, 50);

If realloc fails and returns NULL, the original block (20 bytes) is lost because str now points to NULL.

4. Best Practices:

To avoid memory leaks, always check the result of realloc **before** overwriting the original pointer:

```
char *temp = (char *)realloc(str, 50);
if (temp != NULL) {
    str = temp; // Update pointer only if successful
} else {
    // Handle realloc failure (e.g., free str if not needed
anymore)
}
```

Let's break down the code and explain it step by step:

Initial Context

- str is assumed to be a pointer to a dynamically allocated memory block. It could have been allocated previously using functions like malloc or calloc.
- The goal of this code is to resize the memory block pointed to by str to 50 bytes using the realloc function.

Code Walkthrough

1. **Calling realloc**:

```
char *temp = (char *)realloc(str, 50);
```

- **What it does**:
    - realloc tries to resize the memory block

pointed to by str to 50 bytes.
- If successful, it returns a pointer to the newly allocated memory block.
- If it fails (e.g., due to insufficient memory), it returns NULL.

- **Why assign to temp?**:
  - If realloc fails and returns NULL, the original memory block pointed to by str remains valid.
  - Assigning the result to temp ensures that str does not lose its reference to the original memory block in case of failure.

---

2. **Checking the result of realloc**:

```
if (temp != NULL) {
```

- **What it does**:
  - Checks whether the realloc call was successful by verifying that temp is not NULL.
  - If temp is NULL, the realloc failed, and no changes are made to the str pointer.

---

3. **Updating the pointer on success**:

```
str = temp; // Update pointer only if successful
```

- **What it does**:
  - Updates the original pointer str to point to the newly allocated memory block (temp).
  - This ensures that str now refers to the resized memory block.

---

4. **Handling realloc failure**:

```
} else {
```

```
    // Handle realloc failure (e.g., free str if not needed
anymore)
}
```

- **What it does**:
  - If temp is NULL, it means realloc failed to allocate memory.
  - You might handle the failure in different ways:
    - Log an error or take corrective action.
    - Free the original memory block (str) if it's no longer needed, to avoid memory leaks.
    - Ensure the program can safely continue running.

Summary

- The code uses a **two-step process** for safety:
  1. Attempts to resize the memory with realloc and stores the result in a temporary pointer (temp).
  2. Updates the original pointer (str) only if realloc succeeds.
- **Why is this safe?**:
  - Directly assigning the result of realloc to str without checking can cause memory leaks if realloc fails. This is avoided here by using the temp pointer.

Example of Failure Handling

Here's a more complete version of how you might handle a failure:

```
char *temp = (char *)realloc(str, 50);
if (temp != NULL) {
    str = temp; // Successfully resized
```

```
} else {
    fprintf(stderr, "Memory reallocation failed!\n");
    // Optionally free the original memory if no longer
needed
    free(str);
    str = NULL; // Nullify to prevent dangling pointer
}
```

This approach makes the code robust against memory allocation issues.

Key Points:

1. realloc may:
   - Resize the block in place (no new allocation).
   - Allocate a new block and free the old one.
   - Fail and return NULL.
2. Always validate the return value of realloc to avoid overwriting the original pointer.
3. If realloc fails and the pointer is overwritten without a check, the original block is leaked.

3. **Accessing Freed Memory**

```
char *str = (char *)malloc(30);
free(str);
printf("%s", str); // Undefined behavior
```

Let's break this code and its behavior into clear steps to understand why it leads to **undefined behavior**:

Code Analysis

Step 1: Memory Allocation

- **malloc(30)**: Allocates 30 bytes of memory dynamically from the heap.
- The returned pointer (str) points to the beginning of this allocated memory block.

- At this point:
  - The memory is uninitialized (it contains garbage values).
  - The program has ownership of this block.
  - You can use it for storage after initializing its content.

Step 2: Freeing the Allocated Memory

- **free(str)**: Releases the memory pointed to by str back to the system.
- After calling free, the memory is no longer valid for use.
- The pointer str itself is not modified; it still points to the same memory address, but that memory now belongs to the system.

Step 3: Attempting to Access Freed Memory

- **printf("%s", str)**:
  - The %s format specifier expects a valid null-terminated string.
  - After free(str), the memory pointed to by str is no longer valid or owned by your program.
  - Accessing this memory (read or write) is **undefined behavior** because:
    1. The contents of the memory are unpredictable—it might be garbage, reallocated for other purposes, or inaccessible.
    2. Dereferencing str can lead to:
       - A crash (segmentation fault).
       - Unintended output.
       - Seemingly correct behavior (rare, depending on system state).

Why is it Undefined Behavior?

- **Undefined behavior (UB)** in C occurs when the standard does not prescribe what should happen, meaning anything could happen (including no visible issue, a crash, or corrupted behavior).
- In this case, using str after it has been freed violates the standard because:
    1. The memory has been deallocated.
    2. The pointer is considered **dangling**—it refers to a memory location that is no longer valid.

Best Practices to Avoid UB

1. **Set the pointer to NULL after free**:

```
free(str);
str = NULL;
```

- This ensures str does not point to a freed memory block.
- Attempting to dereference or print NULL would result in a predictable runtime error in many systems.

2. **Always initialize memory explicitly**:
    - Before using %s, ensure the memory contains a valid string:

```
char *str = (char *)malloc(30);
strcpy(str, "Hello, World!");
printf("%s", str); // Safe
free(str);
```

Conclusion

Using a pointer after it has been freed leads to undefined behavior because the program no longer has ownership of the memory. Always nullify pointers after freeing and ensure memory is valid before use.

Best Practices

- Always check if malloc or realloc returned NULL.
- Free memory when no longer needed.
- Avoid using memory after it has been freed.

---

2. Debugging String Errors

Working with strings in C can lead to subtle bugs due to improper memory handling, boundary errors, or invalid pointers. Here are some debugging tips:

Common Errors

1. **Buffer Overflows** Writing beyond the allocated size leads to memory corruption.

```
char buffer[5];
strcpy(buffer, "Overflow"); // Writes beyond the buffer's
limit
```

The code snippet you provided demonstrates a classic example of a **buffer overflow** vulnerability. Let's break it down step by step:

---

1. Declaration of the buffer

```
char buffer[5];
```

- A char array named buffer is declared with a size of 5.
- This means the array can hold up to **5 characters** (including the null terminator \0 required to mark the end of a C string).

2. Usage of strcpy

```
strcpy(buffer, "Overflow");
```

- The strcpy function copies the content of the string "Overflow" (source) into buffer (destination).
- "Overflow" is 9 characters long:
    - **8 characters ("Overflow")** plus the **null terminator (\0)** at the end.
- The total size required to store "Overflow" is **9 bytes**, which exceeds the capacity of the buffer array (5 bytes).

3. What happens during strcpy?

- strcpy starts copying characters one by one from the source string "Overflow" into the destination buffer array:
    - It writes 'O' into buffer[0]
    - It writes 'v' into buffer[1]
    - It writes 'e' into buffer[2]
    - It writes 'r' into buffer[3]
    - It writes 'f' into buffer[4] (**filling the declared size of the buffer**).
- After buffer[4], the copying continues **beyond the bounds of the array**:
    - 'l' is written into buffer[5] (out-of-bounds)
    - 'o' is written into buffer[6] (out-of-bounds)
    - 'w' is written into buffer[7] (out-of-bounds)
    - '\0' is written into buffer[8] (out-of-bounds)

4. Buffer Overflow

- Since buffer was only allocated space for 5 bytes, the remaining characters overwrite **adjacent memory locations**.
- The behavior of accessing memory beyond the allocated buffer is **undefined**:
    - It may corrupt adjacent data or code.
    - It may cause the program to crash.

    - It may create security vulnerabilities (e.g., attackers can exploit this to inject malicious code).

5. What could go wrong?

- **Data Corruption:** If the memory adjacent to buffer contains other variables, their values might be overwritten.
- **Security Risks:** If an attacker carefully crafts input, they can overwrite specific memory locations, potentially gaining control of the program.
- **Program Instability:** Writing beyond the allocated buffer often leads to crashes or unpredictable behavior.

6. Safe Alternative

Instead of strcpy, use safer alternatives like strncpy or dynamic memory allocation:

```
strncpy(buffer, "Overflow", sizeof(buffer) - 1);
buffer[sizeof(buffer) - 1] = '\0'; // Ensure null-termination
```

This limits the copy to only 4 characters ("Over"), leaving space for the null terminator.

Summary

The code demonstrates how using strcpy without proper bounds checking can lead to a buffer overflow. This is why functions like strcpy are discouraged in modern C programming; safer alternatives and bounds checking should always be employed.

2. **Off-by-One Errors** Forgetting the null terminator:

```
char str[5] = "hello"; // No space for '\0', causes undefined
behavior
```

The statement char str[5] = "hello"; contains an issue that can lead to undefined behavior in C. Let's analyze it step by step:

---

1. Understanding String Literals in C

- In C, string literals (e.g., "hello") are null-terminated.
- The null terminator (\0) is automatically appended to the end of the string to mark its termination.
- "hello" occupies **6 bytes** in memory: 5 for the characters h, e, l, l, o, and 1 for the null terminator (\0).

---

2. Declaration of the Array

```
char str[5];
```

- Here, you explicitly define an array str of size 5.
- This means str can hold exactly 5 characters, with no extra space for the null terminator.

---

3. Attempted Initialization

```
str[5] = "hello";
```

- "hello" (including its null terminator, \0) is **6 bytes long**, but you've allocated only 5 bytes for str.
- During initialization, the array str is filled with the characters 'h', 'e', 'l', 'l', and 'o'.
- **No space is left for the null terminator** (\0), which is crucial for identifying the end of a string in C.

---

4. Undefined Behavior

- If you use this array in any string-related operation (e.g., printf("%s", str);), the function will keep reading memory beyond the array bounds in search of a null terminator.

- Since there's no \0 within the allocated space of str, the program may:
    - Read garbage values beyond the array.
    - Access invalid memory locations, leading to a crash.
- This behavior is **undefined** because the C standard does not guarantee what happens when a string lacks a null terminator.

---

5. Correcting the Issue

To avoid undefined behavior, ensure the array has enough space for the null terminator:

```
char str[6] = "hello"; // Correct: Includes space for '\0'
```

Alternatively, let the compiler determine the size automatically:

```
char str[] = "hello"; // Compiler allocates 6 bytes, including
'\0'
```

---

6. Key Takeaways

- Always ensure that strings have enough space for the null terminator.
- When initializing a string in a fixed-size character array, the size of the array must be at least strlen(string) + 1 to accommodate the null terminator.
- Failing to allocate space for \0 can lead to **undefined behavior**, including crashes and data corruption.

---

3. **Dangling Pointers** Using pointers to deallocated memory.

```
char *ptr = (char *)malloc(10);
free(ptr);
strcpy(ptr, "Oops"); // Undefined behavior
```

This code snippet involves **undefined behavior** because it uses a pointer (ptr) to access memory that has already been deallocated. Here's a detailed explanation:

Code Breakdown:

1. **char *ptr = (char *)malloc(10);**
   - This allocates 10 bytes of memory on the heap and assigns the address of the allocated block to the pointer ptr.
   - The memory is uninitialized at this point.
2. **free(ptr);**
   - This deallocates the memory that ptr points to, making it unavailable for use.
   - After this, the memory location pointed to by ptr is no longer valid, and accessing it will result in undefined behavior.
3. **strcpy(ptr, "Oops");**
   - The function strcpy attempts to copy the string "Oops" into the memory pointed to by ptr.
   - However, since the memory was freed in the previous step, ptr is now a **dangling pointer** (i.e., it points to memory that is no longer valid).
   - Accessing or writing to memory that has been freed results in **undefined behavior**.

What is Undefined Behavior?

Undefined behavior means the C standard does not specify what happens when this code runs. Possible consequences include:

- The program might crash.
- The program might appear to work correctly.

- Memory corruption might occur, leading to unpredictable behavior later.

How to Avoid Undefined Behavior

1. **Do not access freed memory:**
   - After freeing a pointer, set it to NULL to ensure you don't accidentally use it.

```
free(ptr);
ptr = NULL;
```

2. **Reallocate memory if needed:**
   - If you need to use the pointer again, reallocate memory before doing so:

```
ptr = (char *)malloc(10);  // Reallocate memory before
using ptr
strcpy(ptr, "Oops");
```

3. **Check for NULL pointers:**
   - Always check that the pointer is not NULL before using it.

Correct Version of the Code

To fix the undefined behavior, allocate memory again after freeing it:

```
char *ptr = (char *)malloc(10);
free(ptr);

ptr = (char *)malloc(10); // Reallocate memory
if (ptr != NULL) {
    strcpy(ptr, "Oops"); // Safe now
}
```

By reassigning ptr to a valid memory block, the program avoids accessing deallocated memory.

Debugging Tools

- **GDB (GNU Debugger)**: Use breakpoints to inspect memory at runtime:

```
gdb program
run
```

- **Valgrind**: Detect memory leaks and invalid accesses:

```
valgrind ./program
```

- **Address Sanitizers**: Enable with GCC:

```
gcc -fsanitize=address -g program.c -o program
```

Debugging Example

Use printf to trace variable states:

```
char buffer[10];
strcpy(buffer, "Debugging");
printf("Buffer contents: %s\n", buffer);
```

This C code snippet has an issue related to buffer overflow, and here's a detailed explanation of its components and implications:

Code Breakdown:

1. **Declaration of buffer:**

```
char buffer[10];
```

   - This declares an array named buffer that can hold up to 10 characters (including the null terminator \0).

2. **Copying the string "Debugging" to buffer:**

```
strcpy(buffer, "Debugging");
```

   - The strcpy function copies the string "Debugging" (a total of 10 characters, as it includes a null terminator) into buffer.

3. **Print the contents of buffer:**

```
printf("Buffer contents: %s\n", buffer);
```

- This prints the contents of buffer as a string.

Key Issue: Buffer Overflow

The string "Debugging" is **exactly 10 characters** long, which matches the size of buffer. However, this introduces a subtle but critical problem:

- When strcpy copies the string "Debugging", it **does not check if the destination buffer has enough space** to hold the string plus its null terminator. While buffer is technically large enough in this case, even slight modifications (e.g., adding more characters) would exceed its bounds, leading to undefined behavior.

Undefined Behavior:

- Writing beyond the bounds of an array (buffer in this case) can:
    1. Overwrite adjacent memory.
    2. Corrupt the program's state.
    3. Cause crashes or unpredictable behavior at runtime.

Recommendations to Avoid Buffer Overflow:

1. **Use safer string functions like strncpy:**

```
strncpy(buffer, "Debugging", sizeof(buffer) - 1);
buffer[sizeof(buffer) - 1] = '\0'; // Ensure null-termination
```

- This copies up to sizeof(buffer) - 1 characters, leaving space for the null terminator.

2. **Validate string length:** Before copying, ensure that the string to be copied fits within the buffer.

3. **Use snprintf for combined formatting and copying:**

```
snprintf(buffer, sizeof(buffer), "Debugging");
```

Corrected Version:

```
#include <stdio.h>
#include <string.h>

int main() {
    char buffer[10];
    strncpy(buffer, "Debugging", sizeof(buffer) - 1);
    buffer[sizeof(buffer) - 1] = '\0'; // Null-terminate to
ensure safety
    printf("Buffer contents: %s\n", buffer);
    return 0;
}
```

This ensures no overflow occurs, making the program safer and more robust.

---

3. Use Cases for Strings

A. Parsing Input

Strings are often used to process user input. For example, parsing commands from a shell:

```
#include <stdio.h>
#include <string.h>
int main() {
    char input[100];
    printf("Enter command: ");
    fgets(input, sizeof(input), stdin);

    char *token = strtok(input, " ");
    while (token != NULL) {
        printf("Token: %s\n", token);
        token = strtok(NULL, " ");
```

```
    }
    return 0;
}
```

OUTPUT
Enter command: hello world this is c
Token: hello
Token: world
Token: this
Token: is
Token: c

The given program is a simple example of tokenizing a string in C using the strtok function. Here's a step-by-step explanation:

Code Walkthrough

1. Header Files

```
#include <stdio.h>
#include <string.h>
```

- **<stdio.h>**: Includes standard input/output functions such as printf and fgets.
- **<string.h>**: Provides string manipulation functions, such as strtok.

---

2. Declaring Variables

```
char input[100];
```

- An array of char is declared to hold the user input. The size is 100, so it can hold up to 99 characters (leaving one for the null terminator).

---

3. Input Collection

```
printf("Enter command: ");
fgets(input, sizeof(input), stdin);
```

- **printf**: Prompts the user to enter a string.
- **fgets**: Reads the input string, including spaces, and stores it in the input array.
    - It reads up to sizeof(input) - 1 characters or until a newline is encountered.
    - It appends a null terminator (\0) to the string.

---

4. Tokenization

```
char *token = strtok(input, " ");
```

- **strtok**: Tokenizes the input string by breaking it into parts (tokens) using a delimiter.
    - First argument: The string to tokenize (here, input).
    - Second argument: The delimiter(s) (here, " " for space).
    - On the first call, strtok finds the first token and returns a pointer to it.
    - Subsequent calls with strtok(NULL, " ") continue tokenizing the same string.

---

5. Token Iteration

```
while (token != NULL) {
    printf("Token: %s\n", token);
    token = strtok(NULL, " ");
}
```

- The while loop iterates through the tokens until strtok returns NULL, indicating there are no more tokens.
- Each token is printed using printf.

---

6. Program Exit

```
return 0;
```

- Ends the program execution.

Example Execution

Input:

```
Enter command: hello world this is C
```

Tokenization Process:

1. strtok("hello world this is C", " ") → Returns "hello".
2. strtok(NULL, " ") → Returns "world".
3. strtok(NULL, " ") → Returns "this".
4. strtok(NULL, " ") → Returns "is".
5. strtok(NULL, " ") → Returns "C".
6. strtok(NULL, " ") → Returns NULL.

Output:

```
Token: hello
Token: world
Token: this
Token: is
Token: C
```

Key Notes

1. **Destructive Function**:
   - strtok modifies the input string by replacing delimiter characters with \0 to terminate tokens.
   - Example: The original string "hello world" becomes "hello\0world" after the first call.
2. **Non-Reentrant**:
   - strtok is not thread-safe. Use strtok_r for

thread-safe applications.

Enhancements

1. **Handling Newlines**:
   - fgets may include a newline character (\n) at the end of the string. Consider removing it:

```
input[strcspn(input, "\n")] = '\0'; // Replace '\n' with '\0' if
it exists
```

2. **Dynamic Buffer**:
   - Instead of a fixed-size input buffer, dynamically allocate memory if the input size is unknown.

B. Encryption and Encoding

Strings are central to text encoding and encryption. A basic Caesar cipher:

```
#include <stdio.h>
void encrypt(char *text, int shift) {
    for (int i = 0; text[i] != '\0'; i++) {
        if (text[i] >= 'a' && text[i] <= 'z') {
            text[i] = (text[i] - 'a' + shift) % 26 + 'a';
        } else if (text[i] >= 'A' && text[i] <= 'Z') {
            text[i] = (text[i] - 'A' + shift) % 26 + 'A';
        }
    }
}

int main() {
    char message[100] = "Hello, World!";
    encrypt(message, 3);
    printf("Encrypted: %s\n", message);
    return 0;
}
```

OUTPUT

```
Encrypted: Khoor, Zruog!
```

This C program encrypts a message using the **Caesar cipher** algorithm, which shifts each letter in the message by a specified number of positions (referred to as the shift). Non-alphabetic characters remain unchanged.

Code Breakdown

1. **Function: encrypt**
   - **Parameters**:
     - char *text: A pointer to the string to be encrypted.
     - int shift: The number of positions each character in the string is shifted.
   - **Logic**:
     - A for loop iterates through each character in the string text until the null terminator (\0), which marks the end of the string.
     - **For lowercase letters** ('a' to 'z'):
       - Convert the character to a 0-based index (text[i] - 'a').
       - Add the shift and wrap around using the modulus operator (% 26).
       - Convert back to the ASCII range by adding 'a'.
     - **For uppercase letters** ('A' to 'Z'):
       - Similar to lowercase, but uses 'A' as the base.
     - **For non-alphabetic characters**:
       - These are skipped and remain unchanged.
2. **Main Function: main**
   - **Initialization**:
     - A string message is defined and initialized with "Hello, World!".
   - **Encryption**:

        - The encrypt function is called with message and a shift value of 3.
    - **Output**:
        - Prints the encrypted message using printf.

Working of the Program

- **Input**: "Hello, World!"
- **Process**:
    - Each alphabetic character is shifted by 3 positions in the alphabet:
        - 'H' becomes 'K'
        - 'e' becomes 'h'
        - 'l' becomes 'o'
        - 'o' becomes 'r'
        - 'W' becomes 'Z'
        - 'r' becomes 'u'
        - 'd' becomes 'g'
    - Non-alphabetic characters (',', ' ', '!') remain unchanged.
- **Output**: "Khoor, Zruog!"

Key Concepts

1. **Character Manipulation**:
    - The program uses ASCII values to shift characters.
    - By subtracting 'a' or 'A', it normalizes the alphabet to a 0-based index, making modulus arithmetic straightforward.
2. **Modulus Arithmetic**:
    - Ensures that the shift wraps around (e.g., shifting 'z' by 3 results in 'c').
3. **Immutable Non-Alphabetic Characters**:
    - Non-alphabetic characters are left as they are.

C. File Handling

Reading and processing strings from files:

```
#include <stdio.h>
int main() {
    FILE *file = fopen("data.txt", "r");
    if (file == NULL) {
        printf("Failed to open file\n");
        return 1;
    }

    char line[100];
    while (fgets(line, sizeof(line), file)) {
        printf("Read: %s", line);
    }
    fclose(file);
    return 0;
}
```

This C program demonstrates how to read data from a file named data.txt and display its contents line by line. Here's a detailed explanation of each part of the code:

---

1. Include the necessary library

```
#include <stdio.h>
```

This includes the standard I/O library, which provides functions like fopen, fgets, fclose, and printf.

---

2. Open the file

```
FILE *file = fopen("data.txt", "r");
```

- FILE *file: This creates a pointer to a FILE object that represents the file being worked with.
- fopen("data.txt", "r"): Opens the file named data.txt in **read mode** ("r"). If the file doesn't exist, fopen returns NULL.

3. Error handling

```
if (file == NULL) {
    printf("Failed to open file\n");
    return 1;
}
```

- If file is NULL, the program displays an error message (Failed to open file) and returns 1 to indicate an error occurred.
- Returning 1 from main signals a non-zero exit code, typically used to indicate an error.

4. Reading the file line by line

```
char line[100];
while (fgets(line, sizeof(line), file)) {
    printf("Read: %s", line);
}
```

- char line[100]: Declares a buffer that can hold up to 99 characters (plus the null terminator) for each line read from the file.
- fgets(line, sizeof(line), file):
    - Reads a single line from the file into the line buffer, up to 99 characters or until a newline is encountered.
    - Returns NULL when there are no more lines to read.
- printf("Read: %s", line):
    - Prints each line read from the file. fgets retains the newline character (\n) at the end of the line (if present).

5. Close the file

```
fclose(file);
```

- Closes the file after reading. This is important to release system resources associated with the file.

---

6. Return success

```
return 0;
```

- Returns 0 to indicate that the program executed successfully.

Example: If data.txt contains the following:

```
Hello, World!
C programming is fun.
```

Program Output:

```
Read: Hello, World!
Read: C programming is fun.
```

Key Points:

1. **File Handling:**
    - fopen: Opens a file.
    - fgets: Reads a line.
    - fclose: Closes a file.
2. **Error Handling:**
    - Check if the file opened successfully.
3. **Buffer Size:**
    - The line buffer is limited to 100 characters. If a line in the file exceeds this length, it will be truncated.

---

4. Exercises with Solutions

Exercise 1: String Reversal

Write a function to reverse a string in-place.

Solution:

```
#include<stdio.h>
#include<string.h>

void reverseString(char str[]) {
    int start = 0, end = strlen(str) - 1;
    char temp;

    while (start < end) {
        temp = str[start];
        str[start] = str[end];
        str[end] = temp;
        start++;
        end--;
    }
}

int main() {
    char str[100];
    printf("Enter a string: ");
    scanf("%s", str);

    reverseString(str);
    printf("Reversed string: %s", str);

    return 0;
}
```

OUTPUT
Enter a string: hello
Reversed string: olleh

This C program reverses a string entered by the user. Let's go through the code step by step:

1. Include Header Files:

```
#include<stdio.h>
```

```
#include<string.h>
```

- stdio.h is included for input/output functions like printf and scanf.
- string.h is included to use string-related functions like strlen.

2. Function Definition:

```
void reverseString(char str[]) {
    int start = 0, end = strlen(str) - 1;
    char temp;

    while (start < end) {
        temp = str[start];
        str[start] = str[end];
        str[end] = temp;
        start++;
        end--;
    }
}
```

- reverseString is a function that reverses the string passed as a parameter (str[]).
- **Parameters:**
    - char str[]: A character array (string) passed to the function.
- **Local Variables:**
    - int start = 0: The index of the first character of the string.
    - int end = strlen(str) - 1: The index of the last character of the string (since strlen(str) gives the length of the string, and indexing starts from 0).
    - char temp: A temporary variable used to swap characters.

- **While Loop:**
  - while (start < end) keeps running as long as the start index is less than the end index.
  - Inside the loop, characters from the start and end positions are swapped:
    - temp = str[start]: Store the character at the start index in temp.
    - str[start] = str[end]: Replace the character at the start index with the character at the end index.
    - str[end] = temp: Place the character from temp (originally at start) into the end position.
  - Then, start++ and end-- are used to move the start index forward and the end index backward, so the next characters will be swapped.

3. Main Function:

```
int main() {
    char str[100];
    printf("Enter a string: ");
    scanf("%s", str);

    reverseString(str);
    printf("Reversed string: %s", str);

    return 0;
}
```

- char str[100]: A character array str is declared with a maximum size of 100. It will hold the user input.
- printf("Enter a string: ");: Prompts the user to enter a string.
- scanf("%s", str);: Reads a string from the user and stores it in str. Note that scanf("%s", str) will only read input until the first space is encountered (so it

doesn't handle multi-word input).

- reverseString(str);: Calls the reverseString function to reverse the string str.
- printf("Reversed string: %s", str);: Prints the reversed string.
- return 0;: Ends the main function and indicates successful program execution.

Example Walkthrough:

Let's say the input string is "hello".

- Initially: str = "hello", start = 0, end = 4 (length of "hello" - 1).
- 1st iteration of the loop:
  - temp = 'h', str[start] = 'o', str[end] = 'h'
  - str = "oellh", start = 1, end = 3.
- 2nd iteration of the loop:
  - temp = 'e', str[start] = 'l', str[end] = 'e'
  - str = "olleh", start = 2, end = 2 (now start equals end, so the loop stops).
- Final output: "Reversed string: olleh".

Summary:

- The program takes a string input, reverses it using a function, and prints the reversed string.

The reverseString function uses a two-pointer technique (start and end) to swap characters until the entire string is reversed

Exercise 2: Palindrome Check

Check if a given string is a palindrome.

Solution:

```
#include <stdio.h>
```

```
#include <string.h>
#include <ctype.h>

// Function to check if a string is a palindrome
int isPalindrome(char *str) {
    int n = strlen(str);
    for (int i = 0; i < n / 2; i++) {
        if (str[i] != str[n - i - 1]) return 0;
    }
    return 1;
}

// Function to remove newline and extra spaces
void preprocessString(char *str) {
    // Remove trailing newline character
    size_t len = strlen(str);
    if (len > 0 && str[len - 1] == '\n') {
        str[len - 1] = '\0';
    }

    // Optional: Convert to lowercase for case-insensitive
check
    for (int i = 0; str[i]; i++) {
        str[i] = tolower(str[i]);
    }
}

int main() {
    char str[100];
    printf("Enter a string: ");
    if (fgets(str, sizeof(str), stdin)) {
        preprocessString(str); // Clean the input
        if (isPalindrome(str)) {
            printf("\"%s\" is a palindrome\n", str);
        } else {
            printf("\"%s\" is not a palindrome\n", str);
        }
```

```
    } else {
        printf("Error reading input\n");
    }
    return 0;
}
```

OUTPUT
Enter a string: wow
"wow" is a palindrome

Let's break down your C code step by step:

1. #include Statements

These are preprocessor directives that include necessary header files:

- #include <stdio.h>: Includes standard input/output functions like printf() and fgets().
- #include <string.h>: Includes functions for string handling, like strlen().
- #include <ctype.h>: Includes functions for character handling, like tolower().

2. isPalindrome Function

This function checks if a string is a palindrome.

```
int isPalindrome(char *str) {
    int n = strlen(str); // Get the length of the string
    for (int i = 0; i < n / 2; i++) { // Loop through the first half
of the string
        if (str[i] != str[n - i - 1]) return 0; // If characters don't
match, return 0 (false)
    }
    return 1; // Return 1 (true) if the string is a palindrome
}
```

- strlen(str) computes the length of the string str.
- A loop runs from the first character to the middle of

the string (n / 2), comparing characters at opposite ends: str[i] and str[n - i - 1].

- If any pair doesn't match, the function returns 0, indicating the string is **not** a palindrome.
- If all pairs match, the function returns 1, meaning the string **is** a palindrome.

3. preprocessString Function

This function prepares the string for palindrome checking by removing trailing newlines and converting characters to lowercase (for case-insensitive comparison).

```
void preprocessString(char *str) {
    size_t len = strlen(str); // Get the length of the string
    if (len > 0 && str[len - 1] == '\n') { // Check if the string
ends with a newline
        str[len - 1] = '\0'; // Replace newline with null
terminator
    }

    // Convert all characters to lowercase
    for (int i = 0; str[i]; i++) {
        str[i] = tolower(str[i]); // Convert each character to
lowercase
    }
}
```

- First, it checks if the string has a newline character (which is added by fgets() when reading input) at the end and removes it by replacing it with the null character ('\0').
- Then, the tolower() function is used to convert each character to lowercase. This ensures that the comparison for palindrome checking is **case-insensitive**.

4. main Function

This is where the program starts executing.

```
int main() {
    char str[100]; // Declare a character array to store the
input string
    printf("Enter a string: ");
    if (fgets(str, sizeof(str), stdin)) { // Read a line of input
from the user
        preprocessString(str); // Clean the input by
removing newline and converting to lowercase
        if (isPalindrome(str)) { // Check if the string is a
palindrome
            printf("\"%s\" is a palindrome\n", str); // If yes,
print that it's a palindrome
        } else {
            printf("\"%s\" is not a palindrome\n", str); // If no,
print that it's not a palindrome
        }
    } else {
        printf("Error reading input\n"); // In case of an input
error
    }
    return 0; // End of the program
}
```

- char str[100]: Declares a character array of size 100 to hold the user input.
- printf("Enter a string: ");: Prompts the user to enter a string.
- fgets(str, sizeof(str), stdin): Reads a line of text from standard input (up to 99 characters, leaving space for the null terminator). This is safer than scanf because

it prevents buffer overflow.
  - If successful, the program proceeds to clean and check the input.
- preprocessString(str): Calls the preprocessing function to clean the string (remove the newline and convert to lowercase).
- isPalindrome(str): Calls the function to check if the string is a palindrome.
  - If the result is 1, the program prints that the string is a palindrome.
  - If the result is 0, the program prints that the string is not a palindrome.
- If fgets fails to read input (e.g., due to an error), the program prints an error message.

Key Concepts

- **Palindrome**: A string that reads the same forward and backward (e.g., "madam").
- **Case-insensitivity**: Ensuring the comparison of letters like 'a' and 'A' is treated the same.
- **String manipulation**: Using strlen() to find the string's length, tolower() to convert characters, and manipulating the string with basic array indexing.

Exercise 3: Find Most Frequent Character

Write a function to find the most frequent character in a string.

Solution:

```
#include <stdio.h>
#include <string.h>
char mostFrequentChar(char *str) {
    int freq[256] = {0};
    for (int i = 0; str[i] != '\0'; i++) {
        freq[(int)str[i]]++;
    }
```

```
    char maxChar = '\0';
    int maxFreq = 0;
    for (int i = 0; i < 256; i++) {
        if (freq[i] > maxFreq) {
            maxFreq = freq[i];
            maxChar = (char)i;
        }
    }
    return maxChar;
}

int main() {
    char text[] = "success";
    printf("Most frequent character: %c\n",
mostFrequentChar(text)); // Outputs: 's'
    return 0;
}
```

This C program finds and prints the most frequent character in a given string. Here's an explanation of how it works:

Code Breakdown

1. Function Declaration

```
char mostFrequentChar(char *str)
```

- This function takes a string (char *str) as input and returns the most frequent character.

---

2. Frequency Array

```
int freq[256] = {0};
```

- An array freq of size 256 is initialized to 0. This array is used to store the frequency of each character.
- The size 256 is chosen because it represents the

possible values of an ASCII character set.

3. Counting Character Frequencies

```
for (int i = 0; str[i] != '\0'; i++) {
    freq[(int)str[i]]++;
}
```

- The for loop iterates through each character in the string until the null terminator (\0) is encountered.
- (int)str[i] converts the character at position i in the string to its ASCII value, which is used as the index for the freq array.
- freq[(int)str[i]]++ increments the count of the character in the frequency array.

4. Finding the Most Frequent Character

```
char maxChar = '\0';
int maxFreq = 0;

for (int i = 0; i < 256; i++) {
    if (freq[i] > maxFreq) {
        maxFreq = freq[i];
        maxChar = (char)i;
    }
}
```

- The variables maxChar and maxFreq are initialized to store the most frequent character and its frequency.
- The for loop iterates through all possible ASCII characters (indices of the freq array).
- If a character's frequency (freq[i]) is greater than the current maximum (maxFreq), the character and its frequency are updated in maxChar and maxFreq.

5. Returning the Most Frequent Character

```
return maxChar;
```

- The function returns the character with the highest frequency.

---

6. Main Function

```
char text[] = "success";
printf("Most frequent character: %c\n",
mostFrequentChar(text));
```

- The string text is defined as "success".
- The mostFrequentChar function is called with this string, and the result is printed.

How the Program Works for "success"

1. **Frequency Calculation**
    - Character counts are:
        - 's': 3
        - 'u': 1
        - 'c': 2
        - 'e': 1
2. **Finding the Maximum**
    - The most frequent character is 's' with a count of 3.
3. **Output**
    - The program outputs:

```
Most frequent character: s
```

Key Points

- **Edge Cases:** If the input string is empty, the function will return '\0'.

- **Ties:** If two characters have the same highest frequency, the one with the smaller ASCII value (earlier in freq) will be returned.

STRUCTURES AND UNIONS IN C

Introduction

In C programming, structures and unions are user-defined data types that allow grouping of variables under a single name. While structures enable the combination of different types of data, unions facilitate the storage of different data types in the same memory location. Understanding these concepts is crucial for managing and organizing complex data in an efficient manner.

Defining Structures

Explanation

A structure is a collection of variables, possibly of different types, grouped together under a single name. This is especially useful when you need to represent a record with multiple attributes.

Syntax

```
struct Tag {
    data_type member1;
    data_type member2;
    // ... more members
};
```

Example

Consider a structure to represent a student:

```
#include <stdio.h>
#include <string.h>
```

```
// Define a structure to represent a student
struct Student {
    char name[50];
    int age;
    float gpa;
};

int main() {
    // Declare a variable of type struct Student
    struct Student student1;

    // Assign values to the members of student1
    strcpy(student1.name, "John Doe");
    student1.age = 20;
    student1.gpa = 3.8;

    // Print the values of the members
    printf("Name: %s\n", student1.name);
    printf("Age: %d\n", student1.age);
    printf("GPA: %.2f\n", student1.gpa);

    return 0;
}
```

OUTPUT
Name: John Doe
Age: 20
GPA: 3.80

Explanation of the Program

1. Header Files:

```
#include <stdio.h>
#include <string.h>
```

- **#include <stdio.h>**: This header file is included to use input-output functions like printf and scanf.

- **#include <string.h>**: This header file is included to use string manipulation functions such as strcpy.

2. Defining the Structure:

```
struct Student {
    char name[50];
    int age;
    float gpa;
};
```

- A structure named Student is defined to represent a student.
- It contains three members:
    - name (a character array of size 50): Stores the student's name.
    - age (an integer): Stores the student's age.
    - gpa (a float): Stores the student's grade point average.

3. Declaring a Structure Variable:

```
struct Student student1;
```

- A variable student1 of type struct Student is declared. This variable will hold information for one student.

4. Assigning Values to Members:

```
strcpy(student1.name, "John Doe");
student1.age = 20;
student1.gpa = 3.8;
```

- **strcpy(student1.name, "John Doe")**: Copies the string "John Doe" into the name member of student1. strcpy is used because name is an array, and direct assignment (e.g., student1.name = "John Doe") is not allowed for arrays in C.
- **student1.age = 20;**: Assigns the integer 20 to the age

member.

- **student1.gpa = 3.8;**: Assigns the floating-point value 3.8 to the gpa member.

5. Printing the Values:

```
printf("Name: %s\n", student1.name);
printf("Age: %d\n", student1.age);
printf("GPA: %.2f\n", student1.gpa);
```

- **printf("Name: %s\n", student1.name);**: Prints the name member using the %s format specifier for strings.
- **printf("Age: %d\n", student1.age);**: Prints the age member using the %d format specifier for integers.
- **printf("GPA: %.2f\n", student1.gpa);**: Prints the gpa member with 2 decimal places using the %.2f format specifier for floating-point numbers.

Key Concepts Illustrated in the Program:

1. **Structures in C**:
    - Structures group related data of different types into a single entity.
    - They are useful for creating custom data types.
2. **String Manipulation**:
    - The strcpy function is used to copy a string into a character array.
3. **Input and Output**:
    - The printf function is used to display the values stored in the structure members.
4. **Accessing Structure Members**:
    - Use the dot operator (.) to access members of a structure variable.

This simple program demonstrates the basics of defining, initializing, and using structures in C.

Accessing Members of Structures

Explanation

Members of a structure can be accessed using the dot operator (.) if you have a structure variable. If you have a pointer to a structure, you use the arrow operator (->).

Example

```
#include <stdio.h>
#include <string.h>

struct Student {
    char name[50];
    int age;
    float gpa;
};

int main() {
    struct Student student1;
    strcpy(student1.name, "Alice Smith");
    student1.age = 21;
    student1.gpa = 3.9;

    // Access and print members using the dot operator
    printf("Name: %s\n", student1.name);
    printf("Age: %d\n", student1.age);
    printf("GPA: %.2f\n", student1.gpa);

    // Using a pointer to the structure
    struct Student *ptr = &student1;
    printf("Pointer Access - Name: %s\n", ptr->name);
    printf("Pointer Access - Age: %d\n", ptr->age);
    printf("Pointer Access - GPA: %.2f\n", ptr->gpa);

    return 0;
}
```

OUTPUT

```
Name: Alice Smith
Age: 21
GPA: 3.90
Pointer Access - Name: Alice Smith
Pointer Access - Age: 21
Pointer Access - GPA: 3.90
```

This C program demonstrates the use of a struct (structure) to define and manage a student record. Here's a step-by-step explanation:

---

1. Structure Definition

```
struct Student {
    char name[50];
    int age;
    float gpa;
};
```

- This defines a structure named Student with three members:
    - name: A character array to store the student's name (up to 49 characters plus a null terminator \0).
    - age: An integer to store the student's age.
    - gpa: A floating-point variable to store the student's GPA.

---

2. Declaring a Structure Variable

```
struct Student student1;
```

- Declares a variable student1 of type struct Student, which will store the details of one student.

---

3. Assigning Values to the Members

```
strcpy(student1.name, "Alice Smith");
student1.age = 21;
```

```
student1.gpa = 3.9;
```

- strcpy is used to copy the string "Alice Smith" into the name field of student1.
- The age field is set to 21.
- The gpa field is set to 3.9.

---

4. Accessing Members with the Dot Operator

```
printf("Name: %s\n", student1.name);
printf("Age: %d\n", student1.age);
printf("GPA: %.2f\n", student1.gpa);
```

- The **dot operator (.)** is used to access individual fields of student1.
- %.2f formats the gpa value to two decimal places.

---

5. Using a Pointer to the Structure

```
struct Student *ptr = &student1;
```

- A pointer ptr is declared and initialized to point to student1 using the address-of operator (&).

---

6. Accessing Members Using the Pointer

```
printf("Pointer Access - Name: %s\n", ptr->name);
printf("Pointer Access - Age: %d\n", ptr->age);
printf("Pointer Access - GPA: %.2f\n", ptr->gpa);
```

- The **arrow operator (->)** is used to access members of the structure through the pointer ptr.

Output Explanation

When the program is executed, the output will be:

```
Name: Alice Smith
Age: 21
GPA: 3.90
Pointer Access - Name: Alice Smith
Pointer Access - Age: 21
Pointer Access - GPA: 3.90
```

- The first three lines use the **dot operator** to access and print the student1 members.
- The last three lines use the **pointer** (ptr) and the arrow operator to achieve the same result.

Key Concepts Demonstrated

1. **Structures**: Used to group related data.
2. **Dot Operator**: Accesses members of a structure variable directly.
3. **Pointer to Structure**: Allows indirect access to the members.
4. **Arrow Operator (->)**: Specifically designed for accessing members via pointers.

This program is a simple demonstration of structure handling and provides a foundation for more complex data management in C.

Nested Structures

Explanation

A structure can contain other structures as members. This is called a nested structure and is useful for representing more complex data.

Example

Consider a university system where a Student has an Address:

```
#include <stdio.h>
#include <string.h>

// Define the Address structure
```

```
struct Address {
    char street[100];
    char city[50];
    int zipcode;
};

// Define the Student structure, which includes an Address
struct Student {
    char name[50];
    int age;
    float gpa;
    struct Address address;
};

int main() {
    // Declare and initialize a Student
    struct Student student1;
    strcpy(student1.name, "Bob Johnson");
    student1.age = 22;
    student1.gpa = 3.7;
    strcpy(student1.address.street, "123 Maple St");
    strcpy(student1.address.city, "Springfield");
    student1.address.zipcode = 12345;

    // Print the student's information including the nested
address
    printf("Name: %s\n", student1.name);
    printf("Age: %d\n", student1.age);
    printf("GPA: %.2f\n", student1.gpa);
    printf("Address: %s, %s, %d\n",
student1.address.street, student1.address.city,
student1.address.zipcode);

    return 0;
}
```

OUTPUT

Name: Bob Johnson

```
Age: 22
GPA: 3.70
Address: 123 Maple St, Springfield, 12345
```

This program defines and demonstrates the use of **nested structures** in C. It models a Student who has associated personal details like name, age, gpa, and a nested structure called Address which contains information about the student's address.

Key Components of the Code:

1. Structure Definitions

- **Address Structure**:

```
struct Address {
    char street[100];
    char city[50];
    int zipcode;
};
```

  - This structure is used to hold details of a physical address:
    - street: The name of the street (string of up to 99 characters).
    - city: The city name (string of up to 49 characters).
    - zipcode: A numerical value representing the postal code.

- **Student Structure**:

```
struct Student {
    char name[50];
    int age;
    float gpa;
    struct Address address;
};
```

- This structure models a student with the following fields:
  - name: Name of the student (string of up to 49 characters).
  - age: Age of the student (integer).
  - gpa: Grade Point Average (floating-point number).
  - address: A nested Address structure that includes the street, city, and zipcode.

2. Initialization and Assignment

- A variable student1 of type struct Student is declared and initialized:

```
struct Student student1;
```

- Values are assigned to each member:
  - Strings (name, street, city) are assigned using strcpy:

```
strcpy(student1.name, "Bob Johnson");
strcpy(student1.address.street, "123 Maple St");
strcpy(student1.address.city, "Springfield");
```

  - Other fields (age, gpa, zipcode) are assigned directly:

```
student1.age = 22;
student1.gpa = 3.7;
student1.address.zipcode = 12345;
```

3. Printing Information

- The printf function displays all the fields of the student1 structure:

```
printf("Name: %s\n", student1.name);
printf("Age: %d\n", student1.age);
```

```
printf("GPA: %.2f\n", student1.gpa);
printf("Address: %s, %s, %d\n", student1.address.street,
student1.address.city, student1.address.zipcode);
```

- The nested address fields (street, city, zipcode) are accessed using the . operator.

4. Output

When you run this program, it outputs:

```
Name: Bob Johnson
Age: 22
GPA: 3.70
Address: 123 Maple St, Springfield, 12345
```

Explanation of Key Concepts:

1. **Nested Structures**:
    - The struct Address is included within struct Student, allowing a Student object to contain all address-related details within a single field.
    - Accessing nested members requires chaining the . operator (e.g., student1.address.street).
2. **String Handling**:
    - Strings in C cannot be assigned directly; strcpy is used to copy string literals into character arrays.
3. **Modular Design**:
    - Separating Address into its own structure makes the code modular, readable, and reusable in case other structures also need address information.

Structures and Functions

Explanation

Structures can be passed to functions by value or by reference (using pointers). Passing by reference is more efficient, especially for large structures.

Example

Passing a structure by reference to a function:

```
#include <stdio.h>
#include <string.h>

struct Student {
    char name[50];
    int age;
    float gpa;
};

void printStudent(struct Student *s) {
    printf("Name: %s\n", s->name);
    printf("Age: %d\n", s->age);
    printf("GPA: %.2f\n", s->gpa);
}

int main() {
    struct Student student1;
    strcpy(student1.name, "Carol White");
    student1.age = 23;
    student1.gpa = 3.5;

    // Pass the address of student1 to the function
    printStudent(&student1);

    return 0;
}
```

OUTPUT
Name: Carol White
Age: 23
GPA: 3.50

This C program demonstrates the use of **structures** and **pointers** to pass a structure to a function. Here's a detailed breakdown of the code:

---

1. Structure Definition

```
struct Student {
    char name[50];
    int age;
    float gpa;
};
```

- A struct named Student is defined.
- It has three members:
    - name (a character array to store the student's name, up to 49 characters plus the null terminator).
    - age (an integer for the student's age).
    - gpa (a floating-point number for the grade point average).

---

2. Function to Print Student Information

```
void printStudent(struct Student *s) {
    printf("Name: %s\n", s->name);
    printf("Age: %d\n", s->age);
    printf("GPA: %.2f\n", s->gpa);
}
```

- The function printStudent takes a pointer to a struct Student as an argument (struct Student *s).
- It accesses the structure members using the **arrow operator (->)**, which is used to dereference a pointer to a structure.

For example:

- s->name accesses the name field of the structure pointed to by s.

- Similarly, s->age and s->gpa access the age and gpa fields.

The function prints:

- The name of the student using %s for strings.
- The age using %d for integers.
- The GPA using %.2f for floating-point numbers formatted to two decimal places.

---

3. Main Function

```
int main() {
    struct Student student1;
    strcpy(student1.name, "Carol White");
    student1.age = 23;
    student1.gpa = 3.5;

    // Pass the address of student1 to the function
    printStudent(&student1);

    return 0;
}
```

- Inside main, a variable student1 of type struct Student is created.
- The structure members are initialized:
  - strcpy(student1.name, "Carol White"); copies the string "Carol White" into the name field.
  - student1.age = 23; assigns the value 23 to the age field.
  - student1.gpa = 3.5; assigns the value 3.5 to the gpa field.
- The address of student1 (&student1) is passed to printStudent, allowing the function to access and print the student's data.

---

4. Output

When you run the program, it prints:

```
Name: Carol White
Age: 23
GPA: 3.50
```

Why Pass a Pointer?

- Efficiency: Passing a pointer avoids copying the entire structure, especially when the structure is large.
- Direct Modification: A pointer allows the function to modify the original structure, if needed.

This program demonstrates good practices in using structures and pointers for modular programming.

Introduction to Unions

Explanation

A union is a user-defined data type similar to a structure. However, in a union, all members share the same memory location. This means only one member can hold a value at any given time. Unions are useful when you need to store different types of data in the same memory location.

Syntax

```
union Tag {
    data_type member1;
    data_type member2;
    // ... more members
};
```

Example

Consider a union to store different types of data for a single entity:

```
#include <stdio.h>
#include <string.h>

union Data {
    int i;
    float f;
    char str[20];
};

int main() {
    union Data data;

    data.i = 10;
    printf("data.i: %d\n", data.i);

    data.f = 220.5;
    printf("data.f: %.1f\n", data.f);

    strcpy(data.str, "C Programming");
    printf("data.str: %s\n", data.str);

    return 0;
}
```

Explanation

In this example, the union Data can store an integer, a float, or a string, but only one at a time. When a new value is assigned to a member, the previous value is overwritten.

This C program demonstrates the usage of a **union** in the C programming language. Let's break it down step by step:

Code Walkthrough

1. Union Definition

```
union Data {
    int i;
    float f;
    char str[20];
```

```
};
```

- A union named Data is defined with three members:
  - An int named i.
  - A float named f.
  - A char array of size 20 named str.

2. Main Function

```
union Data data;
```

- A variable data of type union Data is declared. It will share memory among the members i, f, and str.

---

3. Assigning and Printing Values

First Assignment

```
data.i = 10;
printf("data.i: %d\n", data.i);
```

- The integer 10 is assigned to data.i. The memory allocated for the union now holds the integer value 10.
- The output will be:

```
data.i: 10
```

Second Assignment

```
data.f = 220.5;
printf("data.f: %.1f\n", data.f);
```

- The float 220.5 is assigned to data.f. This overwrites the memory that was holding the value for data.i.
- Since unions share memory for all members, the value of data.i is no longer valid.
- The output will be:

```
data.f: 220.5
```

Third Assignment

```
strcpy(data.str, "C Programming");
printf("data.str: %s\n", data.str);
```

- The string "C Programming" is copied into data.str. This overwrites the memory that was holding the value for data.f.
- Now, the values of data.i and data.f are invalid.
- The output will be:

```
data.str: C Programming
```

Key Points to Note

1. **Memory Sharing**:
   - A union allocates memory equal to the size of its largest member.
   - In this case, the largest member is char str[20], which requires 20 bytes.
   - Hence, the union Data occupies 20 bytes in total.
2. **Overwriting**:
   - Writing to one member overwrites the value of the others because they share the same memory.
3. **Output Behavior**:
   - Only the value of the most recently assigned member will be valid.

Output

When you run the program, you will see:

```
data.i: 10
data.f: 220.5
```

```
data.str: C Programming
```

Real-Life Application

Unions are often used in scenarios where:

- You need to store data of different types but only one type at a time.
- Memory efficiency is critical (e.g., low-level programming, embedded systems).

In-Depth Use Cases and Advanced Concepts

1. Dynamic Memory Allocation with Structures

Dynamic memory allocation is vital for efficient memory management. Using structures with dynamic memory allocation, you can create flexible data structures like linked lists, trees, and more.

Example: Linked List Implementation

```
#include <stdio.h>
#include <stdlib.h>

// Define the structure for a linked list node
struct Node {
    int data;
    struct Node* next;
};

// Function to create a new node
struct Node* createNode(int data) {
    struct Node* newNode = (struct
Node*)malloc(sizeof(struct Node));
    newNode->data = data;
    newNode->next = NULL;
    return newNode;
}
```

```
// Function to insert a node at the beginning of the list
void insertAtBeginning(struct Node** head, int data) {
    struct Node* newNode = createNode(data);
    newNode->next = *head;
    *head = newNode;
}

// Function to print the linked list
void printList(struct Node* head) {
    struct Node* temp = head;
    while (temp != NULL) {
        printf("%d -> ", temp->data);
        temp = temp->next;
    }
    printf("NULL\n");
}

int main() {
    struct Node* head = NULL;

    insertAtBeginning(&head, 10);
    insertAtBeginning(&head, 20);
    insertAtBeginning(&head, 30);

    printList(head);

    return 0;
}
```

This C program demonstrates how to work with a **singly linked list**, including creating nodes, inserting nodes at the beginning of the list, and printing the list. Here's a step-by-step explanation:

---

1. Structure Definition

```
struct Node {
    int data;
    struct Node* next;
```

```
};
```

- This defines a structure Node that represents a node in the linked list.
- Each node has:
    - data: an integer value stored in the node.
    - next: a pointer to the next node in the list (or NULL if it is the last node).

---

2. Create a New Node

```
struct Node* createNode(int data) {
    struct Node* newNode = (struct
Node*)malloc(sizeof(struct Node));
    newNode->data = data;
    newNode->next = NULL;
    return newNode;
}
```

- The createNode function allocates memory for a new node using malloc.
- Initializes the data field with the provided value (data).
- Sets the next pointer to NULL because the new node does not point to any other node initially.

---

3. Insert a Node at the Beginning

```
void insertAtBeginning(struct Node** head, int data) {
    struct Node* newNode = createNode(data);
    newNode->next = *head;
    *head = newNode;
}
```

- This function inserts a new node at the beginning of the linked list.

- head is a **double pointer** because the function modifies the actual head pointer of the list:
  - createNode(data) creates the new node.
  - newNode->next = *head; makes the new node point to the current head node.
  - *head = newNode; updates the head pointer to point to the new node.

---

4. Print the Linked List

```
void printList(struct Node* head) {
    struct Node* temp = head;
    while (temp != NULL) {
        printf("%d -> ", temp->data);
        temp = temp->next;
    }
    printf("NULL\n");
}
```

- This function traverses the list starting from head and prints each node's data followed by an arrow (->).
- Stops when temp becomes NULL, indicating the end of the list.
- Finally, prints NULL to signify the termination of the list.

---

5. main Function

```
int main() {
    struct Node* head = NULL;

    insertAtBeginning(&head, 10);
    insertAtBeginning(&head, 20);
    insertAtBeginning(&head, 30);

    printList(head);
```

```
    return 0;
}
```

- Initializes the head pointer to NULL, indicating an empty list.
- Calls insertAtBeginning three times:
    1. Adds 10 (list becomes 10 -> NULL).
    2. Adds 20 at the beginning (list becomes 20 -> 10 -> NULL).
    3. Adds 30 at the beginning (list becomes 30 -> 20 -> 10 -> NULL).
- Calls printList(head) to display the linked list.

Output

```
30 -> 20 -> 10 -> NULL
```

Key Concepts

1. **Dynamic Memory Allocation**: The malloc function allocates memory at runtime for each new node.
2. **Pointer Manipulation**: Pointers are used to link nodes and modify the head of the list.
3. **Double Pointer**: Used in insertAtBeginning to modify the actual pointer to the head node.

This code showcases the basics of singly linked list operations in C.

2. Nested Structures and Real-World Applications

Nested structures are common in real-world applications where data is hierarchical.

Example: Company Employee Records

```
#include <stdio.h>
#include <string.h>
```

```
// Define a structure for the address
struct Address {
    char street[50];
    char city[50];
    char state[50];
    int zipcode;
};

// Define a structure for the employee
struct Employee {
    char name[50];
    int id;
    struct Address address; // Nested structure
};

int main() {
    struct Employee emp1;

    strcpy(emp1.name, "David Brown");
    emp1.id = 1001;
    strcpy(emp1.address.street, "456 Oak St");
    strcpy(emp1.address.city, "Metropolis");
    strcpy(emp1.address.state, "NY");
    emp1.address.zipcode = 67890;

    printf("Employee Name: %s\n", emp1.name);
    printf("Employee ID: %d\n", emp1.id);
    printf("Address: %s, %s, %s, %d\n",
emp1.address.street, emp1.address.city,
emp1.address.state, emp1.address.zipcode);

    return 0;
}
```

This program demonstrates the use of **nested structures** in C, where one structure (Address) is included as a member of another structure (Employee). Let's break it down step by step:

Code Explanation

1. Define the Address Structure

```
struct Address {
    char street[50];
    char city[50];
    char state[50];
    int zipcode;
};
```

- This structure represents an **address**.
- It contains:
    - street: A string for the street name.
    - city: A string for the city name.
    - state: A string for the state name.
    - zipcode: An integer for the postal code.

---

2. Define the Employee Structure

```
struct Employee {
    char name[50];
struct Employee emp1;
    struct Address address;
};
```

- This structure represents an **employee**.
- It contains:
    - name: A string for the employee's name.
    - id: An integer for the employee's ID.
    - address: A **nested structure** of type struct Address, which stores the employee's address.

---

3. Create an Employee Variable

```
struct Employee emp1;
```

- This declares a variable emp1 of type struct Employee.

---

4. Assign Values to emp1

```
strcpy(emp1.name, "David Brown");
emp1.id = 1001;
strcpy(emp1.address.street, "456 Oak St");
strcpy(emp1.address.city, "Metropolis");
strcpy(emp1.address.state, "NY");
emp1.address.zipcode = 67890;
```

- strcpy is used to copy string values into character arrays:
  - emp1.name: The employee's name is set to "David Brown".
  - emp1.address.street: The street is set to "456 Oak St".
  - emp1.address.city: The city is set to "Metropolis".
  - emp1.address.state: The state is set to "NY".
- emp1.id is directly assigned the value 1001.
- emp1.address.zipcode is directly assigned the value 67890.

---

5. Print the Employee Details

```
printf("Employee Name: %s\n", emp1.name);
printf("Employee ID: %d\n", emp1.id);
printf("Address: %s, %s, %s, %d\n", emp1.address.street,
emp1.address.city, emp1.address.state,
emp1.address.zipcode);
```

- printf is used to display the employee's details, including the nested address fields.

- Each part of the address (street, city, state, zipcode) is accessed using the **dot operator** (.).

Program Output

When the program runs, it produces the following output:

```
Employee Name: David Brown
Employee ID: 1001
Address: 456 Oak St, Metropolis, NY, 67890
```

Key Concepts

1. **Nested Structures**:
   - Structures can contain other structures as members.
   - This helps in organizing related data hierarchically.
2. **Dot Operator (.)**:
   - Used to access members of a structure.
   - For nested structures, you can "chain" the dot operator (e.g., emp1.address.city).
3. **String Handling**:
   - Strings in C are arrays of characters.
   - strcpy is used to copy a string into a character array.

This approach is highly useful for managing complex data in real-world applications, like employee records with hierarchical details.

---

3. Structures and Functions: Passing by Value vs. Reference

When passing structures to functions, you can choose between passing by value (a copy is made) or passing by reference (a pointer is passed).

Example: Comparison

```
#include <stdio.h>
#include <string.h>
```

```
// Define the structure for a student
struct Student {
    char name[50];
    int age;
    float gpa;
};
```

The provided C code defines a structure called Student using the struct keyword. Let's break it down step-by-step:

1. Include Header Files

```
#include <stdio.h>
#include <string.h>
```

- #include <stdio.h>: This is the standard input/output library in C, enabling the program to use functions like printf and scanf.
- #include <string.h>: This library provides functions to manipulate C-style strings (e.g., strcpy, strcmp, etc.). Though not used in the snippet, it might be needed later in the program to work with the name field.

---

2. Define the Student Structure

```
struct Student {
    char name[50];
    int age;
    float gpa;
};
```

- struct is a user-defined data type in C that groups related variables (fields) under one name, enabling you to represent complex entities.

Fields Explained:

1. **char name[50];**

  - Represents the name of the student.
  - It is a character array with a size of 50, which can store up to 49 characters plus a null terminator (\0).
2. **int age;**
  - Stores the age of the student as an integer.
3. **float gpa;**
  - Stores the Grade Point Average (GPA) of the student as a floating-point number.

---

3. Purpose of the Structure

The Student structure is designed to hold information about a student, including:

- Their **name** (as a string),
- Their **age** (as an integer),
- Their **GPA** (as a floating-point number).

This structure can be used to create variables or arrays of students and to perform operations like:

- Reading data about a student,
- Modifying student data,
- Printing the student's details.

When passing structures to functions, passing by value involves copying the entire structure, which can be inefficient for large structures. Passing by reference, on the other hand, involves passing a pointer to the structure, allowing direct modification of the original structure without the overhead of copying.

Passing by Value In this method, a copy of the structure is made, and any modifications to the structure within the function do not affect the original structure.

Example no 2:

```
#include <stdio.h>
#include <string.h>
```

```
struct Student {
    char name[50];
    int age;
    float gpa;
};

void updateStudentByValue(struct Student s) {
    s.age = 25; // Only the copy is modified
}

int main() {
    struct Student student1;
    strcpy(student1.name, "Carol White");
    student1.age = 23;
    student1.gpa = 3.5;

    // Call the function with the structure passed by value
    updateStudentByValue(student1);

    // The original structure remains unchanged
    printf("Name: %s\n", student1.name);
    printf("Age: %d\n", student1.age); // Still 23
    printf("GPA: %.2f\n", student1.gpa);

    return 0;
}
```

OUTPUT

```
Name: Carol White
Age: 23
GPA: 3.50
```

This C program demonstrates **passing a structure by value** to a function and highlights how modifications made to the structure inside the function do not affect the original structure.

Code Explanation

1. **Structure Definition**

```
struct Student {
    char name[50];
    int age;
    float gpa;
};
```

- A structure Student is defined with three members:
    - name: A character array to hold the name.
    - age: An integer for the student's age.
    - gpa: A float for the student's grade point average.

2. **updateStudentByValue Function**

```
void updateStudentByValue(struct Student s) {
    s.age = 25; // Only the copy is modified
}
```

- The function accepts a Student structure as a parameter, passed **by value**.
- Modifies the age field of the **local copy** of the structure (s).

3. **Main Function**

```
struct Student student1;
strcpy(student1.name, "Carol White");
student1.age = 23;
student1.gpa = 3.5;
```

- An instance of Student, student1, is created and initialized:
    - name is set to "Carol White".
    - age is set to 23.
    - gpa is set to 3.5.

```
updateStudentByValue(student1);
```

- The student1 structure is passed to the updateStudentByValue function **by value**.
    - Inside the function, a **copy** of student1 is created (s), and any modifications made to s do not affect the original student1.

4. **Output**

```
printf("Name: %s\n", student1.name);
printf("Age: %d\n", student1.age); // Still 23
printf("GPA: %.2f\n", student1.gpa);
```

- The program prints the original values of student1.
- Since the age of student1 is not modified by the function, it remains 23.

Key Takeaways

1. **Pass-by-Value in C**
    - When you pass a structure by value to a function, the function works with a **copy** of the structure. Changes made to this copy do not affect the original structure.
2. **Behavior Demonstrated**
    - Inside updateStudentByValue, the age is updated to 25, but this change applies only to the local copy s.
    - The original student1 remains unchanged after the function call.
3. **Output of the Program**

```
Name: Carol White
Age: 23
GPA: 3.50
```

- Age remains 23 because the function modifies only the copy, not the original instance.

Passing by Reference In this method, a pointer to the structure is passed, allowing the function to modify the original structure.

Example:

```
#include <stdio.h>
#include <string.h>

struct Student {
    char name[50];
    int age;
    float gpa;
};

void updateStudentByReference(struct Student *s) {
    s->age = 25; // The original structure is modified
}

int main() {
    struct Student student1;
    strcpy(student1.name, "Carol White");
    student1.age = 23;
    student1.gpa = 3.5;

    // Call the function with the structure passed by
reference
    updateStudentByReference(&student1);

    // The original structure is modified
    printf("Name: %s\n", student1.name);
    printf("Age: %d\n", student1.age); // Now 25
    printf("GPA: %.2f\n", student1.gpa);

    return 0;
```

```
}
```

OUTPUT
Name: Carol White
Age: 25
GPA: 3.50

This C program demonstrates how to modify a structure by passing it as a reference to a function. Here's a detailed breakdown:

Code Breakdown

Structure Definition

```
struct Student {
    char name[50];
    int age;
    float gpa;
};
```

- A structure Student is defined with three fields:
  - name (a string with up to 50 characters)
  - age (an integer)
  - gpa (a floating-point number).

Function to Update the Structure

```
void updateStudentByReference(struct Student *s) {
    s->age = 25; // The original structure is modified
}
```

- The function updateStudentByReference takes a pointer to a Student structure as its parameter (struct Student *s).
- The -> operator is used to access the structure's members through the pointer s.
- In this case, the age member is updated to 25.

Main Function

```
int main() {
    struct Student student1;
    strcpy(student1.name, "Carol White");
    student1.age = 23;
    student1.gpa = 3.5;
```

- A Student structure named student1 is declared and initialized:
    - name is set to "Carol White" using strcpy.
    - age is set to 23.
    - gpa is set to 3.5.

Passing the Structure to the Function

```
updateStudentByReference(&student1);
```

- The address of student1 (&student1) is passed to updateStudentByReference.
- Inside the function, the pointer s points to student1.
- Modifications made to s inside the function directly affect the original student1 in memory.

Printing the Modified Structure

```
printf("Name: %s\n", student1.name);
printf("Age: %d\n", student1.age); // Now 25
printf("GPA: %.2f\n", student1.gpa);
```

- After the function call, student1.age is updated to 25 (as modified by updateStudentByReference).
- The program prints the updated age along with the name and gpa, which remain unchanged.

Key Concepts Illustrated

1. **Passing by Reference**
   - By passing the structure's address to the function, changes inside the function persist outside of it.
2. **Pointer Dereferencing**
   - The -> operator is used to access members of a structure through a pointer.
3. **Structure Modification**
   - The program demonstrates how to modify specific members of a structure by reference.

Output

When you run the program, the output will be:

```
Name: Carol White
Age: 25
GPA: 3.50
```

This confirms that the structure was successfully modified by the updateStudentByReference function.

Complex Use Cases of Structures

Example: Inventory Management System

In an inventory management system, you might need to store information about various items, including their name, ID, price, and quantity. Using structures helps in organizing this data effectively.

Example:

```
#include <stdio.h>
#include <string.h>

// Define a structure to represent an item
struct Item {
    int id;
    char name[50];
    float price;
```

```
    int quantity;
};

// Function to display an item's information
void displayItem(struct Item item) {
    printf("ID: %d\n", item.id);
    printf("Name: %s\n", item.name);
    printf("Price: %.2f\n", item.price);
    printf("Quantity: %d\n", item.quantity);
}

int main() {
    struct Item item1, item2;

    // Initialize the first item
    item1.id = 1;
    strcpy(item1.name, "Laptop");
    item1.price = 999.99;
    item1.quantity = 10;

    // Initialize the second item
    item2.id = 2;
    strcpy(item2.name, "Mouse");
    item2.price = 25.50;
    item2.quantity = 50;

    // Display items' information
    displayItem(item1);
    displayItem(item2);

    return 0;
}
```

OUTPUT
ID: 1
Name: Laptop
Price: 999.99
Quantity: 10

```
ID: 2
Name: Mouse
Price: 25.50
Quantity: 50
```

This C program demonstrates the use of structures to manage and display information about items. Here's an explanation of the program's components:

1. Structure Definition

```
struct Item {
    int id;
    char name[50];
    float price;
    int quantity;
};
```

- A structure Item is defined to represent an item's information.
- **Members**:
    - id: an integer to store the item's unique identifier.
    - name: a character array (string) to store the item's name, with a maximum length of 49 characters (50 includes the null terminator).
    - price: a floating-point number to store the item's price.
    - quantity: an integer to store the item's quantity.

2. Function to Display Item Information

```
void displayItem(struct Item item) {
    printf("ID: %d\n", item.id);
    printf("Name: %s\n", item.name);
    printf("Price: %.2f\n", item.price);
    printf("Quantity: %d\n", item.quantity);
}
```

- This function takes a structure of type Item as an argument.
- It prints the details of the passed item using formatted output:
    - %.2f ensures the price is displayed with two decimal places.

3. Main Function

Variable Declarations

```
struct Item item1, item2;
```

- Two variables, item1 and item2, are declared to hold information about two items.

Initialization

```
item1.id = 1;
strcpy(item1.name, "Laptop");
item1.price = 999.99;
item1.quantity = 10;

item2.id = 2;
strcpy(item2.name, "Mouse");
item2.price = 25.50;
item2.quantity = 50;
```

- The members of item1 and item2 are initialized.
- strcpy is used to assign strings to the name field (since direct assignment like item1.name = "Laptop" is not valid for arrays).

Display Items

```
displayItem(item1);
displayItem(item2);
```

- The displayItem function is called twice, once for

each item, to display their information.

Output

When the program is run, it produces the following output:

```
ID: 1
Name: Laptop
Price: 999.99
Quantity: 10
ID: 2
Name: Mouse
Price: 25.50
Quantity: 50
```

Key Points

1. **Encapsulation**: The struct Item groups related data into a single entity, making it easier to manage.
2. **Reusability**: The displayItem function can be reused for any Item object.
3. **Modularity**: Separation of concerns between structure definition, initialization, and display logic.

This program effectively demonstrates a basic use case of structures in C programming.

Memory Sharing and Efficiency

Unions are useful when you need to store different types of data in the same memory location but not simultaneously. This can save memory when you have multiple data types but only one is used at a time.

Example: Variant Data Type

In some applications, you might need a variable that can hold different types of data. A union can be used to define such a variable.

Example:

```
#include <stdio.h>
#include <string.h>
```

```
// Define a union to store variant data types
union Variant {
    int i;
    float f;
    char str[20];
};

int main() {
    union Variant var;

    var.i = 10;
    printf("var.i: %d\n", var.i);

    var.f = 220.5;
    printf("var.f: %.1f\n", var.f);

    strcpy(var.str, "C Programming");
    printf("var.str: %s\n", var.str);

    // Note: Only one member can hold a value at a time.
The previous value is overwritten.

    return 0;
}
```

OUTPUT
var.i: 10
var.f: 220.5
var.str: C Programming

This program demonstrates the use of a **union** in C programming. A **union** is a special data type where all members share the same memory location. This means that only one member of the union can contain a value at any given time, and assigning a new value to one member overwrites the data in the other members.

Code Breakdown:

1. Defining a union

```
union Variant {
    int i;
    float f;
    char str[20];
};
```

- A union named Variant is defined.
- It can hold:
    - An integer (int i),
    - A floating-point number (float f),
    - A string (char str[20]).
- **Key Property**: All members share the same memory. The size of the union will be equal to the size of its largest member.

2. Variable declaration

```
union Variant var;
```

- A variable var of type union Variant is declared.

3. Assigning and accessing values

```
var.i = 10;
printf("var.i: %d\n", var.i);
```

- The integer member i is assigned the value 10.
- The value is printed: var.i: 10.

```
var.f = 220.5;
printf("var.f: %.1f\n", var.f);
```

- The floating-point member f is assigned the value 220.5.
- The value is printed: var.f: 220.5.
- **Important**: Assigning a value to f overwrites the

value in i because they share the same memory.

```
strcpy(var.str, "C Programming");
printf("var.str: %s\n", var.str);
```

- The string member str is assigned "C Programming" using strcpy.
- The value is printed: var.str: C Programming.
- **Important**: Assigning a value to str overwrites the previous value in f.

4. Union property

- Only **one member can store a valid value at a time**.
- Assigning a value to one member **invalidates** the values of other members because they overlap in memory.

5. Output

The program will produce:

```
var.i: 10
var.f: 220.5
var.str: C Programming
```

However:

- After var.f is set, the value of var.i becomes invalid.
- After var.str is set, the value of var.f becomes invalid.

This behavior highlights the memory-sharing nature of unions.

Practical Applications of Unions:

- Used in situations where a variable may hold multiple types of data, but only one at a time.
- Often used in low-level programming, e.g., working with hardware registers or creating variant data structures like tagged unions in protocols.

Advanced Use Cases and Examples

Example: Union with Structures for Efficient Memory Usage

A common use case for unions is when combined with structures to create a flexible and memory-efficient data type.

Example: Packet Header for Networking

In networking, you might need a packet header that can store different types of headers (e.g., TCP, UDP) in the same memory location.

Example:

```
#include <stdio.h>

// Define structures for different header types
struct TCPHeader {
    unsigned short sourcePort;
    unsigned short destPort;
    unsigned int sequenceNumber;
    unsigned int ackNumber;
    unsigned char offset;
    unsigned char reserved;
    unsigned char flags;
    unsigned short window;
    unsigned short checksum;
    unsigned short urgentPointer;
};

struct UDPHeader {
    unsigned short sourcePort;
    unsigned short destPort;
    unsigned short length;
    unsigned short checksum;
};

// Define a union to hold either a TCP or UDP header
union PacketHeader {
    struct TCPHeader tcp;
```

```
    struct UDPHeader udp;
};

// Define a structure to represent a packet
struct Packet {
    unsigned int sourceIP;
    unsigned int destIP;
    union PacketHeader header; // Union member
    unsigned char protocol; // Protocol type (e.g., TCP or
UDP)
};

int main() {
    struct Packet pkt;

    // Initialize a TCP packet
    pkt.sourceIP = 0xC0A80001; // 192.168.0.1
    pkt.destIP = 0xC0A80002; // 192.168.0.2
    pkt.protocol = 6; // TCP

    pkt.header.tcp.sourcePort = 80;
    pkt.header.tcp.destPort = 8080;
    pkt.header.tcp.sequenceNumber = 1;
    pkt.header.tcp.ackNumber = 0;
    pkt.header.tcp.offset = 5;
    pkt.header.tcp.flags = 2; // SYN
    pkt.header.tcp.window = 1024;
    pkt.header.tcp.checksum = 0;
    pkt.header.tcp.urgentPointer = 0;

    printf("TCP Packet: \n");
    printf("Source IP: %x\n", pkt.sourceIP);
    printf("Destination IP: %x\n", pkt.destIP);
    printf("Source Port: %d\n", pkt.header.tcp.sourcePort);
    printf("Destination Port: %d\n",
pkt.header.tcp.destPort);
```

```
    return 0;
}
```

OUTPUT

```
TCP Packet:
Source IP: c0a80001
Destination IP: c0a80002
Source Port: 80
Destination Port: 8080
```

Explanation

In this example, the Packet structure uses a union to store either a TCP header or a UDP header, based on the protocol type. This approach is memory-efficient because the memory allocated for the union is the size of its largest member, ensuring no wasted space when storing different headers.

This program is a C implementation designed to represent network packets, specifically TCP and UDP packets, using structures, unions, and basic protocol properties. Below is a detailed explanation of each component and the overall program:

Key Components:

1. **Structures for TCP and UDP Headers:**
    - **struct TCPHeader:** Represents the key fields of a TCP (Transmission Control Protocol) header. It includes fields like sourcePort, destPort, sequenceNumber, etc., all of which are essential in establishing and maintaining a TCP connection.
    - **struct UDPHeader:** Represents the key fields of a UDP (User Datagram Protocol) header. UDP has fewer fields compared to TCP, primarily for simplicity and speed.
2. **Union for Packet Header:**
    - **union PacketHeader:** This union allows a packet to contain either a TCP header or

a UDP header but not both simultaneously. It optimizes memory usage by reusing the same memory location for different header types.

3. **Packet Structure:**
   - **struct Packet:** Represents an entire packet and includes:
     - sourceIP and destIP (source and destination IP addresses).
     - header (the union for the packet header, either TCP or UDP).
     - protocol (to specify whether the packet is TCP or UDP).
4. **Main Function:**
   - Initializes a Packet instance (pkt) as a TCP packet.
   - Sets its fields (e.g., sourceIP, destIP, and TCP-specific fields like sourcePort, destPort).
   - Prints out the details of the packet.

Line-by-Line Breakdown:

Structure Definitions:

```
struct TCPHeader { /* Fields in a TCP header */ };
struct UDPHeader { /* Fields in a UDP header */ };
```

- These structures define the data layout for TCP and UDP headers, matching their real-world specifications.

Union for Headers:

```
union PacketHeader {
    struct TCPHeader tcp;
    struct UDPHeader udp;
};
```

- Ensures that a packet contains either a TCP header or

a UDP header but uses only enough memory for the larger of the two.

Packet Structure:

```
struct Packet {
    unsigned int sourceIP;
    unsigned int destIP;
    union PacketHeader header;
    unsigned char protocol;
};
```

- Combines the IP addresses, protocol type, and the packet's header into one unified structure.

Initialization:

```
pkt.sourceIP = 0xC0A80001; // 192.168.0.1
pkt.destIP = 0xC0A80002; // 192.168.0.2
pkt.protocol = 6; // TCP
```

- Initializes the source and destination IPs in hexadecimal format (common in networking).
- Sets protocol to 6, which corresponds to TCP in the Internet Protocol.

TCP Header Initialization:

```
pkt.header.tcp.sourcePort = 80;
pkt.header.tcp.destPort = 8080;
pkt.header.tcp.sequenceNumber = 1;
pkt.header.tcp.flags = 2; // SYN
```

- Fills in the fields of the TCP header (e.g., source/destination ports, sequence number, and control flags).

Printing Packet Details:

```
printf("Source IP: %x\n", pkt.sourceIP);
```

```
printf("Destination Port: %d\n", pkt.header.tcp.destPort);
```

- Displays the key details of the TCP packet using printf.

Output:

When you run the program, it initializes a TCP packet with the specified fields and prints:

```
TCP Packet:
Source IP: c0a80001
Destination IP: c0a80002
Source Port: 80
Destination Port: 8080
```

Key Concepts Highlighted:

1. **Use of Unions:** Demonstrates efficient memory management when handling different packet types.
2. **Networking Basics:** Encodes and prints common fields used in TCP/IP networking.
3. **Bitwise Fields:** Flags in TCP headers are often handled using bitwise operations, though this program simplifies it with a single byte.

This program forms the foundation for understanding network protocol representation in low-level programming.

Complex Nested Structures and Use Cases

Nested structures can represent highly complex data in an organized manner. This is particularly useful in applications such as database systems, graphical user interfaces (GUIs), and simulation models.

Example: University Database

Consider a university database that stores information about students, courses, and enrollments.

Example:

```
#include <stdio.h>
#include <string.h>

// Define a structure to represent a course
struct Course {
    char courseID[10];
    char courseName[100];
    int credits;
};

// Define a structure to represent an enrollment
struct Enrollment {
    struct Course course;
    char grade[2];
};

// Define a structure to represent a student
struct Student {
    char studentID[10];
    char name[50];
    int year;
    struct Enrollment enrollments[10]; // Array of nested
structures
};

int main() {
    struct Student student1;

    // Initialize the student
    strcpy(student1.studentID, "S12345");
    strcpy(student1.name, "John Doe");
    student1.year = 2;

    // Initialize the enrollments
    strcpy(student1.enrollments[0].course.courseID,
"CSE101");
    strcpy(student1.enrollments[0].course.courseName,
```

```
"Introduction to Computer Science");
    student1.enrollments[0].course.credits = 3;
    strcpy(student1.enrollments[0].grade, "A");

    strcpy(student1.enrollments[1].course.courseID,
"MAT201");
    strcpy(student1.enrollments[1].course.courseName,
"Calculus II");
    student1.enrollments[1].course.credits = 4;
    strcpy(student1.enrollments[1].grade, "B");

    // Print the student's information
    printf("Student ID: %s\n", student1.studentID);
    printf("Name: %s\n", student1.name);
    printf("Year: %d\n", student1.year);

    // Print details of courses the student is enrolled in
    printf("\nEnrollments:\n");
    for (int i = 0; i < 2; i++) { // Loop through enrollments
(adjusted to the initialized count)
        printf("  Course ID: %s\n",
student1.enrollments[i].course.courseID);
        printf("  Course Name: %s\n",
student1.enrollments[i].course.courseName);
        printf("  Credits: %d\n",
student1.enrollments[i].course.credits);
        printf("  Grade: %s\n",
student1.enrollments[i].grade);
        printf("\n");
    }

    return 0;
}
```

OUTPUT
Student ID: S12345
Name: John Doe
Year: 2

```
Enrollments:
  Course ID: CSE101
  Course Name: Introduction to Computer Science
  Credits: 3
  Grade: A

  Course ID: MAT201
  Course Name: Calculus II
  Credits: 4
  Grade: B
```

This C program demonstrates the use of **nested structures** to organize data for a student and their course enrollments. Here's a detailed explanation of each part of the code:

---

1. Defining the Structures

struct Course

- Represents a course.
- Contains:
  - courseID: A string for the course identifier.
  - courseName: A string for the course name.
  - credits: An integer for the number of credits the course carries.

struct Enrollment

- Represents an enrollment in a course.
- Contains:
  - course: A struct Course to hold details of the enrolled course.
  - grade: A string to store the grade achieved in the course.

struct Student

- Represents a student.
- Contains:
  - studentID: A string for the student's ID.

  - name: A string for the student's name.
  - year: An integer representing the year the student is currently in.
  - enrollments: An array of struct Enrollment to hold the list of courses the student is enrolled in, up to 10 courses.

---

2. main() Function

Initializing the student1 Structure

- student1 is declared as a struct Student.
- The fields of student1 are initialized:
  - studentID is set to "S12345".
  - name is set to "John Doe".
  - year is set to 2.

Initializing Enrollments

- Two enrollments are added for student1:
  - **First Enrollment (CSE101)**
    - Course ID: "CSE101"
    - Course Name: "Introduction to Computer Science"
    - Credits: 3
    - Grade: "A"
  - **Second Enrollment (MAT201)**
    - Course ID: "MAT201"
    - Course Name: "Calculus II"
    - Credits: 4
    - Grade: "B"

Printing Student Information

- Basic student details are printed:
  - studentID, name, and year.

Printing Enrollment Details

- A loop iterates through the enrollments array to print details of each enrolled course:

- Course ID, Course Name, Credits, and Grade.

Key Features and Concepts

1. **Nested Structures**:
   - struct Student contains an array of struct Enrollment.
   - struct Enrollment contains a nested struct Course.
2. **Initialization**:
   - Strings are initialized using strcpy.
   - Integer fields are directly assigned values.
3. **Array of Structures**:
   - The enrollments array stores multiple enrollments for the student.
   - A fixed size of 10 is used for demonstration.
4. **Loop for Iteration**:
   - The for loop iterates over the first 2 enrollments (only these are initialized).

How to Extend This Program

- Add more enrollments to the array and adjust the loop limit accordingly.
- Use dynamic allocation if the number of enrollments varies.
- Add input functions to make the program interactive for real-time data entry.

Here is a tabular comparison of Structure and Union in C:

Feature	Structure	Union
Definition	A structure is a user-defined data type that groups related variables of different types under one name.	A union is a user-defined data type where all members share the same memory location.
Memory Allocation	Each member of a	All members share

	structure has its own memory allocation.	the same memory space, so the size of the union is determined by its largest member.
Size	The size of a structure is the sum of the sizes of all its members (plus any padding).	The size of a union is the size of its largest member.
Accessing Members	All members can be accessed and stored simultaneously.	Only one member can hold a value at any given time; assigning a value to one member overwrites the others.
Use Case	Used when you need to group related data and access all members independently.	Used when you need to store multiple types of data in the same memory location but only one type at a time.
Initialization	All members can be initialized independently.	Only the first member can be initialized at the time of declaration.
Example	**c\nstruct Example {\n int a;\n float b;\n};\n**	**c\nunion Example {\n int a;\n float b;\n};\n**
Flexibility	More flexible as all members can store data simultaneously.	Less flexible since only one member can store data at a time.
Memory Efficiency	Less memory-efficient compared to a union.	More memory-efficient when you need to use only one member at a time.
Overhead	More overhead due to separate memory allocation for each member.	Minimal overhead as all members share the same memory.

FILE HANDLING IN C

File handling is a critical aspect of C programming, allowing developers to read from and write to files for storing data permanently. This functionality is provided through a set of functions defined in the <stdio.h> library.

---

1. Opening, Reading, and Writing to Files

To perform file operations, a **file pointer** (FILE *) is used. This pointer refers to a file structure that holds information about the file being accessed.

Opening a File (fopen)

The fopen function opens a file and returns a pointer to the FILE structure. Its syntax is:

```
FILE *fopen(const char *filename, const char *mode);
```

- filename: Name or path of the file.
- mode: Specifies the type of operation.

File Modes

The most commonly used file modes are:

Mode	Description
r	Open an existing file for reading. File must exist.
w	Open a file for writing. If the file exists, it is overwritten; otherwise, created.
a	Open a file for appending data. Creates the file if it does not exist.
r+	Open a file for both reading and writing. File must exist.

w+	Open a file for reading and writing. Overwrites if the file exists; creates otherwise.
a+	Open a file for reading and appending.

Closing a File (fclose)

Every opened file must be closed using the fclose function to free system resources:

```
int fclose(FILE *stream);
```

---

2. Reading and Writing

Reading from a File (fread and fgets)

- fgets: Reads a string from the file.
- fread: Reads binary data.

Writing to a File (fprintf, fwrite)

- fprintf: Writes formatted data to a file.
- fwrite: Writes binary data.

Example: Reading and Writing Text Files

```
#include <stdio.h>

int main() {
    FILE *file;

    // Writing to a file
    file = fopen("example.txt", "w");
    if (file == NULL) {
        printf("Error opening file.\n");
        return 1;
    }
    fprintf(file, "Hello, file handling in C!\n");
    fclose(file);

    // Reading from a file
    file = fopen("example.txt", "r");
    if (file == NULL) {
```

```
        printf("Error opening file.\n");
        return 1;
    }
    char line[100];
    while (fgets(line, sizeof(line), file) != NULL) {
        printf("%s", line);
    }
    fclose(file);

    return 0;
}
```

The given C program demonstrates basic file handling operations, such as writing to and reading from a file.

Here's a breakdown of the program:

1. **Opening the file for writing** (fopen("example.txt", "w")):
   - The fopen() function is used to open a file. In this case, "example.txt" is opened in "write" mode ("w"). If the file doesn't exist, it will be created. If it already exists, its contents will be erased.
   - If the file fails to open (e.g., due to permission issues or incorrect path), fopen() returns NULL, and an error message is printed, terminating the program with return 1.
2. **Writing to the file** (fprintf(file, "Hello, file handling in C!\n")):
   - The fprintf() function writes formatted text to the file, similar to printf() but for files. In this case, it writes "Hello, file handling in C!" followed by a newline to example.txt.
3. **Closing the file after writing** (fclose(file)):
   - After writing to the file, fclose() is called to close the file and release the associated resources.

4. **Opening the file for reading** (fopen("example.txt", "r")):
    - The file "example.txt" is opened again, but this time in "read" mode ("r"). If the file does not exist or cannot be opened for reading, it returns NULL, and an error message is printed.
5. **Reading from the file** (fgets(line, sizeof(line), file)):
    - The fgets() function is used to read a line of text from the file. It reads up to sizeof(line) - 1 characters, storing them in the line array. The function returns NULL when the end of the file is reached.
    - The program prints each line read from the file using printf("%s", line).
6. **Closing the file after reading** (fclose(file)):
    - Once reading is complete, the file is closed with fclose() to free the file pointer.

Summary:

The program first writes a line of text to a file (example.txt) and then reads the file's contents and prints them to the console. File handling functions used:

- fopen(): Opens a file for reading or writing.
- fprintf(): Writes formatted data to a file.
- fgets(): Reads a line from the file.
- fclose(): Closes the file.

---

3. Handling Binary Files

Binary files store data in a binary format, offering faster access and more compact storage compared to text files.

fwrite and fread These functions handle binary data. They write or read data blocks:

```
size_t fwrite(const void *ptr, size_t size, size_t count, FILE
*stream);
```

```
size_t fread(void *ptr, size_t size, size_t count, FILE
*stream);
```

Example: Reading and Writing Binary Files

```
#include <stdio.h>

typedef struct {
    char name[50];
    int age;
} Person;

int main() {
    FILE *file;
    Person person = {"John Doe", 30};

    // Writing binary data
    file = fopen("data.bin", "wb");
    if (file == NULL) {
        printf("Error opening file.\n");
        return 1;
    }
    fwrite(&person, sizeof(Person), 1, file);
    fclose(file);

    // Reading binary data
    file = fopen("data.bin", "rb");
    if (file == NULL) {
        printf("Error opening file.\n");
        return 1;
    }
    Person readPerson;
    fread(&readPerson, sizeof(Person), 1, file);
    fclose(file);

    printf("Name: %s, Age: %d\n", readPerson.name,
readPerson.age);
```

```
    return 0;
}
```

This C program demonstrates how to write and read binary data to and from a file using structures. Here's a step-by-step explanation of what each part does:

1. Structure Definition:

```
typedef struct {
    char name[50];
    int age;
} Person;
```

- A Person structure is defined that contains two fields:
  - name: a character array (string) that can hold up to 50 characters (including the null terminator).
  - age: an integer to store the person's age.

2. Main Function:

```
int main() {
    FILE *file;
    Person person = {"John Doe", 30};
```

- A file pointer file is declared.
- A Person structure person is initialized with the values "John Doe" for the name and 30 for the age.

3. Writing Data to a Binary File:

```
file = fopen("data.bin", "wb");
if (file == NULL) {
    printf("Error opening file.\n");
    return 1;
}
fwrite(&person, sizeof(Person), 1, file);
fclose(file);
```

- The file data.bin is opened in **write-binary** mode ("wb"), which means the file is opened for writing in binary format. If the file cannot be opened (e.g., due to permission issues), an error message is displayed, and the program exits.
- The fwrite function is used to write the contents of the person structure into the file:
    - &person: the address of the person structure (to pass the structure by reference).
    - sizeof(Person): the size of the structure to write.
    - 1: the number of elements to write (in this case, 1 Person structure).
- Finally, the file is closed with fclose(file) to ensure the data is properly written and resources are freed.

4. Reading Data from the Binary File:

```
file = fopen("data.bin", "rb");
if (file == NULL) {
    printf("Error opening file.\n");
    return 1;
}
Person readPerson;
fread(&readPerson, sizeof(Person), 1, file);
fclose(file);
```

- The file data.bin is opened in **read-binary** mode ("rb"), which means the file is opened for reading in binary format. If the file cannot be opened, an error message is displayed, and the program exits.
- A new Person structure readPerson is declared to hold the data read from the file.
- The fread function is used to read the contents of the file into readPerson:

  - &readPerson: the address of the readPerson structure (to store the data).
  - sizeof(Person): the size of the structure to read.
  - 1: the number of elements to read (in this case, 1 Person structure).
- The file is closed with fclose(file) after reading.

5. Displaying the Read Data:

```
printf("Name: %s, Age: %d\n", readPerson.name,
readPerson.age);
```

- The printf function is used to display the name and age fields of the readPerson structure, which were read from the file.

Summary:

- This program demonstrates how to use file handling functions (fopen, fwrite, fread, fclose) to work with binary data in C.
- It writes a structure (Person) to a binary file, reads the structure back from the file, and then prints the contents of the structure.

---

4. File Operations

fseek: Sets the file position to a specific location.

```
int fseek(FILE *stream, long offset, int origin);
```

- origin: SEEK_SET (beginning), SEEK_CUR (current position), or SEEK_END (end).

Example:

```
#include <stdio.h>

int main() {
```

```
    FILE *file = fopen("example.txt", "r");
    if (file == NULL) {
        printf("Error opening file.\n");
        return 1;
    }

    fseek(file, 5, SEEK_SET); // Move to 5th byte from the
beginning
    char ch = fgetc(file);   // Read character at that position
    printf("Character at 6th position: %c\n", ch);

    fclose(file);
    return 0;
}
```

This C program reads a file called example.txt and performs the following operations:

1. **File Opening**:
   - The program attempts to open the file example.txt in **read mode** ("r") using the fopen function.
   - If the file cannot be opened (e.g., if the file doesn't exist), fopen will return NULL, and the program prints an error message and exits with a return value of 1.
2. **fseek Usage**:
   - The fseek(file, 5, SEEK_SET) function moves the file pointer to the 5th byte from the beginning of the file (SEEK_SET specifies that the position is relative to the start of the file).
   - The second argument 5 specifies the offset, so the file pointer is positioned at the 6th byte (since file positions are 0-based, i.e., position 0 is the first byte).
3. **Reading a Character**:
   - The program then uses fgetc(file) to read the character at the current position (which was moved to the 6th byte in the file).

    - The character is stored in the variable ch.

4. **Output**:
    - The program then prints the character at the 6th position in the file using printf. It outputs a message like Character at 6th position: [ch], where [ch] is the character read from the file.
5. **File Closing**:
    - Finally, the file is closed using fclose(file) to release the resources associated with the file.

Example:

The output of the program depends on the contents of the example.txt file.

For example, if the file example.txt contains the following text:

```
Hello, world!
```

The program moves the file pointer to the 6th byte (the comma ,), then reads and prints the character at that position.

Output:

```
Character at 6th position: ,
```

If the file example.txt contains something else, the output would reflect the character at the 6th byte of that file. If the file is smaller than 6 bytes, the program will attempt to read an invalid byte, which may result in undefined behavior or an error, depending on the system and implementation.

---

5. Error Handling in File Operations

File operations can fail, so error handling is essential. Use:

- **ferror**: Checks for an error.
- **perror**: Prints error messages.
- **feof**: Detects the end of a file.

Example: Error Handling

```
#include <stdio.h>

int main() {
    FILE *file = fopen("nonexistent.txt", "r");
    if (file == NULL) {
        perror("Error opening file");
        return 1;
    }

    char line[100];
    if (fgets(line, sizeof(line), file) == NULL) {
        if (feof(file)) {
            printf("End of file reached.\n");
        } else if (ferror(file)) {
            perror("Error reading file");
        }
    }

    fclose(file);
    return 0;
}
```

This C program attempts to open a file named "nonexistent.txt" for reading and handle any potential errors that occur during file opening or reading. Here's a step-by-step explanation of the code:

1. Opening the File:

```
FILE *file = fopen("nonexistent.txt", "r");
```

- The program uses fopen to try to open the file "nonexistent.txt" in **read mode** ("r").
- If the file exists, the pointer file will point to the file; if it does not exist or there is any other issue, fopen will return NULL.

2. Error Handling for File Opening:

```
if (file == NULL) {
```

```
    perror("Error opening file");
    return 1;
}
```

- If fopen fails (i.e., file is NULL), the program enters this if block.
- The perror function prints a system error message that corresponds to the reason why the file couldn't be opened (such as "No such file or directory").
- The program then returns 1, which indicates an error, and the execution ends.

3. Reading the File:

```
char line[100];
if (fgets(line, sizeof(line), file) == NULL) {
```

- The program attempts to read a line from the file using fgets, storing the content into the line array.
- fgets reads a string from the file until a newline character or the end of the file is encountered. It also limits the number of characters read to the size of line (100 characters in this case).
- If fgets returns NULL, it indicates that no line was read, which could be due to the end of the file (EOF) or an error.

4. Error Handling for Reading the File:

```
if (feof(file)) {
    printf("End of file reached.\n");
} else if (ferror(file)) {
    perror("Error reading file");
}
```

- If fgets returns NULL, the program checks whether

the end of the file (EOF) has been reached using feof.

- If feof(file) is true, it prints "End of file reached." indicating that there was no more content to read.
- If ferror(file) is true, it indicates a read error (e.g., a hardware issue), and perror is used to print the error message.

5. Closing the File:

```
fclose(file);
```

- Regardless of whether the reading was successful or not, the program calls fclose to close the file and release any resources associated with it.

6. Program Termination:

```
return 0;
```

- If the file was opened successfully and the program completes its operations, it returns 0, indicating successful execution.

Summary of Possible Scenarios:

- If "nonexistent.txt" doesn't exist, the program will print an error message from perror and terminate.
- If the file exists but is empty, fgets will return NULL, and the program will print "End of file reached.".
- If there is an error while reading (e.g., disk failure), perror("Error reading file") will be printed.

Summary of Key Functions:

Function	Purpose
fopen	Opens a file
fclose	Closes a file

fwrite	Writes binary data
fread	Reads binary data
fseek	Moves the file pointer
fgets	Reads a line of text
fprintf	Writes formatted text
ferror	Checks for an error
perror	Prints an error message

Function	Purpose	Usage	Return Value	Common Use Case
fopen()	Opens a file for reading, writing, or appending.	FILE *fopen(const char *filename, const char *mode);	Returns a file pointer (FILE *) on success, NULL on failure.	Opening a file for reading, writing, or appending.
fclose()	Closes an open file.	int fclose(FILE *stream);	Returns 0 on success, EOF on error.	Closing a file after reading/writing operations are done.
fwrite()	Writes data to a file.	size_t fwrite(const void *ptr, size_t size, size_t count, FILE *stream);	Returns the number of items successfully written.	Writing binary data to a file.
fread()	Reads data from a file.	size_t fread(void *ptr, size_t size, size_t count, FILE *stream);	Returns the number of items successfully read.	Reading binary data from a file.
fseek()	Moves the file pointer to a specific location in a file.	int fseek(FILE *stream, long offset, int whence);	Returns 0 on success, non-zero on error.	Moving the file pointer (e.g., to read from a specific position).
fgets()	Reads a line from a file.	char *fgets(char *str, int n, FILE *stream);	Returns the string on success, NULL on error or EOF.	Reading a line of text from a file.
fprintf()	Writes formatted text to a file (similar to printf(), but to a file).	int fprintf(FILE *stream, const char *format, ...);	Returns the number of characters written, or a negative value on error.	Writing formatted data to a file.
ferror()	Checks for errors in a file stream.	int ferror(FILE *stream);	Returns non-zero if an error occurred, 0 if no error.	Checking if an error occurred during reading or writing.
perror()	Prints a descriptive error message to stderr based on the global errno.	void perror(const char *s);	No return value.	Printing an error message based on errno.

Key Differences:

- **fopen() vs fclose()**: fopen() is used to open a file, while fclose() is used to close it.
- **fwrite() vs fread()**: fwrite() is used for writing data to a file, while fread() is used for reading data.

- **fseek() vs fgets()**: fseek() changes the position of the file pointer, whereas fgets() reads a line from the file.
- **fprintf() vs fwrite()**: fprintf() writes formatted text to a file, while fwrite() writes raw binary data.
- **ferror() vs perror()**: ferror() checks for errors in a file stream, while perror() prints a human-readable error message based on error.

DYNAMIC MEMORY ALLOCATION IN C

Dynamic memory allocation plays a crucial role in C programming for managing memory effectively during runtime. In contrast to static memory allocation, where the size of memory is known at compile-time, dynamic memory allocation provides flexibility by allocating memory at runtime. This is especially important for creating data structures like linked lists, dynamic arrays, and trees, where the size is not known in advance.

The primary dynamic memory allocation functions in C are:

malloc()

calloc()

realloc()

free()

1. malloc() – Memory Allocation

The malloc() function is used to allocate a block of memory of a specified size. It does not initialize the memory, which means the contents of the allocated memory block are undetermined (garbage values).

Detailed Syntax:

```
void *malloc(size_t size);
```

- size: The number of bytes to allocate for the memory block.

- Returns: A pointer of type void * (generic pointer), which can be cast to the desired type (e.g., int *, char *, etc.). If memory allocation fails, it returns NULL.

Extended Example with Error Handling:

```
#include <stdio.h>
#include <stdlib.h>
#include <stdint.h>
int main() {
    int *arr;
    int n = 100000;  // Requesting a large block of memory

    // Check for potential overflow in size calculation
    if (n > 0 && (n > (SIZE_MAX / sizeof(int)))) {
        fprintf(stderr, "Size overflow, cannot allocate
memory! Exiting...\n");
        return 1;
    }

    // Allocating memory for 100,000 integers
    arr = (int*) malloc(n * sizeof(int));
    if (arr == NULL) {  // Memory allocation failed
        fprintf(stderr, "Memory allocation failed! Exiting...
\n");
        return 1;  // Return a non-zero value to indicate
failure
    }

    // Initialize the memory block
    for (int i = 0; i < n; i++) {
        arr[i] = i;
    }

    // Do something with arr
    // Example: Print first 5 values for checking
    for (int i = 0; i < 5; i++) {
        printf("arr[%d] = %d\n", i, arr[i]);
```

```
    }

    free(arr); // Free the allocated memory when done
    arr = NULL; // Set the pointer to NULL to avoid
dangling pointer

    return 0;
}
```

OUTPUT
arr[0] = 0
arr[1] = 1
arr[2] = 2
arr[3] = 3
arr[4] = 4

This C program demonstrates dynamic memory allocation using malloc and proper memory management with free. Let's break down the code step by step:

1. Header Files

```
#include <stdio.h>
#include <stdlib.h>
```

- stdio.h: Used for input/output operations like printing to the console (printf, fprintf).
- stdlib.h: Provides the functions for memory management (malloc, free), and program termination (exit).

2. Declaring the Array and Size

```
int *arr;
int n = 100000; // Requesting a large block of memory
```

- arr is declared as a pointer to int. This pointer will be used to point to the dynamically allocated array.
- n is set to 100000, representing the number of elements in the array.

3. Memory Allocation with malloc

```
arr = (int*) malloc(n * sizeof(int)); // Allocates memory for
100,000 integers
```

- malloc(n * sizeof(int)) allocates memory for n integers. The sizeof(int) ensures that the correct amount of memory is allocated for each int element.
- The malloc function returns a pointer to the allocated memory, which is then cast to an int* (pointer to integer), and stored in arr.

4. Error Handling for Memory Allocation

```
if (arr == NULL) { // Memory allocation failed
    fprintf(stderr, "Memory allocation failed! Exiting...\n");
    return 1; // Return a non-zero value to indicate failure
}
```

- malloc returns NULL if memory allocation fails. This block checks if arr is NULL and prints an error message to the standard error stream (stderr).
- If the allocation fails, the program exits with a return value of 1, indicating failure.

5. Initializing the Array

```
for (int i = 0; i < n; i++) {
    arr[i] = i;
}
```

- A for loop is used to initialize each element of the array. Each element arr[i] is set to its index value (i), so arr[0] = 0, arr[1] = 1, and so on up to arr[99999] = 99999.

6. Memory Cleanup

```
free(arr); // Free the allocated memory when done
```

- After the array is no longer needed, the free function is called to release the dynamically allocated memory. This prevents memory leaks, which occur if memory is allocated but not properly freed.

7. Program Exit

```
return 0;
```

- The program ends by returning 0 to indicate successful completion.

Key Concepts:

- **Dynamic Memory Allocation**: The malloc function allocates memory at runtime based on the size needed (n * sizeof(int)), instead of using a fixed-size array. This is useful when the array size isn't known at compile time.
- **Error Handling**: If memory allocation fails (e.g., due to insufficient system resources), the program handles it by printing an error message and exiting.
- **Memory Management**: It is essential to free dynamically allocated memory using free to avoid memory leaks, which can degrade performance or crash the program.

This program shows basic dynamic memory management in C and ensures proper allocation and deallocation of memory.

Key Insights on malloc():

- Memory allocation failure can happen if the system runs out of memory. Always check the return value of malloc() for NULL to detect allocation failure.
- It's a good practice to check if the allocation succeeds and to handle errors gracefully, particularly when allocating large amounts of memory.

2. calloc() – Contiguous Allocation

Unlike malloc(), the calloc() function initializes the allocated memory to zero. This is particularly useful when allocating memory for structures or arrays where you want to ensure that no garbage values are present. The calloc() function is used to allocate memory for an array of elements. Unlike malloc(), it initializes the memory to zero before returning the pointer. This can be useful in cases where you want to ensure that the memory block is initialized.

Detailed Syntax:

```
void *calloc(size_t num, size_t size);
```

- num: The number of elements.
- size: The size of each element.
- Returns: A pointer to the allocated memory, or NULL if the allocation fails.

Example with calloc() to Handle Arrays of Structures:

```
#include <stdio.h>
#include <stdlib.h>

struct Person {
    char name[100];
    int age;
};

int main() {
    int n = 3;
    struct Person *people;

    // Allocating memory for 3 'Person' structures and
initializing to zero
    people = (struct Person*) calloc(n, sizeof(struct Person));

    if (people == NULL) {
```

```
        fprintf(stderr, "Memory allocation failed!\n");
        return 1;
    }

    // Initialize and print
    for (int i = 0; i < n; i++) {
        snprintf(people[i].name, sizeof(people[i].name),
"Person %d", i + 1);
        people[i].age = 20 + i;
        printf("Name: %s, Age: %d\n", people[i].name,
people[i].age);
    }

    free(people);  // Don't forget to free the memory
    return 0;
}
```

OUTPUT
Name: Person 1, Age: 20
Name: Person 2, Age: 21
Name: Person 3, Age: 22

This C program demonstrates how to dynamically allocate memory for an array of structures and initialize and manipulate the data within them. Here's a detailed breakdown:

1. Structure Definition:

```
struct Person {
    char name[100];
    int age;
};
```

- A structure Person is defined with two members:
    - name is a character array (string) with a size of 100 characters.
    - age is an integer representing the age of the person.

2. Memory Allocation:

```
people = (struct Person*) calloc(n, sizeof(struct Person));
```

- The calloc function is used to allocate memory dynamically for an array of n elements (in this case, 3).
- Each element is of type struct Person, so sizeof(struct Person) gives the memory required for one Person object.
- calloc initializes the allocated memory to zero, which means each Person's name array will be initialized to empty strings, and age will be set to 0.
- If the memory allocation fails, people will be NULL, and the program will print an error message and exit.

3. Initialization and Printing:

```
for (int i = 0; i < n; i++) {
    snprintf(people[i].name, sizeof(people[i].name),
"Person %d", i + 1);
    people[i].age = 20 + i;
    printf("Name: %s, Age: %d\n", people[i].name,
people[i].age);
}
```

- A loop runs n times (3 iterations).
- For each iteration:
    - snprintf is used to safely write the string "Person 1", "Person 2", etc., into the name field of each Person. This ensures the string fits within the name array.
    - The age field is set to 20 + i, so the ages will be 20, 21, and 22 for the 3 people.
- The printf function is used to print the name and age of each person.

4. Freeing Allocated Memory:

```
free(people);
```

- After using the dynamically allocated memory, it's important to free it using free() to avoid memory leaks.

Key Concepts:

- **Dynamic Memory Allocation:** calloc is used for allocating memory at runtime instead of at compile time.
- **Memory Initialization:** calloc also initializes the allocated memory to zero, unlike malloc.
- **Pointer to Struct:** The people pointer is used to reference the dynamically allocated array of struct Person objects.
- **Safety:** snprintf ensures that you don't exceed the size of the name array, avoiding buffer overflow.
- **Memory Deallocation:** free ensures that memory is released when no longer needed

Important Notes:

- **calloc() vs malloc()**: The key difference between calloc() and malloc() is initialization. While malloc() doesn't initialize the allocated memory, calloc() ensures that all memory is set to zero.
- calloc() takes two arguments: the number of elements and the size of each element. In contrast, malloc() takes a single argument for the total number of bytes to allocate.

---

3. realloc() – Reallocation

The realloc() function allows resizing a previously allocated memory block. This is extremely useful when the size of the allocated memory needs to grow or shrink dynamically.

Example:

Imagine a scenario where you initially allocate memory for 5 integers but later need to expand it to hold 10 integers:

```
#include <stdio.h>
#include <stdlib.h>

int main() {
    int *arr;
    int n = 5;

    arr = (int*) malloc(n * sizeof(int));  // Initial allocation
for 5 integers
    if (arr == NULL) {
        fprintf(stderr, "Memory allocation failed!\n");
        return 1;
    }

    // Fill the initial array
    for (int i = 0; i < n; i++) {
        arr[i] = i * 10;
    }

    // Reallocate the memory for 10 integers
    arr = (int*) realloc(arr, 10 * sizeof(int));
    if (arr == NULL) {
        fprintf(stderr, "Reallocation failed!\n");
        return 1;
    }

    // Initialize the new portion of the array
    for (int i = 5; i < 10; i++) {
        arr[i] = i * 10;
    }

    // Print the values after reallocation
    for (int i = 0; i < 10; i++) {
        printf("%d ", arr[i]);
```

```
    }

    free(arr); // Don't forget to free the memory
    return 0;
}
```

OUTPUT
0 10 20 30 40 50 60 70 80 90

This C program demonstrates dynamic memory allocation using malloc and realloc. Here's a step-by-step explanation:

1. Initial Memory Allocation (malloc):

```
arr = (int*) malloc(n * sizeof(int));
```

- malloc is used to allocate memory for n integers (5 integers in this case).
- The sizeof(int) is multiplied by n to allocate enough memory for 5 integers. In this case, n = 5, so the total memory allocated is 5 * sizeof(int).
- The pointer arr holds the address of this dynamically allocated memory.

If memory allocation fails (i.e., the pointer arr is NULL), the program prints an error message and exits with a non-zero value (1).

2. Initializing the Array:

```
for (int i = 0; i < n; i++) {
    arr[i] = i * 10;
}
```

- The program initializes the allocated array with values: 0, 10, 20, 30, 40.
- The loop iterates through the first 5 elements, and each element is assigned a value equal to its index multiplied by 10.

3. Reallocating Memory (realloc):

```
arr = (int*) realloc(arr, 10 * sizeof(int));
```

- The realloc function is used to resize the previously allocated memory. Here, the size is increased to accommodate 10 integers instead of 5.
- The pointer arr is reassigned to the new memory block returned by realloc.

If reallocation fails (i.e., the pointer arr is NULL after realloc), the program prints an error message and exits.

4. Initializing the New Portion of the Array:

```
for (int i = 5; i < 10; i++) {
    arr[i] = i * 10;
}
```

- After reallocation, the array now has space for 10 integers. The new indices (from 5 to 9) are initialized with values 50, 60, 70, 80, 90.
- This step ensures that the newly allocated portion of the array is populated with values.

5. Printing the Array:

```
for (int i = 0; i < 10; i++) {
    printf("%d ", arr[i]);
}
```

- The program prints all 10 values in the array. It will print: 0 10 20 30 40 50 60 70 80 90.

6. Freeing the Allocated Memory:

```
free(arr);
```

- Finally, the memory allocated for the array is freed using the free function to avoid memory leaks. This step ensures that the dynamically allocated memory is returned to the system after its use.

Summary:

- The program allocates memory for 5 integers, initializes them, reallocates memory to accommodate 10 integers, initializes the new elements, prints all elements, and then frees the memory.
- It's important to check whether malloc and realloc were successful, and to always free dynamically allocated memory when it's no longer needed.

Key Insights on realloc():

- **When realloc() succeeds**: It returns a pointer to the new memory block. This pointer might be different from the original pointer if the memory was moved to a different location.
- **When realloc() fails**: It returns NULL, and the original memory block is left untouched. In this case, it's crucial to **not lose the original pointer** before calling realloc().

Handling realloc() safely:

You should store the return value of realloc() in a temporary pointer variable to avoid losing the original memory block if reallocation fails.

```
int *temp = (int*) realloc(arr, 10 * sizeof(int));
if (temp == NULL) {
    free(arr);  // Free the original memory if reallocation
fails
    fprintf(stderr, "Memory reallocation failed!\n");
    return 1;
}
arr = temp;
```

4. free() – Memory Deallocation

The free() function releases previously allocated memory back to the system. After freeing memory, the pointer becomes a **dangling pointer**, which refers to a memory location that has been deallocated and should no longer be accessed. The free() function is used to release memory that was previously allocated dynamically by malloc(), calloc(), or realloc(). Once memory is freed, the pointer becomes a **dangling pointer**, meaning it points to a memory location that is no longer valid.

Detailed Syntax:

```
void free(void *ptr);
```

- ptr: The pointer to the dynamically allocated memory that needs to be deallocated.
- Returns: Nothing (void).

Example:

```
#include <stdio.h>
#include <stdlib.h>

int main() {
    int *arr;

    arr = (int*) malloc(5 * sizeof(int)); // Allocate memory
for 5 integers
    if (arr == NULL) {
        fprintf(stderr, "Memory allocation failed!\n");
        return 1;
    }

    // Use the memory...

    free(arr); // Release memory

    // After free, do not use 'arr' again. It is a dangling
pointer.
```

```
    // Accessing 'arr' after freeing it leads to undefined
behavior.

    return 0;
}
```

This C program demonstrates dynamic memory allocation using malloc() and how to safely release memory using free(). Here's a detailed explanation of the code:

Code Walkthrough:

1. **Header Files**:
    - #include <stdio.h>: This includes the standard input/output library for printing error messages to the console.
    - #include <stdlib.h>: This includes the standard library for memory management functions, such as malloc() and free().
2. **Main Function**:

```
int *arr;
```

- int *arr; declares a pointer arr of type int* that will point to dynamically allocated memory for storing integers.

3. **Memory Allocation**:

```
arr = (int*) malloc(5 * sizeof(int)); // Allocate memory for
5 integers
```

- malloc(5 * sizeof(int)): This allocates memory dynamically for 5 integers. sizeof(int) gives the size of one integer in bytes, so malloc allocates enough space to hold 5 integers.
- (int*) casts the returned void* pointer to an int* pointer so it can be used to store integers.

4. **Memory Allocation Check**:

```
if (arr == NULL) {
```

```
    fprintf(stderr, "Memory allocation failed!\n");
    return 1;
}
```

- After memory allocation, it checks if arr is NULL. If malloc fails to allocate memory (due to insufficient memory or other reasons), it returns NULL. In this case, an error message is printed, and the program exits with a status of 1 to indicate failure.

5. **Memory Usage** (commented):
   - In this section, the program could use the allocated memory (e.g., by assigning values to the array elements), but this part is left empty in the code.
6. **Freeing Memory**:

```
free(arr); // Release memory
```

- The free() function is used to release the dynamically allocated memory back to the operating system. It ensures that the program does not waste memory and prevents memory leaks.

7. **Warning on Dangling Pointer**:
   - After free(arr);, the pointer arr still holds the same memory address, but the memory at that address is now deallocated. This is known as a "dangling pointer."
   - **Important**: Accessing the memory through arr after calling free is undefined behavior and can lead to crashes or unpredictable behavior. To avoid this, you should set arr to NULL after freeing it:

```
arr = NULL;
```

This ensures that further access attempts will be caught, as NULL pointers are easier to check than invalid pointers.

Key Concepts:

- **Dynamic Memory Allocation**: Using malloc to allocate memory during runtime, as opposed to static memory allocation where the memory size is determined at compile time.
- **Memory Management**: It's crucial to free dynamically allocated memory using free() to avoid memory leaks.
- **Dangling Pointer**: After freeing memory, pointers that still reference that memory are considered "dangling" and must not be used. It's best practice to set the pointer to NULL after calling free().

In summary, the program demonstrates allocating and freeing dynamic memory while emphasizing the importance of handling pointers correctly after freeing memory to avoid undefined behavior.

Important Notes on free():

- **Avoid double freeing**: Calling free() twice on the same pointer can cause undefined behavior.
- **Dangling pointers**: After calling free(), the pointer is invalid, and you should avoid using it. A common practice is to set the pointer to NULL after freeing it:

```
free(arr);
arr = NULL;  // Avoid dangling pointer
```

Memory Leaks and How to Avoid Them

A **memory leak** happens when memory is allocated but never deallocated, leading to wasted memory over time. The program may eventually run out of memory if it continually allocates memory without freeing it.

Example of Memory Leak:

```
#include <stdio.h>
#include <stdlib.h>

int main() {
    int *arr;

    arr = (int*) malloc(100 * sizeof(int));  // Allocate
memory
    // Forgot to free memory

    return 0;  // Memory leak occurs because 'arr' was never
freed
}
```

In this C program, a memory leak occurs due to the lack of proper memory deallocation. Here's a step-by-step breakdown of what's happening:

1. **Memory Allocation:**

```
arr = (int*) malloc(100 * sizeof(int));
```

    - The program allocates memory for an array of 100 integers using the malloc function.
    - malloc returns a pointer to the first byte of the allocated memory, which is stored in the arr pointer. Each integer typically requires 4 bytes, so 100 * sizeof(int) allocates memory for 100 integers (400 bytes on most systems).
    - However, the return type of malloc is void*, so it's cast to int* for compatibility with the arr pointer type.

2. **Missing free Function Call:**
    - The program does **not** call the free function to release the allocated memory.
    - When you use malloc, memory is allocated

from the heap, and it remains allocated until the program terminates or it is explicitly freed using free.

- Since free is not called in this program, the allocated memory will not be released, causing a **memory leak**.

3. **Memory Leak:**
   - A **memory leak** occurs when dynamically allocated memory is not properly deallocated. Over time, if this issue persists, it can lead to reduced available memory, which can cause the program or the system to run out of memory.

How to Fix It:

To avoid the memory leak, the program should call free to release the allocated memory before exiting. For example:

```
#include <stdio.h>
#include <stdlib.h>

int main() {
   int *arr;

   arr = (int*) malloc(100 * sizeof(int)); // Allocate
memory

   // Use the allocated memory here

   free(arr); // Free memory to avoid memory leak

   return 0;
}
```

The free(arr) statement deallocates the memory that was allocated by malloc, ensuring no memory is leaked.

Key Points:

- Always free dynamically allocated memory when you're done using it.

- Failing to do so leads to memory leaks, which can cause programs to consume excessive memory over time.

How to Avoid Memory Leaks:

- **Always call free() when you're done with dynamically allocated memory**.
- **Use memory management tools**: Programs like **Valgrind** can help detect memory leaks by checking for memory that is allocated but never freed.
- **Set pointers to NULL** after freeing memory to avoid accidental dereferencing.

Memory Fragmentation and Strategies for Managing It

Memory fragmentation can be a serious problem, especially when dealing with many allocations and deallocations over time. Fragmentation occurs when free memory becomes scattered in small chunks that are too small to be used for large allocations.

Types of Fragmentation:

1. **External Fragmentation**: Occurs when there is enough total free memory but it's divided into small, non-contiguous blocks, making it impossible to allocate large contiguous blocks.
2. **Internal Fragmentation**: Occurs when allocated memory is larger than needed, wasting space inside the allocated blocks.

Strategies for Managing Fragmentation:

- **Memory pools**: A memory pool is a pre-allocated block of memory that is divided into smaller chunks for use by the program. This minimizes fragmentation since memory is allocated from a contiguous block.
- **Efficient use of realloc()**: By resizing memory in

increments (rather than doubling or halving the size), fragmentation can be reduced.

Tools for Debugging and Preventing Memory Issues

1. **Valgrind**: A powerful tool for detecting memory leaks, memory corruption, and undefined memory usage in C and C++ programs.
   - To run a program with Valgrind:

```
valgrind --leak-check=full ./your_program
```

   - Valgrind will provide detailed reports on memory leaks and errors in memory allocation.
2. **AddressSanitizer**: A runtime memory error detector that can be used with GCC or Clang to detect issues like memory leaks, out-of-bounds access, and use-after-free.
   - Compile with:

```
gcc -fsanitize=address -g your_program.c -o your_program
```

   - Run the program as usual and AddressSanitizer will report memory issues.

Here's a comparison of malloc(), calloc(), realloc(), and free() in C in tabular form:

Function	Purpose	Syntax	Memory Initialization	Return Value	Usage Scenario
malloc()	Allocates a block of memory	void* malloc(size_t size);	No initialization	Returns a pointer to the allocated memory or NULL on failure.	Used to allocate a specific amount of memory dynamically.
calloc()	Allocates memory for an array of elements	void* calloc(size_t num, size_t size);	Initializes memory to 0	Returns a pointer to the allocated memory or NULL on failure.	Used to allocate memory for an array and initialize it to zero.
realloc()	Resizes a previously allocated memory block	void* realloc(void* ptr, size_t size);	Memory contents remain, but may be changed	Returns a pointer to the resized block or NULL on failure.	Used when resizing a previously allocated memory block (e.g., array).
free()	Frees previously allocated memory	void free(void* ptr);	N/A	Does not return a value.	Used to release memory that was previously allocated by malloc(), calloc(), or realloc().

Key Differences:

- **Memory Initialization:**
  - malloc() does **not** initialize the memory, leaving it with garbage values.

    - calloc() initializes the memory to 0 (for all bytes).
- **Memory Resizing:**
    - realloc() changes the size of a previously allocated memory block and moves the data to a new location if necessary.
- **Memory Deallocation:**
    - free() is used to deallocate the memory that was previously allocated by malloc(), calloc(), or realloc().

LINKED LISTS IN C

Linked lists are linear data structures composed of nodes connected by pointers, where each node holds data and a reference to the next node. Unlike arrays, linked lists do not require contiguous memory allocation, making it easier to insert or delete elements dynamically. In a singly linked list, each node only points to the next node in the sequence, creating a one-way list.

1. Representation of Singly Linked Lists in Memory

In a singly linked list, each node contains:

- **Data**: Stores the information or value of the node.
- **Next pointer**: Points to the next node in the list.

Here's a structure definition for a node in C:

```
#include <stdio.h>
#include <stdlib.h>

struct Node {
    int data;
    struct Node* next;
};
```

- data is an integer, which could be any data type.
- next is a pointer to the next node in the list.

2. Basic Operations and Code

A. Traversal

Traversing a linked list means visiting each node and accessing its data. Here's how to do it in C.

```
void traverseList(struct Node* head) {
```

```
    struct Node* current = head;
    while (current != NULL) {
        printf("%d -> ", current->data);
        current = current->next;
    }
    printf("NULL\n");
}
```

Explanation

1. **Initialize**: We start from the head node (first node in the list).
2. **Loop**: Move through each node until current becomes NULL, meaning the end of the list.
3. **Print**: Access and print each node's data.

B. Searching

Searching in a linked list involves looking for a specific value in the nodes.

```
int search(struct Node* head, int key) {
    struct Node* current = head;
    while (current != NULL) {
        if (current->data == key) {
            return 1; // Found
        }
        current = current->next;
    }
    return 0; // Not found
}
```

Explanation

1. **Start at head**: Begin with the head node.
2. **Check each node**: Traverse each node, comparing data to key.
3. **Return result**: If key matches data, return 1 (true); otherwise, return 0 if not found.

C. Insertion

There are multiple ways to insert a node in a linked list:

- At the beginning
- At the end
- After a specified node

Let's look at insertion at the beginning and at the end.

i. Insertion at the Beginning

```
void insertAtBeginning(struct Node** head, int new_data)
{
    struct Node* new_node = (struct
Node*)malloc(sizeof(struct Node));
    new_node->data = new_data;
    new_node->next = *head;
    *head = new_node;
}
```

Explanation

1. **Allocate memory**: Create a new node and assign memory.
2. **Assign data**: Store new_data in the new node.
3. **Link new node**: Set the next of the new node to the current head.
4. **Update head**: Make the new node the head of the list.

ii. Insertion at the End

```
void insertAtEnd(struct Node** head, int new_data) {
    struct Node* new_node = (struct
Node*)malloc(sizeof(struct Node));
    struct Node* last = *head;

    new_node->data = new_data;
    new_node->next = NULL;
```

```
    if (*head == NULL) {
        *head = new_node;
        return;
    }

    while (last->next != NULL) {
        last = last->next;
    }
    last->next = new_node;
}
```

Explanation

1. **Allocate memory**: Create a new node.
2. **Assign data**: Store new_data in the new node and set its next to NULL.
3. **Traverse to the end**: Loop through nodes until reaching the last node.
4. **Link new node**: Set next of the last node to the new node.

D. Deletion

To delete a node, we find the node, unlink it, and free its memory.

i. Deletion of a Node by Value

```
void deleteNode(struct Node** head, int key) {
    struct Node *temp = *head, *prev = NULL;
    if (temp != NULL && temp->data == key) {
        *head = temp->next;
        free(temp);
        return;
    }
    while (temp != NULL && temp->data != key) {
```

```
        prev = temp;
        temp = temp->next;
    }
    if (temp == NULL) return;
    prev->next = temp->next;
    free(temp);
}
```

Explanation

1. **Check head node**: If the head node has the key, unlink and delete it.
2. **Traverse**: Move through each node to find key.
3. **Unlink**: If found, unlink temp from the list by adjusting the previous node's next.
4. **Free memory**: Release the memory of temp.

3. Real-Life Example: Playlist in a Music Player

Consider a playlist of songs where each song points to the next one. A singly linked list is useful here because:

- You can **traverse** the playlist sequentially.
- **Insert** songs at the beginning, end, or in between.
- **Delete** songs by title.

Each song can be represented as a node with data (song title) and next (pointer to the next song). Traversing displays all song titles, while insertion and deletion allow adding or removing songs dynamically.

Complete C Program Example

Here's a C program implementing a linked list with the operations discussed:

```
#include <stdio.h>
#include <stdlib.h>
struct Node {
    int data;
```

```
    struct Node* next;
};
// Functions
void traverseList(struct Node* head);
void insertAtBeginning(struct Node** head, int new_data);
void insertAtEnd(struct Node** head, int new_data);
int search(struct Node* head, int key);
void deleteNode(struct Node** head, int key);
int main() {
    struct Node* head = NULL;
    insertAtBeginning(&head, 3);
    insertAtEnd(&head, 5);
    insertAtEnd(&head, 7);
    printf("List after insertion: ");
    traverseList(head);
    printf("Searching for 5 in the list: %s\n", search(head,
5) ? "Found" : "Not Found");
    deleteNode(&head, 3);
    printf("List after deletion of 3: ");
    traverseList(head);
    return 0;
}
void traverseList(struct Node* head) {
    struct Node* current = head;
    while (current != NULL) {
        printf("%d -> ", current->data);
        current = current->next;
    }
    printf("NULL\n");
}
void insertAtBeginning(struct Node** head, int new_data)
```

```
{
    struct Node* new_node = (struct
Node*)malloc(sizeof(struct Node));
    new_node->data = new_data;
    new_node->next = *head;
    *head = new_node;
}
void insertAtEnd(struct Node** head, int new_data) {
    struct Node* new_node = (struct
Node*)malloc(sizeof(struct Node));
    struct Node* last = *head;
    new_node->data = new_data;
    new_node->next = NULL;
    if (*head == NULL) {
        *head = new_node;
        return;
    }
    while (last->next != NULL) {
        last = last->next;
    }
    last->next = new_node;
}
int search(struct Node* head, int key) {
    struct Node* current = head;
    while (current != NULL) {
        if (current->data == key) {
            return 1;
        }
        current = current->next;
    }
    return 0;
```

```
}
void deleteNode(struct Node** head, int key) {
    struct Node *temp = *head, *prev = NULL;
    if (temp != NULL && temp->data == key) {
        *head = temp->next;
        free(temp);
        return;
    }
    while (temp != NULL && temp->data != key) {
        prev = temp;
        temp = temp->next;
    }
    if (temp == NULL) return;
    prev->next = temp->next;
    free(temp);
}
```

This C code demonstrates basic operations on a singly linked list, including insertion, deletion, traversal, and searching. Let's break down each part of the code to understand its functionality.

1. Structure Definition

```
struct Node {
    int data;
    struct Node* next;
};
```

- Here, a Node structure is defined to represent each element of the linked list.
- Each Node has an integer data to store the value and a pointer next to point to the next node in the list.

2. Function Declarations

The following function prototypes declare the various operations that will be implemented on the linked list:

```
void traverseList(struct Node* head);
void insertAtBeginning(struct Node** head, int new_data);
void insertAtEnd(struct Node** head, int new_data);
int search(struct Node* head, int key);
void deleteNode(struct Node** head, int key);
```

- **traverseList**: Prints all elements in the list.
- **insertAtBeginning**: Inserts a new node at the start of the list.
- **insertAtEnd**: Inserts a new node at the end of the list.
- **search**: Checks if a value exists in the list.
- **deleteNode**: Removes a node with a specified value from the list.

3. main Function

```
int main() {
    struct Node* head = NULL;
    insertAtBeginning(&head, 3);
    insertAtEnd(&head, 5);
    insertAtEnd(&head, 7);
    printf("List after insertion: ");
    traverseList(head);
    printf("Searching for 5 in the list: %s\n", search(head,
5) ? "Found" : "Not Found");

    deleteNode(&head, 3);
    printf("List after deletion of 3: ");
    traverseList(head);
    return 0;
```

```
}
```

- Initializes the list by setting head to NULL.
- Inserts values 3, 5, and 7 into the list.
- Traverses and displays the list after insertion.
- Searches for the value 5 and prints if it was found.
- Deletes the node containing 3 and traverses the list again to display the updated state.

4. traverseList Function

```
void traverseList(struct Node* head) {
    struct Node* current = head;
    while (current != NULL) {
        printf("%d -> ", current->data);
        current = current->next;
    }
    printf("NULL\n");
}
```

- Traverses the linked list from head to the end.
- Prints each node's data, followed by " -> ", and ends with "NULL" to signify the end of the list.

5. insertAtBeginning Function

```
void insertAtBeginning(struct Node** head, int new_data)
{
    struct Node* new_node = (struct
Node*)malloc(sizeof(struct Node));
    new_node->data = new_data;
    new_node->next = *head;
    *head = new_node;
}
```

- Creates a new node with the specified new_data.
- Sets the new node's next pointer to the current head.
- Updates head to point to the new node, making it the first element in the list.

6. insertAtEnd Function

```
void insertAtEnd(struct Node** head, int new_data) {
    struct Node* new_node = (struct
Node*)malloc(sizeof(struct Node));
    struct Node* last = *head;
    new_node->data = new_data;
    new_node->next = NULL;
    if (*head == NULL) {
        *head = new_node;
        return;
    }
    while (last->next != NULL) {
        last = last->next;
    }
    last->next = new_node;
}
```

- Creates a new node with the given new_data.
- If the list is empty (i.e., head is NULL), the new node becomes the head.
- Otherwise, it traverses to the end of the list and sets the next pointer of the last node to the new node.

7. search Function

```
int search(struct Node* head, int key) {
    struct Node* current = head;
```

```
    while (current != NULL) {
        if (current->data == key) {
            return 1;
        }
        current = current->next;
    }
    return 0;
}
```

- Traverses the list and compares each node's data with the key.
- If a node with data == key is found, it returns 1 (true).
- If the key is not found, it returns 0 (false).

8. deleteNode Function

```
void deleteNode(struct Node** head, int key) {
    struct Node *temp = *head, *prev = NULL;
    if (temp != NULL && temp->data == key) {
        *head = temp->next;
        free(temp);
        return;
    }
    while (temp != NULL && temp->data != key) {
        prev = temp;
        temp = temp->next;
    }
    if (temp == NULL) return;
    prev->next = temp->next;
    free(temp);
}
```

- First checks if the node to be deleted is the head node.
- If head contains the key, it updates head to the next node and frees the memory of the current head.
- If the key is not in the head, it traverses the list while keeping track of the previous node.
- When it finds the node to delete, it updates the next pointer of the previous node to skip the temp node.
- Frees the memory for the deleted node.

This program showcases a simple linked list with insertion, deletion, searching, and traversal functions. The code is easy to adapt to other scenarios, such as managing tasks, browser history, or even playlists, making linked lists an essential concept in computer science and real-life applications.

Linked Representation of Stack and Queue

In data structures, **linked lists** are used to represent dynamic collections that can grow or shrink in size. Unlike arrays, they don't require a fixed size. Let's go through the representation of stacks and queues using linked lists, header nodes, and some other complex structures like doubly and circular linked lists.

Stack Representation Using a Linked List

A **stack** is a Last-In-First-Out (LIFO) data structure, which means the last element added is the first one to be removed. The main operations are:

- **Push**: Add an element to the top of the stack.
- **Pop**: Remove the element from the top of the stack.

Structure Definition

```
#include <stdio.h>
#include <stdlib.h>
// Node structure
struct Node {
    int data;
```

```
    struct Node* next;
};
// Stack structure using linked list
struct Stack {
    struct Node* top;  // Points to the top of the stack
};
```

Push Operation

To push an element onto the stack:

1. Create a new node.
2. Set its data and make it point to the current top node.
3. Update the top pointer to this new node.

```
void push(struct Stack* stack, int value) {
    struct Node* newNode = (struct
Node*)malloc(sizeof(struct Node));
    if (!newNode) {
        printf("Heap overflow\n");
        return;
    }
    newNode->data = value;
    newNode->next = stack->top;
    stack->top = newNode;
    printf("%d pushed to stack\n", value);
}
```

Pop Operation

To pop an element:

1. Check if the stack is empty.
2. If not, store the top node's data, update the top pointer to the next node, and free the old top node.

```
int pop(struct Stack* stack) {
    if (stack->top == NULL) {
```

```
        printf("Stack Underflow\n");
        return -1;
    }
    struct Node* temp = stack->top;
    int popped = temp->data;
    stack->top = stack->top->next;
    free(temp);
    return popped;
}
```

Complexity Analysis

- **Push and Pop**: O(1), since both operations only involve a constant amount of work regardless of stack size.

Queue Representation Using a Linked List

A **queue** is a First-In-First-Out (FIFO) data structure. The main operations are:

- **Enqueue**: Add an element to the rear.
- **Dequeue**: Remove an element from the front.

Structure Definition

```
struct Queue {
    struct Node* front;  // Points to the front of the queue
    struct Node* rear;   // Points to the rear of the queue
};
```

Enqueue Operation

To enqueue an element:

1. Create a new node and assign data.
2. If the queue is empty, make the front and rear point to the new node.
3. Else, link the rear node to the new node and update the rear pointer.

```
void enqueue(struct Queue* queue, int value) {
    struct Node* newNode = (struct
Node*)malloc(sizeof(struct Node));
    newNode->data = value;
    newNode->next = NULL;
    if (queue->rear == NULL) {
        queue->front = queue->rear = newNode;
    } else {
        queue->rear->next = newNode;
        queue->rear = newNode;
    }
    printf("%d enqueued to queue\n", value);
}
```

Dequeue Operation

To dequeue an element:

1. Check if the queue is empty.
2. If not, move the front pointer to the next node and free the old front node.

```
int dequeue(struct Queue* queue) {
    if (queue->front == NULL) {
        printf("Queue Underflow\n");
        return -1;
    }
    struct Node* temp = queue->front;
    int value = temp->data;
    queue->front = queue->front->next;
    if (queue->front == NULL) {
        queue->rear = NULL;
    }
    free(temp);
    return value;
}
```

Complexity Analysis

- **Enqueue and Dequeue**: O(1).

Doubly Linked List

A **doubly linked list** is a linked list where each node points to both the previous and the next node, making it easier to traverse in both directions.

Node Structure

```
struct DNode {
    int data;
    struct DNode* prev;
    struct DNode* next;
};
```

Insert at the Beginning

```
void insertAtBeginning(struct DNode** head, int value) {
    struct DNode* newNode = (struct
DNode*)malloc(sizeof(struct DNode));
    newNode->data = value;
    newNode->prev = NULL;
    newNode->next = *head;
    if (*head != NULL) {
        (*head)->prev = newNode;
    }
    *head = newNode;
}
```

Delete from End

```
void deleteFromEnd(struct DNode** head) {
    if (*head == NULL) return;
    struct DNode* temp = *head;
    while (temp->next != NULL) {
        temp = temp->next;
```

```
    }
    if (temp->prev) {
        temp->prev->next = NULL;
    } else {
        *head = NULL;
    }
    free(temp);
}
```

Complexity Analysis

- **Insertion and Deletion**: O(1) if the node is known, O(n) if traversal is required.

Circular Linked List

A **circular linked list** connects the last node back to the head node, forming a circle. It's useful for applications requiring circular data traversal, like round-robin scheduling.

Insert at End

```
void insertAtEndCircular(struct Node** head, int value) {
    struct Node* newNode = (struct
Node*)malloc(sizeof(struct Node));
    newNode->data = value;
    if (*head == NULL) {
        *head = newNode;
        newNode->next = *head;
    } else {
        struct Node* temp = *head;
        while (temp->next != *head) {
            temp = temp->next;
        }
        temp->next = newNode;
        newNode->next = *head;
```

```
    }
}
```

Delete from Beginning

```
void deleteFromBeginningCircular(struct Node** head) {
    if (*head == NULL) return;
    struct Node* temp = *head;
    struct Node* last = *head;
    while (last->next != *head) {
        last = last->next;
    }
    *head = (*head)->next;
    last->next = *head;
    free(temp);
}
```

Complexity Analysis

- **Insertion and Deletion**: O(1)for beginning/end, O(n) if a specific position is needed.

Real-Life Examples

1. **Stack (Undo feature)**: In text editors, the "Undo" operation is a stack where the last edit is the first one to be undone.
2. **Queue (Customer service)**: A customer service center uses a queue to attend the first customer who came in.

EXAMPLE WITH STEP-BY-STEP EXPLANATION

1. Stack Implementation Using Linked List

A stack operates on a Last-In-First-Out (LIFO) basis, meaning that the last item added is the first to be removed.

```
#include <stdio.h>
#include <stdlib.h>
```

```
// Define the structure of a Node
struct Node {
    int data;
    struct Node* next;
};

// Define the structure of a Stack
struct Stack {
    struct Node* top;  // Pointer to the top node
};

// Function to initialize the stack
struct Stack* createStack() {
    struct Stack* stack = (struct Stack*)malloc(sizeof(struct
Stack));
    stack->top = NULL;  // Initialize top as NULL
    return stack;
}

// Push operation to add an element to the stack
void push(struct Stack* stack, int value) {
    struct Node* newNode = (struct
Node*)malloc(sizeof(struct Node));
    newNode->data = value;
    newNode->next = stack->top;
    stack->top = newNode;
    printf("%d pushed to stack\n", value);
}

// Pop operation to remove the top element from the stack
int pop(struct Stack* stack) {
    if (stack->top == NULL) {
        printf("Stack Underflow\n");
        return -1;
    }
    struct Node* temp = stack->top;
```

```
    int popped = temp->data;
    stack->top = stack->top->next;
    free(temp);
    return popped;
}

// Peek operation to view the top element without
removing it
int peek(struct Stack* stack) {
    if (stack->top == NULL) {
        printf("Stack is empty\n");
        return -1;
    }
    return stack->top->data;
}

// Driver code
int main() {
    struct Stack* stack = createStack();
    push(stack, 10);
    push(stack, 20);
    push(stack, 30);

    printf("%d popped from stack\n", pop(stack));
    printf("Top element is %d\n", peek(stack));

    return 0;
}
```

OUTPUT

```
10 pushed to stack
20 pushed to stack
30 pushed to stack
30 popped from stack
Top element is 20
```

Explanation:

1. **Node Structure**: Defines a Node with data and a next pointer.
2. **Stack Structure**: Points to the top of the stack.
3. **Push**: Adds an element to the top.
4. **Pop**: Removes the top element and returns its value.
5. **Peek**: Returns the top element without removing it.

Let's go through this C program step-by-step. This program implements a simple stack using a linked list.

1. Defining the Node Structure

```
struct Node {
    int data;
    struct Node* next;
};
```

- This defines a Node structure with two members:
    - data: an integer to hold the data for the node.
    - next: a pointer to the next node in the stack (linked list).

2. Defining the Stack Structure

```
struct Stack {
    struct Node* top;  // Pointer to the top node
};
```

- This defines a Stack structure with one member:
    - top: a pointer to the Node at the top of the stack.

3. Creating a Stack

```
struct Stack* createStack() {
    struct Stack* stack = (struct
Stack*)malloc(sizeof(struct Stack));
    stack->top = NULL;  // Initialize top as NULL
    return stack;
}
```

- createStack is a function that initializes a new stack:
    - It allocates memory for a Stack structure.
    - Sets the top pointer to NULL, indicating the stack is initially empty.
    - Returns a pointer to the newly created stack.

4. Push Operation

```
void push(struct Stack* stack, int value) {
    struct Node* newNode = (struct
Node*)malloc(sizeof(struct Node));
    newNode->data = value;
    newNode->next = stack->top;
    stack->top = newNode;
    printf("%d pushed to stack\n", value);
}
```

- push adds a new element (node) to the stack:
    - Allocates memory for a new Node.
    - Sets the data of the new node to value.
    - Points the next of the new node to the current top of the stack.
    - Updates the top pointer in the stack to this new node, making it the top element.
    - Prints a message confirming the value pushed to the stack.

5. Pop Operation

```
int pop(struct Stack* stack) {
    if (stack->top == NULL) {
        printf("Stack Underflow\n");
        return -1;
    }
    struct Node* temp = stack->top;
    int popped = temp->data;
    stack->top = stack->top->next;
```

```
    free(temp);
    return popped;
}
```

- pop removes the top element from the stack:
    - Checks if top is NULL (meaning the stack is empty) and, if so, displays "Stack Underflow" and returns -1.
    - If not empty, it:
        - Stores the top node's data in popped.
        - Advances the top pointer to the next node.
        - Frees the memory of the removed node.
        - Returns the data of the popped node.

6. Peek Operation

```
int peek(struct Stack* stack) {
    if (stack->top == NULL) {
        printf("Stack is empty\n");
        return -1;
    }
    return stack->top->data;
}
```

- peek shows the value of the top element without removing it:
    - Checks if top is NULL. If so, it displays "Stack is empty" and returns -1.
    - Otherwise, it returns the data of the top node.

7. Driver Code (main function)

```
int main() {
    struct Stack* stack = createStack();
    push(stack, 10);
```

```
    push(stack, 20);
    push(stack, 30);

    printf("%d popped from stack\n", pop(stack));
    printf("Top element is %d\n", peek(stack));

    return 0;
}
```

- This part tests the stack functions:
    - Creates a new stack.
    - Pushes the values 10, 20, and 30 onto the stack.
    - Pops the top element (expected to pop 30).
    - Prints the top element after popping (expected to be 20).

---

2. Queue Implementation Using Linked List

A queue operates on a First-In-First-Out (FIFO) basis, meaning that the first item added is the first to be removed.

```
#include <stdio.h>
#include <stdlib.h>

// Define the structure of a Node
struct Node {
    int data;
    struct Node* next;
};

// Define the structure of a Queue
struct Queue {
    struct Node* front;
    struct Node* rear;
};

// Function to initialize the queue
```

```
struct Queue* createQueue() {
    struct Queue* queue = (struct
Queue*)malloc(sizeof(struct Queue));
    queue->front = queue->rear = NULL;
    return queue;
}

// Enqueue operation to add an element to the rear of the
queue
void enqueue(struct Queue* queue, int value) {
    struct Node* newNode = (struct
Node*)malloc(sizeof(struct Node));
    newNode->data = value;
    newNode->next = NULL;
    if (queue->rear == NULL) {
        queue->front = queue->rear = newNode;
        return;
    }
    queue->rear->next = newNode;
    queue->rear = newNode;
    printf("%d enqueued to queue\n", value);
}

// Dequeue operation to remove an element from the front
of the queue
int dequeue(struct Queue* queue) {
    if (queue->front == NULL) {
        printf("Queue Underflow\n");
        return -1;
    }
    struct Node* temp = queue->front;
    int value = temp->data;
    queue->front = queue->front->next;
    if (queue->front == NULL) queue->rear = NULL;
    free(temp);
    return value;
```

```
}

// Driver code
int main() {
    struct Queue* queue = createQueue();
    enqueue(queue, 10);
    enqueue(queue, 20);
    enqueue(queue, 30);

    printf("%d dequeued from queue\n", dequeue(queue));
    return 0;
}
```

OUTPUT

```
20 enqueued to queue
30 enqueued to queue
10 dequeued from queue
```

Explanation:

Node and Queue Structures: front points to the first element, and rear points to the last.

Enqueue: Adds an element to the rear of the queue.

Dequeue: Removes the element at the front.

1. Structure Definitions

The code defines two structures:

- **Node**: Represents a single element in the queue, storing an integer data and a pointer next that links to the next node in the queue.

```
struct Node {
    int data;
    struct Node* next;
};
```

- **Queue**: Represents the entire queue with two

pointers:
  - front points to the first node in the queue.
  - rear points to the last node in the queue.

```
struct Queue {
    struct Node* front;
    struct Node* rear;
};
```

2. Queue Initialization with createQueue

The function createQueue() initializes an empty queue. It allocates memory for a Queue structure and sets both front and rear pointers to NULL, indicating an empty queue.

```
struct Queue* createQueue() {
    struct Queue* queue = (struct
Queue*)malloc(sizeof(struct Queue));
    queue->front = queue->rear = NULL;
    return queue;
}
```

3. Enqueue Operation with enqueue

The enqueue() function adds a new element to the end (rear) of the queue.

```
void enqueue(struct Queue* queue, int value) {
    struct Node* newNode = (struct
Node*)malloc(sizeof(struct Node));
    newNode->data = value;
    newNode->next = NULL;
```

- **Step 1**: Allocate memory for a new node and set its data to the value provided and its next pointer to NULL.
- **Step 2**: If the queue is empty (i.e., rear is NULL), set both front and rear pointers to the new node, making this the first element in the queue.

```
if (queue->rear == NULL) {
    queue->front = queue->rear = newNode;
    return;
}
```

- **Step 3**: If the queue is not empty, link the current rear node's next pointer to the new node, then update the rear pointer to the new node.

```
queue->rear->next = newNode;
queue->rear = newNode;
printf("%d enqueued to queue\n", value);
```

4. Dequeue Operation with dequeue

The dequeue() function removes an element from the front of the queue.

```
int dequeue(struct Queue* queue) {
    if (queue->front == NULL) {
        printf("Queue Underflow\n");
        return -1;
    }
```

- **Step 1**: Check if the queue is empty by testing if front is NULL. If it is empty, print "Queue Underflow" and return -1.
- **Step 2**: If the queue is not empty, store the front node in a temporary pointer temp, save its data in a variable value, and move the front pointer to the next node.

```
struct Node* temp = queue->front;
int value = temp->data;
queue->front = queue->front->next;
```

- **Step 3**: If the queue becomes empty after dequeuing,

set rear to NULL.

```
if (queue->front == NULL) queue->rear = NULL;
```

- **Step 4**: Free the memory of the dequeued node and return the value.

```
free(temp);
return value;
```

5. Driver Code in main

The main() function tests the enqueue and dequeue operations.

```
int main() {
    struct Queue* queue = createQueue();
    enqueue(queue, 10);
    enqueue(queue, 20);
    enqueue(queue, 30);

    printf("%d dequeued from queue\n",
dequeue(queue));
    return 0;
}
```

- **Step 1**: Initialize an empty queue using createQueue().
- **Step 2**: Enqueue three elements (10, 20, and 30), which will print confirmation messages.
- **Step 3**: Dequeue one element (the first enqueued element 10) and print the dequeued value.

---

3. Doubly Linked List

A doubly linked list allows traversal in both directions, with each node pointing to the next and previous nodes.

```
#include <stdio.h>
#include <stdlib.h>

// Define the structure of a Doubly Linked List Node
struct DNode {
    int data;
    struct DNode* prev;
    struct DNode* next;
};

// Insert at the beginning of the list
void insertAtBeginning(struct DNode** head, int value) {
    struct DNode* newNode = (struct
DNode*)malloc(sizeof(struct DNode));
    newNode->data = value;
    newNode->prev = NULL;
    newNode->next = *head;
    if (*head != NULL) (*head)->prev = newNode;
    *head = newNode;
}

// Insert at the end of the list
void insertAtEnd(struct DNode** head, int value) {
    struct DNode* newNode = (struct
DNode*)malloc(sizeof(struct DNode));
    newNode->data = value;
    newNode->next = NULL;
    if (*head == NULL) {
        newNode->prev = NULL;
        *head = newNode;
        return;
    }
    struct DNode* last = *head;
    while (last->next != NULL) last = last->next;
    last->next = newNode;
    newNode->prev = last;
```

```
}

// Print the list
void printList(struct DNode* node) {
    struct DNode* last;
    while (node != NULL) {
        printf("%d ", node->data);
        last = node;
        node = node->next;
    }
    printf("\n");
}

// Driver code
int main() {
    struct DNode* head = NULL;
    insertAtBeginning(&head, 10);
    insertAtEnd(&head, 20);
    insertAtEnd(&head, 30);

    printf("Doubly linked list: ");
    printList(head);

    return 0;
}
```

OUTPUT

```
Doubly linked list: 10 20 30
```

Explanation:

1. **Insert at Beginning**: Adds a new node at the start.
2. **Insert at End**: Traverses to the end to add a new node there.
3. **Print List**: Traverses the list and prints each element.

Here's a step-by-step explanation of the code:

1. **Including Header Files:**

```
#include <stdio.h>
```

```
#include <stdlib.h>
```

- stdio.h is included for input and output functions (like printf).
- stdlib.h is included for memory allocation functions (like malloc).

2. **Defining the Doubly Linked List Node Structure**:

```
struct DNode {
    int data;
    struct DNode* prev;
    struct DNode* next;
};
```

- The DNode structure represents a node in the doubly linked list.
- data stores the integer value of the node.
- prev is a pointer to the previous node in the list.
- next is a pointer to the next node in the list.

3. **Inserting a Node at the Beginning of the List**:

```
void insertAtBeginning(struct DNode** head, int value) {
    struct DNode* newNode = (struct
DNode*)malloc(sizeof(struct DNode));
    newNode->data = value;
    newNode->prev = NULL;
    newNode->next = *head;
    if (*head != NULL) (*head)->prev = newNode;
    *head = newNode;
}
```

- A new node is created using malloc to allocate memory.
- data is set to value, and prev is set to NULL because this will be the first node.

- next points to the current head node, so it connects the new node to the existing list.
- If the list is not empty, the old head node's prev pointer is updated to point to the new node.
- Finally, head is updated to point to this new node, making it the first node in the list.

4. **Inserting a Node at the End of the List**:

```
void insertAtEnd(struct DNode** head, int value) {
    struct DNode* newNode = (struct
DNode*)malloc(sizeof(struct DNode));
    newNode->data = value;
    newNode->next = NULL;
    if (*head == NULL) {
        newNode->prev = NULL;
        *head = newNode;
        return;
    }
    struct DNode* last = *head;
    while (last->next != NULL) last = last->next;
    last->next = newNode;
    newNode->prev = last;
}
```

- A new node is created with data set to value and next set to NULL since it will be the last node.
- If the list is empty, the new node becomes the head, and its prev is set to NULL.
- If the list isn't empty, it traverses the list to find the last node.
- The last node's next pointer is updated to point to the new node, and the new node's prev pointer is set to the last node.

5. **Printing the List**:

```
void printList(struct DNode* node) {
    struct DNode* last;
    while (node != NULL) {
        printf("%d ", node->data);
        last = node;
        node = node->next;
    }
    printf("\n");
}
```

- The function takes the head node as input and iterates through the list.
- It prints the data of each node, followed by a space.
- After reaching the end of the list, it prints a newline.

6. **Main Function (Driver Code)**:

```
int main() {
    struct DNode* head = NULL;
    insertAtBeginning(&head, 10);
    insertAtEnd(&head, 20);
    insertAtEnd(&head, 30);

    printf("Doubly linked list: ");
    printList(head);

    return 0;
}
```

- The head pointer is initialized to NULL, representing an empty list.
- insertAtBeginning(&head, 10) inserts 10 at the beginning of the list.
- insertAtEnd(&head, 20) and insertAtEnd(&head, 30) add 20 and 30 at the end.

- Finally, printList(head) prints the entire list, resulting in 10 20 30.

---

4. Circular Linked List

In a circular linked list, the last node points back to the head node, forming a circular structure.

```
#include <stdio.h>
#include <stdlib.h>

// Define the structure of a Circular Linked List Node
struct Node {
    int data;
    struct Node* next;
};

// Insert at the end of the circular linked list
void insertAtEndCircular(struct Node** head, int value) {
    struct Node* newNode = (struct
Node*)malloc(sizeof(struct Node));
    newNode->data = value;
    newNode->next = *head;
    if (*head == NULL) {
        newNode->next = newNode;
        *head = newNode;
    } else {
        struct Node* temp = *head;
        while (temp->next != *head) {
            temp = temp->next;
        }
        temp->next = newNode;
        newNode->next = *head;
    }
}

// Print the circular linked list
void printCircularList(struct Node* head) {
```

```
    if (head == NULL) return;
    struct Node* temp = head;
    do {
        printf("%d ", temp->data);
        temp = temp->next;
    } while (temp != head);
    printf("\n");
}

// Driver code
int main() {
    struct Node* head = NULL;
    insertAtEndCircular(&head, 10);
    insertAtEndCircular(&head, 20);
    insertAtEndCircular(&head, 30);

    printf("Circular linked list: ");
    printCircularList(head);

    return 0;
}
```

OUTPUT

```
Circular linked list: 10 20 30
```

Explanation:

1. **Insert at End**: Traverses to the last node and links it to the new node, then points the new node back to the head.
2. **Print Circular List**: Loops through the list starting from the head and stops once it completes a full cycle.

This C program creates and manages a circular linked list, which is a linked list where the last node links back to the first node, creating a circular structure. The program includes two primary functions: one for inserting a node at the end of the circular linked list and one for printing the list.

Here's a step-by-step breakdown of the code:

Step 1: Define the Node Structure

```
struct Node {
    int data;
    struct Node* next;
};
```

- Here, a Node structure is defined, representing each node in the circular linked list.
- Each Node has an integer data field (data) and a pointer to the next node (next).

Step 2: Define the insertAtEndCircular Function

```
void insertAtEndCircular(struct Node** head, int
value) {
    struct Node* newNode = (struct
Node*)malloc(sizeof(struct Node));
    newNode->data = value;
    newNode->next = *head;
```

- This function inserts a new node with the specified value at the end of the circular linked list.
- A new node (newNode) is created and initialized with the given value. newNode->next is initially set to *head.

Step 2a: Check if the List is Empty

```
        if (*head == NULL) {
            newNode->next = newNode;
            *head = newNode;
        }
```

- If the head of the list is NULL, it means the list is

currently empty.

- In this case, newNode->next is set to point to itself, creating a self-loop.
- The head pointer is updated to point to newNode, making it the first node in the list.

Step 2b: Insert the Node at the End if the List is Not Empty

```
    else {
        struct Node* temp = *head;
        while (temp->next != *head) {
            temp = temp->next;
        }
        temp->next = newNode;
        newNode->next = *head;
    }
}
```

- If the list is not empty, a temporary pointer (temp) is set to head and iterates through the list until it finds the last node (the node whose next points to head).
- Once the last node is found, its next pointer is updated to newNode.
- newNode->next is then set to point to head, maintaining the circular structure of the list.

Step 3: Define the printCircularList Function

```
void printCircularList(struct Node* head) {
    if (head == NULL) return;
    struct Node* temp = head;
    do {
        printf("%d ", temp->data);
        temp = temp->next;
    } while (temp != head);
    printf("\n");
```

```
}
```

- This function prints all the nodes in the circular linked list.
- It checks if the list is empty (head == NULL). If it is, it returns immediately without printing anything.
- If the list is not empty, a temporary pointer (temp) is set to head.
- A do-while loop is used to traverse and print the data of each node until temp comes back to head.
- The loop ensures that each node is printed once, even in a circular structure.

Step 4: Driver Code (main Function)

```
int main() {
    struct Node* head = NULL;
    insertAtEndCircular(&head, 10);
    insertAtEndCircular(&head, 20);
    insertAtEndCircular(&head, 30);

    printf("Circular linked list: ");
    printCircularList(head);

    return 0;
}
```

- The main function initializes head as NULL, meaning the list is initially empty.
- It calls insertAtEndCircular three times, inserting the values 10, 20, and 30 at the end of the circular linked list.
- Finally, it calls printCircularList to display the elements of the list.

This output confirms that each value was added to the

end of the list and that the circular linked list was traversed correctly, printing each node's value.

SUMMARY

Linked lists are dynamic data structures consisting of nodes connected in sequence. Each node holds data and a reference to the next node, making linked lists adaptable for memory management.

Key Types and Operations:

1. **Singly Linked List**: Nodes link in one direction, ending with NULL. Key operations include:
    - **Traversal**: Moving through each node sequentially.
    - **Searching**: Looking for a specific value.
    - **Insertion**: Adding nodes at various positions.
    - **Deletion**: Removing nodes by adjusting pointers.
2. **Stack and Queue with Linked Lists**:
    - **Stack**: Linked list allows for efficient push and pop operations.
    - **Queue**: Enqueueing at the end and dequeuing from the front enables efficient queue management.
3. **Header Nodes**: An additional node at the start of the list, simplifying insertion and deletion operations by reducing edge cases.
4. **Doubly Linked List**: Each node has pointers to both the next and previous nodes, allowing bidirectional traversal. It simplifies operations like insertion and deletion, but has additional memory overhead.
5. **Circular Linked List**: The last node points back to the head, creating a circular structure that facilitates continuous traversal and enables efficient insertion and deletion at both ends.

Complexity Analysis

Linked lists provide efficient O(1) insertion and deletion

with some variations, while traversal and search can take O(n) in the worst case. Their flexibility makes them essential in memory-efficient applications, especially where dynamic allocation is critical.

SORTING, HASHING, AND GRAPHS

1. Introduction to Sorting, Hashing, and Graphs

Overview

Sorting, hashing, and graphs are foundational concepts in computer science, vital for efficient data manipulation, retrieval, and structuring. Each serves a unique purpose:

- **Sorting** organizes data into a specified order, often for ease of access or improved processing speed.
- **Hashing** enables quick data retrieval by mapping data to specific addresses in a structure known as a hash table, drastically improving lookup times.
- **Graphs** provide a means to model relationships between data entities, allowing complex networks and connectivity to be represented and analyzed efficiently.

Importance of Efficient Data Manipulation and Representation

In modern applications, the need to handle vast amounts of data quickly is crucial. Efficient data manipulation and representation help achieve:

1. **Faster Processing:** Well-organized data structures like sorted lists, hash tables, and graphs make it quicker to search, insert, delete, or update data.
2. **Reduced Complexity:** Data representation techniques such as graphs simplify complex problems, such as finding the shortest path or detecting cycles, by using algorithms tailored for

network-like structures.

3. **Optimized Memory Usage:** Efficient algorithms and data structures minimize memory usage and avoid unnecessary duplication, which is essential in large-scale applications.

---

2. Sorting

Sorting arranges data in a specific order, either ascending or descending, which improves the accessibility and processing of that data.

Common Sorting Algorithms

- **Bubble Sort:** A simple algorithm that repeatedly steps through the list, compares adjacent elements, and swaps them if they are in the wrong order.
- **Merge Sort:** A divide-and-conquer algorithm that divides the list into smaller sublists, sorts each sublist, and then merges them back together.
- **Quick Sort:** Also a divide-and-conquer approach but selects a 'pivot' element and partitions the list into elements less than or greater than the pivot.
- **Heap Sort:** Based on the binary heap data structure, it sorts by first constructing a heap and then repeatedly extracting the maximum or minimum element.

Feature	Bubble Sort	Merge Sort	Quick Sort	Heap Sort
Algorithm Type	Comparison-based, Exchanging	Comparison-based, Divide & Conquer	Comparison-based, Divide & Conquer	Comparison-based, Selection
Complexity (Best)	O(n)	O(n log n)	O(n log n)	O(n log n)
Complexity (Avg)	$O(n^2)$	O(n log n)	O(n log n)	O(n log n)
Complexity (Worst)	$O(n^2)$	O(n log n)	$O(n^2)$	O(n log n)
Stability	Stable	Stable	Unstable	Unstable
In-place	Yes	No (requires extra space)	Yes	Yes
Method	Swaps adjacent elements	Recursively divides and merges	Partitions around a pivot	Builds a max-heap and repeatedly extracts the max element
Adaptability	Not adaptive	Not adaptive	Partially adaptive	Not adaptive
Best Use Case	Small datasets or nearly sorted data	Linked lists, large datasets	General-purpose, with random pivoting	Priority queues, scheduling
Parallelization	Hard to parallelize	Easy to parallelize	Hard to parallelize	Difficult to parallelize

Applications of Sorting

- **Database Management:** Efficient sorting algorithms are used to order records, facilitating faster search and retrieval.
- **File Systems:** Sorting is crucial in organizing and retrieving files.
- **Data Analysis:** Sorting enables meaningful data aggregation and the identification of trends.

3. Hashing

Hashing involves mapping data to a fixed-size hash table, enabling quick data retrieval. The hash function takes an input and returns an address in the hash table, where the data can be stored or retrieved.

Key Aspects of Hashing

- **Hash Functions:** Determines the address in the table. A good hash function minimizes collisions, where two data elements map to the same address.
- **Collision Resolution:** Techniques like chaining, linear probing, and double hashing resolve collisions when they occur.
- **Load Factor:** Represents the ratio of the number of elements to the table's capacity and helps determine when to resize the table.

Concept	Hash Functions	Collision Resolution	Load Factor
Definition	A function that maps data to a fixed-size integer, called a hash code or hash value.	Techniques to handle situations when two keys map to the same hash value (i.e., collisions).	Ratio that indicates how full a hash table is, calculated as (number of elements) / (total capacity).
Purpose	To transform data into a specific location within a hash table for quick retrieval.	To manage and resolve conflicts in hash tables when multiple keys produce the same hash index.	To measure the efficiency and space utilization of a hash table, helping determine when to resize it.
Importance	Ensures data is distributed evenly to optimize retrieval and	Ensures that collisions do not lead to data loss or degrade	Provides a threshold for resizing to maintain efficient

	storage in a hash table.	the performance of hash tables.	performance and avoid excessive collisions.
Key Parameters	Quality of distribution, speed of computation, and avoidance of collisions.	Techniques such as open addressing, chaining, and rehashing.	Threshold values that dictate when to resize (e.g., 0.7 for load factor).
Example	A hash function might map names to indexes in an array for quick lookup.	If "Alice" and "Bob" both hash to index 5, collision resolution strategies will determine where to store "Bob."	If a hash table has 70 elements in a capacity of 100, the load factor is 0.7, which may prompt resizing.
Common Techniques	Modular hashing, multiplicative hashing, and universal hashing.	Separate chaining, linear probing, quadratic probing, and double hashing.	Adjusted by increasing the table size when the load factor exceeds a certain limit.

Applications of Hashing

- **Database Indexing:** Allows for the fast retrieval of database entries.
- **Password Management:** Passwords are often hashed before storing, so even if the database is accessed, passwords remain secure.
- **Caches:** Hash tables are often used in caching to store and quickly retrieve frequently accessed data.

4. Graphs

Graphs are structures made up of nodes (or vertices) connected by edges. They model relationships between entities, capturing complex network relationships in data.

Types of Graphs

- **Directed and Undirected Graphs:** In directed graphs, edges have direction, while undirected graphs have bi-directional edges.
- **Weighted Graphs:** Edges carry weights, useful in representing things like distances or costs.
- **Trees:** A special type of acyclic, undirected graph with a hierarchical structure, commonly used in data representation.

Key Graph Algorithms

- **Depth-First Search (DFS):** Traverses a graph by exploring as far down a branch as possible before backtracking.
- **Breadth-First Search (BFS):** Traverses the graph layer-by-layer, exploring all neighbors of a node before moving deeper.
- **Dijkstra's Algorithm:** Finds the shortest path in a weighted graph, widely used in routing and navigation.
- **Prim's and Kruskal's Algorithms:** Used to find the minimum spanning tree in weighted graphs, useful for network optimization.

DIFFRENCES BETWEEN THEM

Aspect	Depth-First Search (DFS)	Breadth-First Search (BFS)	Dijkstra's Algorithm	Prim's and Kruskal's Algorithms
Purpose	Traverses or searches graphs and trees.	Traverses or searches graphs and trees.	Finds the shortest path from a source node to all other nodes.	Finds the minimum spanning tree (MST) in a weighted, undirected graph.
Traversal Type	Depth-first (follows one path until the end, then backtracks)	Breadth-first (explores all neighbors level-by-level)	Shortest path traversal	MST construction
Approach	Recursive or stack-based	Queue-based	Greedy algorithm	Greedy algorithm
Optimality	Not optimal for finding the shortest path	Not optimal for finding the shortest path	Finds optimal shortest path	Finds optimal MST
Data Structure Used	Stack (explicit or implicit recursion)	Queue	Priority Queue	Priority Queue (Prim's), Edge List (Kruskal's)
Complexity	O(V+E)	O(V+E)	O((V+E)logV) using a priority queue	O(ElogV) for both Prim's and Kruskal's
Application	Pathfinding, connectivity checks	Shortest path in unweighted graphs, connectivity checks	Shortest path in weighted graphs	Network design, circuit layout (MST applications)
Graph Type	Works on both directed and undirected graphs	Works on both directed and undirected graphs	Works on weighted graphs	Works on weighted, undirected graphs
Example of Use	Solving mazes, cycle detection	Social networking sites, finding shortest paths in trees	GPS navigation, routing algorithms	Telecommunications, designing minimum-cost networks

Applications of Graphs

- **Social Networks:** Represent relationships between users.
- **Pathfinding:** Used in GPS and game development to determine optimal routes.
- **Network Analysis:** Graphs help in analyzing

connections and traffic in computer and transport networks.

1. Definition and Purpose of Sorting Algorithms

Sorting algorithms are methods used to arrange elements in a particular order (ascending or descending) to simplify data management and retrieval. They are fundamental in computer science because sorted data allows faster searching, easier manipulation, and improved readability.

---

2. Types of Sorting Algorithms

a. Selection Sort

Objective: Selection Sort repeatedly finds the smallest (or largest) element from the unsorted part and moves it to the sorted part.

Properties:

- **Time Complexity**: O(n^2)
- **Space Complexity**: O(1) (in-place sorting)
- **Stable**: No

Best Use Cases: Useful when working with small datasets or when memory usage is critical since it's an in-place sorting algorithm.

Real-Life Example: Selecting the lowest-cost product from a list, one by one, until the list is ordered.

C Code:

```
#include <stdio.h>

void selectionSort(int arr[], int n) {
    for (int i = 0; i < n - 1; i++) {
        int min_idx = i;
        for (int j = i + 1; j < n; j++)
            if (arr[j] < arr[min_idx])
                min_idx = j;
        int temp = arr[min_idx];
        arr[min_idx] = arr[i];
```

```
            arr[i] = temp;
        }
    }

void printArray(int arr[], int n) {
    for (int i = 0; i < n; i++)
        printf("%d ", arr[i]);
    printf("\n");
}

int main() {
    int arr[] = {64, 25, 12, 22, 11};
    int n = sizeof(arr)/sizeof(arr[0]);
    selectionSort(arr, n);
    printf("Sorted array: \n");
    printArray(arr, n);
    return 0;
}
```

OUTPUT

```
Sorted array:
11 12 22 25 64
```

Code Explanation

Here's a step-by-step explanation of how this C program works to sort an array using the **Selection Sort** algorithm.

Code Breakdown

1. **selectionSort(int arr[], int n) Function**:
    - This function performs selection sort on an integer array arr of size n.
2. **Outer Loop (for)**:

```
for (int i = 0; i < n - 1; i++)
```

- This loop iterates through the array from the first element to the second-last element.

- For each iteration of i, the smallest element in the unsorted part of the array (from i to n-1) is selected and placed in the current position i.

3. **Finding the Minimum Element (inner loop)**:

```
int min_idx = i;
for (int j = i + 1; j < n; j++)
    if (arr[j] < arr[min_idx])
        min_idx = j;
```

- min_idx is initialized to i, meaning we assume the current element is the smallest in the unsorted portion of the array.
- The inner loop iterates through the remaining unsorted portion (from i + 1 to n - 1) to find the actual minimum element's index.
- If arr[j] is found to be smaller than arr[min_idx], min_idx is updated to j.

4. **Swapping the Elements**:

```
int temp = arr[min_idx];
arr[min_idx] = arr[i];
arr[i] = temp;
```

- After finding the minimum element's index, min_idx, we swap this element with the element at the i position.
- This places the smallest element from the unsorted portion into its correct position, i.

5. **Sorting Process**:
    - This process continues, moving from the start of the array toward the end. Each pass ensures that the smallest remaining unsorted element is placed in its correct position.

  - By the end of the loop, the array is sorted in ascending order.

printArray(int arr[], int n) Function

- This helper function prints each element of the array arr with a space in between, followed by a new line.

main() Function

1. **Initialize Array**:

```
int arr[] = {64, 25, 12, 22, 11};
```

  - An array arr with five elements is created for sorting.

2. **Calculate the Number of Elements**:

```
int n = sizeof(arr) / sizeof(arr[0]);
```

  - n is calculated as the size of the array in bytes divided by the size of one element to get the number of elements in arr.

3. **Sort the Array**:

```
selectionSort(arr, n);
```

  - The selectionSort() function is called with arr and n, sorting the array in place.

4. **Print the Sorted Array**:

```
printf("Sorted array: \n");
printArray(arr, n);
```

  - The program outputs the sorted array using printArray().

Example Walkthrough

Given array: {64, 25, 12, 22, 11}

Iteration 1 (i = 0):

- Find the minimum element in [64, 25, 12, 22, 11]. The minimum is 11.
- Swap 11 and 64.
- Array becomes: {11, 25, 12, 22, 64}.

Iteration 2 (i = 1):

- Find the minimum element in [25, 12, 22, 64]. The minimum is 12.
- Swap 12 and 25.
- Array becomes: {11, 12, 25, 22, 64}.

Iteration 3 (i = 2):

- Find the minimum element in [25, 22, 64]. The minimum is 22.
- Swap 22 and 25.
- Array becomes: {11, 12, 22, 25, 64}.

Iteration 4 (i = 3):

- Find the minimum element in [25, 64]. The minimum is 25 (already in place).
- No swap needed.
- Final array: {11, 12, 22, 25, 64}.

---

b. Bubble Sort

Objective: Bubble Sort repeatedly steps through the list, compares adjacent elements, and swaps them if they are in the wrong order.

Properties:

- **Time Complexity**: O(n^2), O(n) in best case (if the array is already sorted)
- **Space Complexity**: O(1)
- **Stable**: Yes

Best Use Cases: Suitable for small or mostly sorted datasets; it's an easy-to-understand and implement algorithm but inefficient for large datasets.

Real-Life Example: Imagine blowing bubbles in water; the largest ones quickly rise to the top, similar to how the largest numbers "bubble up" to the end of the list.

C Code:

```
#include <stdio.h>

void bubbleSort(int arr[], int n) {
    for (int i = 0; i < n - 1; i++) {
        for (int j = 0; j < n - i - 1; j++) {
            if (arr[j] > arr[j + 1]) {
                int temp = arr[j];
                arr[j] = arr[j + 1];
                arr[j + 1] = temp;
            }
        }
    }
}

void printArray(int arr[], int n) {
    for (int i = 0; i < n; i++)
        printf("%d ", arr[i]);
    printf("\n");
}

int main() {
    int arr[] = {64, 34, 25, 12, 22, 11, 90};
    int n = sizeof(arr)/sizeof(arr[0]);
    bubbleSort(arr, n);
    printf("Sorted array: \n");
    printArray(arr, n);
    return 0;
}
```

OUTPUT

```
Sorted array:
11 12 22 25 34 64 90
```

Code Explanation

This C program implements the Bubble Sort algorithm to sort an array of integers in ascending order. Here's a breakdown of each part:

Code Breakdown

1. **Including Libraries:**

```
#include <stdio.h>
```

The #include <stdio.h> directive imports the standard input-output library, which allows the program to use functions like printf.

2. **Bubble Sort Function Definition:**

```
void bubbleSort(int arr[], int n) {
    for (int i = 0; i < n - 1; i++) {
        for (int j = 0; j < n - i - 1; j++) {
            if (arr[j] > arr[j + 1]) {
                int temp = arr[j];
                arr[j] = arr[j + 1];
                arr[j + 1] = temp;
            }
        }
    }
}
```

- **Function Purpose**: This function performs the Bubble Sort on the input array arr of length n.
- **Outer Loop (i)**: The loop for (int i = 0; i < n - 1; i++) goes through each element, repeating the sorting pass n - 1 times. As each pass guarantees that the largest remaining unsorted element bubbles up to its correct

position, the number of passes required decreases with each iteration.

- **Inner Loop (j)**: The inner loop for (int j = 0; j < n - i - 1; j ++) compares adjacent elements in the array. With each pass, the inner loop goes up to n - i - 1 to avoid re-sorting already sorted elements at the end of the array.
- **Swapping Elements**: If arr[j] > arr[j + 1], it means the current element is larger than the next element, so they are swapped. The temporary variable temp is used to hold arr[j] while swapping values.

3. **Print Array Function:**

```
void printArray(int arr[], int n) {
    for (int i = 0; i < n; i++)
        printf("%d ", arr[i]);
    printf("\n");
}
```

- This function prints the elements of the array arr of length n. The for loop iterates through each element and prints it, followed by a space. Finally, printf("\n"); adds a newline after the array.

4. **Main Function:**

```
int main() {
    int arr[] = {64, 34, 25, 12, 22, 11, 90};
    int n = sizeof(arr)/sizeof(arr[0]);
    bubbleSort(arr, n);
    printf("Sorted array: \n");
    printArray(arr, n);
    return 0;
}
```

- **Array Initialization**: An array arr with 7 integers is initialized with some unsorted values.

- **Calculating Array Length**: int n = sizeof(arr)/ sizeof(arr[0]); calculates the number of elements in arr. sizeof(arr) gives the total bytes of the array, and sizeof(arr[0]) gives the bytes of one integer. Dividing these provides the number of elements.
- **Sorting the Array**: The bubbleSort(arr, n); function is called to sort the array.
- **Printing the Sorted Array**: printf("Sorted array: \n"); prints a header, and printArray(arr, n); prints the sorted array.

---

c. Insertion Sort

Objective: Insertion Sort builds the sorted array one item at a time by repeatedly picking the next element and inserting it into its correct position.

Properties:

- **Time Complexity**: O(n^2), O(n) for nearly sorted data
- **Space Complexity**: O(1)
- **Stable**: Yes

Best Use Cases: Effective for small or nearly sorted datasets; it's simple and has good performance in these cases.

Real-Life Example: Arranging a hand of playing cards by picking and placing each card in its correct position among already sorted cards.

C Code:

```
#include <stdio.h>

void insertionSort(int arr[], int n) {
    for (int i = 1; i < n; i++) {
        int key = arr[i];
        int j = i - 1;
        while (j >= 0 && arr[j] > key) {
            arr[j + 1] = arr[j];
```

```
            j = j - 1;
        }
        arr[j + 1] = key;
    }
}

void printArray(int arr[], int n) {
    for (int i = 0; i < n; i++)
        printf("%d ", arr[i]);
    printf("\n");
}

int main() {
    int arr[] = {12, 11, 13, 5, 6};
    int n = sizeof(arr)/sizeof(arr[0]);
    insertionSort(arr, n);
    printArray(arr, n);
    return 0;
}
```

Code Explanation:

Let's break down this C program, which performs insertion sort on an array and then prints the sorted array.

1. Importing Standard I/O Library

```
#include <stdio.h>
```

This line includes the standard input-output library in C, which is necessary for using printf.

2. Insertion Sort Function

```
void insertionSort(int arr[], int n) {
    for (int i = 1; i < n; i++) {
        int key = arr[i];
        int j = i - 1;
        while (j >= 0 && arr[j] > key) {
            arr[j + 1] = arr[j];
```

```
            j = j - 1;
        }
        arr[j + 1] = key;
    }
}
```

This function performs insertion sort on the array arr of length n.

- **Outer Loop** (for loop): This loop iterates over each element starting from arr[1] (the second element) to arr[n-1] (last element).
    - **key** stores the value of arr[i], which is the element currently being positioned in the sorted part of the array.
    - **j = i - 1;**: j points to the last element in the sorted part of the array (the portion from arr[0] to arr[i-1]).
- **Inner Loop** (while loop): This loop shifts elements in the sorted part of the array that are larger than key to the right, creating a place for the key.
    - **Condition** (j >= 0 && arr[j] > key): The loop continues as long as j is non-negative and arr[j] is greater than key.
    - **arr[j + 1] = arr[j];**: Moves arr[j] one position to the right.
    - **j = j - 1;**: Decrements j to compare the next element to the left with key.
- **Insert key in the Correct Position**: After the inner loop, arr[j + 1] = key; places key in the correct position within the sorted part of the array.

3. Print Array Function

```
void printArray(int arr[], int n) {
    for (int i = 0; i < n; i++)
        printf("%d ", arr[i]);
    printf("\n");
```

```
}
```

This function prints the elements of the array arr. It loops through each element and prints it, followed by a space, and then moves to a new line.

4. Main Function

```
int main() {
    int arr[] = {12, 11, 13, 5, 6};
    int n = sizeof(arr)/sizeof(arr[0]);
    insertionSort(arr, n);
    printArray(arr, n);
    return 0;
}
```

This is the main entry point of the program.

- **Define the Array**: int arr[] = {12, 11, 13, 5, 6}; initializes an array of five integers.
- **Calculate Length**: int n = sizeof(arr)/sizeof(arr[0]); calculates the length of the array arr.
- **Sort the Array**: insertionSort(arr, n); calls the insertionSort function to sort arr.
- **Print Sorted Array**: printArray(arr, n); calls the printArray function to print the sorted array.
- **Return 0**: return 0; indicates the program has ended successfully.

---

d. Quick Sort

Objective: Quick Sort selects a pivot and partitions the array around it, sorting elements relative to the pivot recursively.

Properties:

- **Time Complexity**: O(nlogn) on average, O(n^2) worst case

- **Space Complexity**: O(logn)
- **Stable**: No

Best Use Cases: Ideal for large datasets and generally faster than other O(n2)O(n^2)O(n2) algorithms. It's particularly useful when memory overhead needs to be low.

Real-Life Example: Organizing a library by choosing a middle book as a pivot and separating books with authors' names earlier and later in the alphabet.

C Code:

```
#include <stdio.h>

void swap(int* a, int* b) {
    int t = *a;
    *a = *b;
    *b = t;
}

int partition(int arr[], int low, int high) {
    int pivot = arr[high];
    int i = (low - 1);
    for (int j = low; j <= high - 1; j++) {
        if (arr[j] < pivot) {
            i++;
            swap(&arr[i], &arr[j]);
        }
    }
    swap(&arr[i + 1], &arr[high]);
    return (i + 1);
}

void quickSort(int arr[], int low, int high) {
    if (low < high) {
        int pi = partition(arr, low, high);
        quickSort(arr, low, pi - 1);
        quickSort(arr, pi + 1, high);
    }
```

```
}

void printArray(int arr[], int n) {
    for (int i = 0; i < n; i++)
        printf("%d ", arr[i]);
    printf("\n");
}

int main() {
    int arr[] = {10, 7, 8, 9, 1, 5};
    int n = sizeof(arr)/sizeof(arr[0]);
    quickSort(arr, 0, n - 1);
    printf("Sorted array: \n");
    printArray(arr, n);
    return 0;
}
```

OUTPUT

```
Sorted array:
1 5 7 8 9 10
```

Code Explanation

This program implements the QuickSort algorithm in C. Let's go through it step-by-step.

Code Breakdown:

1. **Libraries and Function Declarations**:
    - #include <stdio.h>: Includes the standard input/output library for using printf.
    - The program defines several functions: swap, partition, quickSort, and printArray.
2. **swap Function**:
    - **Purpose**: Swaps the values of two integers.
    - **Parameters**: Pointers to two integers (int* a, int* b).
    - **Logic**: Uses a temporary variable t to hold the value of *a, then swaps the values of *a and

*b.

```
void swap(int* a, int* b) {
    int t = *a;
    *a = *b;
    *b = t;
}
```

3. **partition Function**:
    - **Purpose**: Partitions the array around a "pivot" element and returns the partition index.
    - **Parameters**: Array arr[], and two indices low and high.
    - **Logic**:
        - The pivot element is chosen as the last element (arr[high]).
        - A variable i is initialized to low - 1 to mark the boundary of elements smaller than the pivot.
        - The loop iterates from low to high - 1, checking if each element is less than the pivot.
            - If arr[j] < pivot, it increments i and swaps arr[i] and arr[j] to place the smaller element on the left.
        - After the loop, the pivot is swapped with arr[i + 1] to place it in its correct sorted position.
        - Returns the index i + 1, the final position of the pivot.

```
int partition(int arr[], int low, int high) {
    int pivot = arr[high];
    int i = (low - 1);
    for (int j = low; j <= high - 1; j++) {
        if (arr[j] < pivot) {
```

```
            i++;
            swap(&arr[i], &arr[j]);
        }
    }
    swap(&arr[i + 1], &arr[high]);
    return (i + 1);
}
```

4. **quickSort Function**:
    - **Purpose**: Recursively sorts the array using the QuickSort algorithm.
    - **Parameters**: Array arr[], and two indices low and high.
    - **Logic**:
        - If low < high, the array has more than one element and needs sorting.
        - Calls partition to partition the array and get the pivot index pi.
        - Recursively applies QuickSort to the left and right sub-arrays split by pi.

```
void quickSort(int arr[], int low, int high) {
    if (low < high) {
        int pi = partition(arr, low, high);
        quickSort(arr, low, pi - 1);
        quickSort(arr, pi + 1, high);
    }
}
```

5. **printArray Function**:
    - **Purpose**: Prints all elements of the array.
    - **Parameters**: Array arr[] and its size n.
    - **Logic**: Loops through each element in arr[] and prints it with a space.

```
void printArray(int arr[], int n) {
    for (int i = 0; i < n; i++)
```

```
        printf("%d ", arr[i]);
    printf("\n");
}
```

6. **main Function**:
    - **Purpose**: The entry point of the program where the QuickSort algorithm is applied to a test array.
    - **Steps**:
        - Initializes arr[] with sample data and calculates its length n.
        - Calls quickSort on the entire array.
        - Prints the sorted array using printArray.

```
int main() {
    int arr[] = {10, 7, 8, 9, 1, 5};
    int n = sizeof(arr)/sizeof(arr[0]);
    quickSort(arr, 0, n - 1);
    printf("Sorted array: \n");
    printArray(arr, n);
    return 0;
}
```

Step-by-Step Execution:

1. **Initialize and Sort**: The main function initializes an array and calls quickSort.
2. **Partitioning and Recursive Sorting**:
    - quickSort recursively partitions the array and sorts subarrays around each pivot.
3. **Final Output**: After sorting, printArray displays the sorted array as output.

---

e. Merge Sort

Objective: Merge Sort divides the array into halves, sorts each half, and merges them back together in sorted order.

Properties:

- **Time Complexity**: O(nlogn)O(n \log n)O(nlogn)
- **Space Complexity**: O(n)O(n)O(n)
- **Stable**: Yes

Best Use Cases: Great for large datasets or linked lists and when stable sorting is required.

Real-Life Example: Sorting cards by splitting them into smaller piles, organizing each pile, and then merging them back together in order.

C Code:

```
#include <stdio.h>
#include <stdlib.h>

void merge(int arr[], int l, int m, int r) {
    int n1 = m - l + 1;
    int n2 = r - m;

    int L[n1], R[n2];
    for (int i = 0; i < n1; i++)
        L[i] = arr[l + i];
    for (int j = 0; j < n2; j++)
        R[j] = arr[m + 1 + j];

    int i = 0, j = 0, k = l;
    while (i < n1 && j < n2) {
        if (L[i] <= R[j]) {
            arr[k] = L[i];
            i++;
        } else {
            arr[k] = R[j];
            j++;
        }
        k++;
    }
    while (i < n1) {
```

```
        arr[k] = L[i];
        i++;
        k++;
    }
    while (j < n2) {
        arr[k] = R[j];
        j++;
        k++;
    }
}

void mergeSort(int arr[], int l, int r) {
    if (l < r) {
        int m = l + (r - l) / 2;
        mergeSort(arr, l, m);
        mergeSort(arr, m + 1, r);
        merge(arr, l, m, r);
    }
}

void printArray(int arr[], int n) {
    for (int i = 0; i < n; i++)
        printf("%d ", arr[i]);
    printf("\n");
}

int main() {
    int arr[] = {12, 11, 13, 5, 6, 7};
    int n = sizeof(arr)/sizeof(arr[0]);
    mergeSort(arr, 0, n - 1);
    printf("Sorted array: \n");
    printArray(arr, n);
    return 0;
}
```

OUTPUT

```
Sorted array:
5 6 7 11 12 13
```

Code Explanation:

This C program implements the merge sort algorithm, a recursive, divide-and-conquer sorting algorithm. Let's break it down step by step.

Step 1: Define merge() function

The merge function is responsible for merging two halves of an array in sorted order.

1. **Initialize Array Sizes**:

```
int n1 = m - l + 1;
int n2 = r - m;
```

Here, n1 and n2 are the sizes of the left and right subarrays, calculated from the midpoint m.

2. **Create Temporary Arrays**:

```
int L[n1], R[n2];
```

Two temporary arrays, L and R, hold the left and right halves of the array arr.

3. **Copy Data to Temp Arrays**:

```
for (int i = 0; i < n1; i++)
    L[i] = arr[l + i];
for (int j = 0; j < n2; j++)
    R[j] = arr[m + 1 + j];
```

This copies the elements of arr into the L and R arrays.

4. **Merge the Arrays Back into arr**:
    - The while loop compares elements of L and R:

```
while (i < n1 && j < n2) {
    if (L[i] <= R[j]) {
```

```
        arr[k] = L[i];
        i++;
    } else {
        arr[k] = R[j];
        j++;
    }
    k++;
}
```

If L[i] is less than or equal to R[j], it copies L[i] into arr and increments i. Otherwise, it copies R[j] and increments j.

- **Copy Remaining Elements**:

```
while (i < n1) {
    arr[k] = L[i];
    i++;
    k++;
}
while (j < n2) {
    arr[k] = R[j];
    j++;
    k++;
}
```

After the main merging loop, this ensures any leftover elements from L or R are added to arr.

Step 2: Define mergeSort() function

The mergeSort function is a recursive function that divides the array and sorts the two halves.

1. **Check Base Case**:

```
if (l < r) {
    int m = l + (r - l) / 2;
```

The function checks if l is less than r (meaning more than one element). If so, it calculates the midpoint m.

2. **Recursively Sort the Two Halves**:

```
mergeSort(arr, l, m);
mergeSort(arr, m + 1, r);
```

This divides the array into two halves, sorting each half.

3. **Merge the Sorted Halves**:

```
merge(arr, l, m, r);
```

After both halves are sorted, they are merged back together in sorted order using the merge function.

Step 3: Define printArray() function

The printArray function simply prints each element in the array.

1. **Print Each Element**:

```
for (int i = 0; i < n; i++)
    printf("%d ", arr[i]);
printf("\n");
```

Loops through each element in the array and prints it, with a space in between each element.

Step 4: Main Function

The main function is the entry point of the program.

1. **Initialize Array**:

```
int arr[] = {12, 11, 13, 5, 6, 7};
int n = sizeof(arr)/sizeof(arr[0]);
```

Creates an array of integers and calculates its length.

2. **Sort Array Using Merge Sort**:

```
mergeSort(arr, 0, n - 1);
```

Calls mergeSort with the entire array range (from index 0 to n - 1).

3. **Print Sorted Array**:

```
printf("Sorted array: \n");
printArray(arr, n);
```

Finally, it prints the sorted array using printArray.

Overall Flow

1. mergeSort recursively splits the array in half until single-element arrays remain.
2. merge merges these small arrays back together in sorted order.
3. After the entire array is sorted, printArray displays the sorted array.

---

f. Heap Sort

Objective: Heap Sort uses a binary heap data structure to organize elements, building a max heap and then swapping the root with the last item.

Properties:

- **Time Complexity**: O(nlogn)
- **Space Complexity**: O(1)
- **Stable**: No

Best Use Cases: Suitable for scenarios requiring an in-place O(nlogn)O(n \log n)O(nlogn) sorting algorithm, such as systems where space efficiency is crucial.

Real-Life Example: Priority queues in operating systems use heap structures for scheduling tasks.

C Code:

```
#include <stdio.h>

void heapify(int arr[], int n, int i) {
    int largest = i;
    int left = 2 * i + 1;
    int right = 2 * i + 2;
```

```
    if (left < n && arr[left] > arr[largest])
        largest = left;

    if (right < n && arr[right] > arr[largest])
        largest = right;

    if (largest != i) {
        int temp = arr[i];
        arr[i] = arr[largest];
        arr[largest] = temp;
        heapify(arr, n, largest);
    }
}

void heapSort(int arr[], int n) {
    for (int i = n / 2 - 1; i >= 0; i--)
        heapify(arr, n, i);

    for (int i = n - 1; i > 0; i--) {
        int temp = arr[0];
        arr[0] = arr[i];
        arr[i] = temp;
        heapify(arr, i, 0);
    }
}

void printArray(int arr[], int n) {
    for (int i = 0; i < n; i++)
        printf("%d ", arr[i]);
    printf("\n");
}

int main() {
    int arr[] = {12, 11, 13, 5, 6, 7};
    int n = sizeof(arr)/sizeof(arr[0]);
    heapSort(arr, n);
    printf("Sorted array: \n");
```

```
    printArray(arr, n);
    return 0;
}
```

OUTPUT

```
Sorted array:
5 6 7 11 12 13
```

Code Explanation:

This code demonstrates the implementation of the **Heap Sort** algorithm in C, which uses a binary heap data structure. Let's walk through the code step-by-step.

1. Understanding heapify Function

The heapify function is a key component of heap sort, which is responsible for creating a **max-heap** from a subtree rooted at index i.

Here's a breakdown of the function:

```
void heapify(int arr[], int n, int i) {
    int largest = i;          // Initialize largest as root
    int left = 2 * i + 1;      // Left child index
    int right = 2 * i + 2;     // Right child index

    if (left < n && arr[left] > arr[largest])
        largest = left;        // Update largest if left child is
greater

    if (right < n && arr[right] > arr[largest])
        largest = right;       // Update largest if right child is
greater

    if (largest != i) {
        int temp = arr[i];
        arr[i] = arr[largest];
        arr[largest] = temp;    // Swap root with largest child

        heapify(arr, n, largest); // Recursively heapify the
```

```
affected subtree
    }
}
```

Explanation:

- **Purpose**: heapify ensures that the subtree rooted at index i satisfies the max-heap property.
- **Working**:
    1. The initial assumption is that the largest element is the root (i).
    2. Then it checks if the left or right child is greater than the root. If so, it updates largest.
    3. If largest has changed, it swaps the root with the largest child and calls heapify recursively for the new subtree rooted at the child to fix any violations.

2. Understanding heapSort Function

The heapSort function sorts the array by first building a max-heap and then extracting elements one by one to place them in sorted order.

```
void heapSort(int arr[], int n) {
    for (int i = n / 2 - 1; i >= 0; i--)
        heapify(arr, n, i);     // Build max heap from bottom-
up

    for (int i = n - 1; i > 0; i--) {
        int temp = arr[0];
        arr[0] = arr[i];
        arr[i] = temp;        // Swap the root (max element)
with the last element

        heapify(arr, i, 0);     // Heapify the reduced heap
    }
}
```

Explanation:

1. **Build Max-Heap**:
    - The first loop (for (int i = n / 2 - 1; i >= 0; i--)) starts from the last non-leaf node and applies heapify to create a max-heap.
2. **Heap Sort Process**:
    - After building the max-heap, the function enters the second loop, where:
        - The largest element (root of the heap) is swapped with the last element in the heap.
        - The heapify function is called on the reduced heap (excluding the last element, now sorted) to maintain the max-heap property for the rest of the unsorted array.

3. Understanding printArray Function

The printArray function simply prints each element in the array.

```
void printArray(int arr[], int n) {
    for (int i = 0; i < n; i++)
        printf("%d ", arr[i]);
    printf("\n");
}
```

Explanation:

- This function takes an array and its length as inputs, then iterates through the array, printing each element followed by a space.

4. main Function

This function initializes an array, calls heapSort, and prints the sorted array.

```
int main() {
    int arr[] = {12, 11, 13, 5, 6, 7};
    int n = sizeof(arr)/sizeof(arr[0]);
    heapSort(arr, n);
```

```
    printf("Sorted array: \n");
    printArray(arr, n);
    return 0;
}
```

Explanation:

1. The array arr[] = {12, 11, 13, 5, 6, 7} is defined.
2. n is calculated as the length of the array.
3. heapSort(arr, n) sorts the array.
4. The sorted array is then printed.

Execution of the Code

Let's break down what happens when the code runs with the given input {12, 11, 13, 5, 6, 7}:

1. **Build Max-Heap**:
    - Starting from the last non-leaf node, the heapify process arranges elements to satisfy the max-heap property.
    - Resulting max-heap: {13, 12, 7, 5, 6, 11}.
2. **Sorting**:
    - The largest element (root of the heap) is moved to the end.
    - heapify is applied to the reduced heap to continue sorting.
    - After all iterations, the sorted array becomes {5, 6, 7, 11, 12, 13}.

---

3. Performance and Comparison

Algorithm	Time Complexity	Space Complexity	Stable	Best Use Cases
Selection Sort	O(n^2)	O(1)	No	Small arrays, low memory requirements
Bubble Sort	O(n^2)	O(1)	Yes	Small, mostly sorted arrays
Insertion Sort	O(n^2)	O(1)	Yes	Small, nearly sorted arrays
Quick Sort	O(n log n)	O(logn)	No	Large, random datasets
Merge Sort	O(nlogn)	O(n)	Yes	Large datasets, stability required

Heap Sort	O(nlogn)	O(1)	No	Large datasets, memory efficiency

4. When to Use Which Algorithm

- **Selection Sort**: When simplicity and minimal memory usage are essential.
- **Bubble Sort**: Suitable for educational purposes or if the data is almost sorted.
- **Insertion Sort**: Ideal for small or nearly sorted datasets.
- **Quick Sort**: Best for general-purpose sorting with random data due to average-case performance.
- **Merge Sort**: Excellent choice when stability is essential, especially for linked lists.
- **Heap Sort**: Useful when constant space and an O(n logn) sort are needed.

1. Definition and Purpose of Hashing

Hashing is a technique used to map data (keys) to specific positions (indices) in a data structure, typically an array. This mapping is achieved using a hash function, which converts data into a hash code or hash value, often used as an index in a hash table. The purpose of hashing is to enable fast data retrieval, insertion, and deletion, making it useful in scenarios where speed and efficiency are crucial.

2. Hash Functions

A **hash function** is a mathematical function that takes an input (or 'key') and returns an integer, called a hash code or hash value. This hash code is then used as an index in a hash table to store the corresponding data.

Example of a Hash Function in C:

```
#include <stdio.h>
#define TABLE_SIZE 10

int hashFunction(int key) {
    return key % TABLE_SIZE;  // Simple modulo-based
```

```
hash function
}

int main() {
    int key = 25;
    int index = hashFunction(key);
    printf("The index for key %d is %d\n", key, index);
    return 0;
}
```

OUTPUT

```
The index for key 25 is 5
```

In this example, the hash function is key % TABLE_SIZE, which maps each key to a position in an array of size TABLE_SIZE.

This C program demonstrates a simple hash function that calculates the index of a given key within a hash table of a fixed size. Let's go through it step-by-step:

Code Analysis

1. **Header File Inclusion**

```
#include <stdio.h>
```

- This line includes the stdio.h library, which allows us to use input-output functions like printf to display output.

2. **Macro Definition**

```
#define TABLE_SIZE 10
```

- #define is a preprocessor directive that defines a constant named TABLE_SIZE with a value of 10. This value represents the size of our hash table.
- Setting TABLE_SIZE to 10 means the hash table will have 10 slots (from index 0 to 9).

3. **Hash Function Definition**

```
int hashFunction(int key) {
    return key % TABLE_SIZE; // Simple modulo-based
hash function
}
```

- This function, hashFunction, takes an integer key as input.
- It returns the result of key % TABLE_SIZE, which is the remainder when key is divided by TABLE_SIZE.
- This operation ensures that the returned index is always within the range of 0 to TABLE_SIZE - 1 (0 to 9 in this case).
- This is a basic hash function used to "map" a key to a particular index in the hash table.

4. **Main Function**

```
int main() {
    int key = 25;
    int index = hashFunction(key);
    printf("The index for key %d is %d\n", key, index);
    return 0;
}
```

- The main function is the entry point of the program.
- **Step-by-Step Execution in main:**
    - **Step 1:** int key = 25;
        - An integer variable key is initialized with the value 25. This is the key we want to hash.
    - **Step 2:** int index = hashFunction(key);
        - This line calls hashFunction with key as the argument.

    - Inside hashFunction, key % TABLE_SIZE is calculated: 25 % 10=525 \, \% \, 10 = 525%10=5
    - The function returns 5, which is assigned to index.
  - **Step 3:** printf("The index for key %d is %d\n", key, index);
    - The printf function outputs the key and its corresponding index: "The index for key 25 is 5".
  - **Step 4:** return 0;
    - The program terminates successfully, returning 0 to indicate successful execution.

3. Properties of a Good Hash Function

A good hash function should:

- **Distribute keys uniformly** across the hash table to minimize collisions.
- **Be efficient to compute** to ensure fast operations.
- **Minimize clustering**, which can slow down operations.
- **Use all information** in the key to produce a unique hash for each distinct input when possible.

4. Collision Resolution Techniques

Since hash functions may map multiple keys to the same index, collisions can occur. Various techniques can resolve these collisions:

a. Chaining

Chaining stores multiple items at the same index by using linked lists. When a collision occurs, the new element is added to the linked list at the hashed index.

Example Code for Chaining in C:

```
#include <stdio.h>
```

```
#include <stdlib.h>

#define TABLE_SIZE 10

typedef struct Node {
    int key;
    struct Node* next;
} Node;

Node* hashTable[TABLE_SIZE];

int hashFunction(int key) {
    return key % TABLE_SIZE;
}

void insert(int key) {
    int index = hashFunction(key);
    Node* newNode = (Node*)malloc(sizeof(Node));
    newNode->key = key;
    newNode->next = hashTable[index];
    hashTable[index] = newNode;
}

void display() {
    for (int i = 0; i < TABLE_SIZE; i++) {
        Node* temp = hashTable[i];
        printf("Index %d: ", i);
        while (temp) {
          printf("%d -> ", temp->key);
          temp = temp->next;
        }
        printf("NULL\n");
    }
}

int main() {
    insert(12);
    insert(22);
```

```
    insert(32);
    display();
    return 0;
}
```

OUTPUT

```
Index 0: NULL
Index 1: NULL
Index 2: 32 -> 22 -> 12 -> NULL
Index 3: NULL
Index 4: NULL
Index 5: NULL
Index 6: NULL
Index 7: NULL
Index 8: NULL
Index 9: NULL
```

Code Explanation:

In this example, inserting keys 12, 22, and 32 will result in the same index (if TABLE_SIZE is 10), but they'll be stored in a linked list at that index.

This C code demonstrates a basic implementation of a hash table with chaining for collision resolution. Let's go through it step by step:

Step 1: Include Standard Libraries

```
#include <stdio.h>
#include <stdlib.h>
```

- stdio.h is included for input/output functions like printf.
- stdlib.h is included for memory allocation functions like malloc.

Step 2: Define Constants and Structures

```
#define TABLE_SIZE 10

typedef struct Node {
    int key;
    struct Node* next;
} Node;
```

- TABLE_SIZE is set to 10, defining the size of the hash table.
- Node is a structure used for chaining elements in each bucket of the hash table. It contains:
    - int key: The key to store in the hash table.
    - Node* next: A pointer to the next node in the chain.

Step 3: Initialize the Hash Table

```
Node* hashTable[TABLE_SIZE];
```

- An array hashTable of pointers to Node is created with a size of TABLE_SIZE. Each entry will act as the head of a linked list for chaining.

Step 4: Define the Hash Function

```
int hashFunction(int key) {
    return key % TABLE_SIZE;
}
```

- hashFunction takes an integer key as input and returns an index in the hash table by calculating key % TABLE_SIZE.
- This function helps distribute keys into the table by mapping each key to a particular index.

Step 5: Insert Function

```
void insert(int key) {
    int index = hashFunction(key);
```

```
    Node* newNode = (Node*)malloc(sizeof(Node));
    newNode->key = key;
    newNode->next = hashTable[index];
    hashTable[index] = newNode;
}
```

- insert takes an integer key and places it in the hash table:
    - It first calculates the index using hashFunction.
    - It allocates memory for a new Node, sets its key, and points it to the current head node at hashTable[index].
    - hashTable[index] is updated to point to newNode, making it the new head of the chain for that index.
- This method implements *chaining* to handle collisions by linking multiple keys that map to the same index.

Step 6: Display Function

```
void display() {
    for (int i = 0; i < TABLE_SIZE; i++) {
        Node* temp = hashTable[i];
        printf("Index %d: ", i);
        while (temp) {
            printf("%d -> ", temp->key);
            temp = temp->next;
        }
        printf("NULL\n");
    }
}
```

- display prints the contents of the hash table:
    - It iterates over each index from 0 to TABLE_SIZE - 1.

- For each index, it follows the chain of Nodes (if any) and prints each key.
- If no keys are present at an index, it just prints NULL.

Step 7: Main Function

```
int main() {
    insert(12);
    insert(22);
    insert(32);
    display();
    return 0;
}
```

- The main function:
    - Calls insert to add keys 12, 22, and 32 to the hash table.
    - Calls display to print the entire hash table and observe where each key is stored.

Explanation of Key Behavior

- The hash function key % TABLE_SIZE will yield the same index for keys 12, 22, and 32, so they will be added to the same linked list at hashTable[2].
- When display is called, the output for Index 2 will show the chain of keys 32 -> 22 -> 12 -> NULL, indicating how collisions are handled by chaining.

b. Open Addressing

In open addressing, collisions are resolved by finding another open slot in the array using a probing method. Open addressing avoids linked lists by storing all entries within the hash table.

i. Linear Probing

In linear probing, when a collision occurs, the algorithm checks the next consecutive slot in the table (index + 1) until it finds an empty slot.

Example Code for Linear Probing in C:

```
#include <stdio.h>
#define TABLE_SIZE 10

int hashTable[TABLE_SIZE] = {0}; // Initialize hash table
with 0

int hashFunction(int key) {
    return key % TABLE_SIZE;
}

void insert(int key) {
    int index = hashFunction(key);
    while (hashTable[index] != 0) {
        index = (index + 1) % TABLE_SIZE;  // Move to next
index
    }
    hashTable[index] = key;
}

void display() {
    for (int i = 0; i < TABLE_SIZE; i++) {
        printf("Index %d: %d\n", i, hashTable[i]);
    }
}

int main() {
    insert(12);
    insert(22);
    insert(32);
    display();
    return 0;
}
```

OUTPUT

```
Index 0: 0
Index 1: 0
Index 2: 12
Index 3: 22
Index 4: 32
Index 5: 0
Index 6: 0
Index 7: 0
Index 8: 0
Index 9: 0
```

This C code implements a simple hash table with open addressing using linear probing for collision resolution. Let me break it down step by step.

1. Header File Inclusion

```
#include <stdio.h>
```

- The stdio.h header file is included to allow input/output operations, such as using printf to display output.

2. Constant Definition

```
#define TABLE_SIZE 10
```

- A constant TABLE_SIZE is defined with the value 10. This represents the size of the hash table, i.e., the number of slots in the table.

3. Hash Table Declaration

```
int hashTable[TABLE_SIZE] = {0}; // Initialize hash table
with 0
```

- This creates an array hashTable of size TABLE_SIZE (10). The array is initialized to 0, meaning all slots in the hash table are initially empty.

4. Hash Function

```
int hashFunction(int key) {
    return key % TABLE_SIZE;
}
```

- The hashFunction takes an integer key and returns the remainder when key is divided by TABLE_SIZE (10). This is a simple modulo operation used to map the key to an index in the hash table. The result of this function is the index where the key should ideally be stored in the table.

5. Insert Function

```
void insert(int key) {
    int index = hashFunction(key); // Calculate the index
for the key
    while (hashTable[index] != 0) { // If the index is
occupied (not empty)
        index = (index + 1) % TABLE_SIZE;  // Move to the
next index (linear probing)
    }
    hashTable[index] = key; // Insert the key at the empty
index
}
```

- The insert function adds a key to the hash table. Here's how it works:
    1. It first calculates the index where the key should be stored using the hashFunction.
    2. It checks if the slot at that index is already occupied (i.e., the value is not 0). If it's occupied, it moves to the next index using linear probing.
        - Linear probing means checking the next index (index + 1) and wrapping around using modulo (%

TABLE_SIZE) if the index exceeds the table size.

3. The key is inserted into the first available slot.

6. Display Function

```
void display() {
    for (int i = 0; i < TABLE_SIZE; i++) { // Loop through all
the indices
        printf("Index %d: %d\n", i, hashTable[i]); // Print
each index and its corresponding value
    }
}
```

- The display function prints the contents of the hash table. It loops through all indices from 0 to TABLE_SIZE - 1 and prints the index and the corresponding value stored in the hash table.

7. Main Function

```
int main() {
    insert(12); // Insert key 12 into the hash table
    insert(22); // Insert key 22 into the hash table
    insert(32); // Insert key 32 into the hash table
    display();  // Display the contents of the hash table
    return 0;   // Return 0 to indicate successful completion
}
```

- In the main function:
    1. Three keys (12, 22, and 32) are inserted into the hash table using the insert function.
    2. After inserting the keys, the display function is called to show the contents of the hash table.
    3. The program then ends with a return 0 statement indicating successful execution.

Step-by-Step Execution:

1. **Insert Key 12:**
   - Hash function: 12 % 10 = 2
   - Slot at index 2 is empty (0), so 12 is inserted at index 2.
2. **Insert Key 22:**
   - Hash function: 22 % 10 = 2
   - Slot at index 2 is already occupied by 12.
   - Linear probing: The next index is 3, which is empty, so 22 is inserted at index 3.
3. **Insert Key 32:**
   - Hash function: 32 % 10 = 2
   - Slot at index 2 is occupied by 12, and slot at index 3 is occupied by 22.
   - Linear probing: The next index is 4, which is empty, so 32 is inserted at index 4.
4. **Display Hash Table:**
   - After the insertions, the hash table looks like this:

```
Index 0: 0
Index 1: 0
Index 2: 12
Index 3: 22
Index 4: 32
Index 5: 0
Index 6: 0
Index 7: 0
Index 8: 0
Index 9: 0
```

- The keys 12, 22, and 32 are stored in indices 2, 3, and 4, respectively, and all other slots are empty (0).

ii. Quadratic Probing

Quadratic probing resolves collisions by checking indices according to a quadratic function, such as (index + i^2) % TABLE_SIZE.

iii. Double Hashing

Double hashing uses a second hash function to determine the step size in case of a collision, making it less prone to clustering.

5. Real-Life Examples of Hashing

- **Databases**: Hashing is used in databases for indexing, which allows for quick access to data by reducing the time complexity to O(1).
- **Password Storage**: Hashing is used to securely store passwords by converting them into hash codes, making it difficult to retrieve the original passwords.
- **Caching**: Hashing is used in caching algorithms to store and retrieve cached data efficiently.
- **Data Deduplication**: Hashing is used to identify and remove duplicate files in data storage systems by comparing hash values.

6. Applications of Hashing

- **Symbol Tables in Compilers**: Hash tables are used to store information about variables and functions, allowing quick lookup and storage.
- **File Systems**: Hash functions are used in file systems to store file metadata efficiently.
- **Load Balancing**: Hashing algorithms help distribute tasks across servers by mapping requests to specific servers.
- **Cryptographic Hashing**: Hash functions are essential in cryptography, used to encrypt information for secure communication.

Graph Basics and Terminologies

1. **Vertex (Node)**: A fundamental unit in a graph that represents an object. For example, in a social network, each person is a vertex.
2. **Edge**: A connection between two vertices. In an undirected graph, edges have no direction, while in directed graphs, edges have direction.
3. **Degree**:
    - **Degree of a Vertex**: The number of edges connected to a vertex.
    - **In-degree**: The number of incoming edges to a vertex (for directed graphs).
    - **Out-degree**: The number of outgoing edges from a vertex (for directed graphs).
4. **Path**: A sequence of vertices connected by edges. For example, in a graph with vertices A,B,CA, B, CA,B,C, a path could be A→B→CA \rightarrow B \rightarrow CA→B→C.
5. **Cycle**: A path where the starting and ending vertices are the same.

Graph Representations

1. Adjacency Matrix

An adjacency matrix represents a graph with a 2D array. Each element (i,j)(i, j)(i,j) of the matrix indicates whether there's an edge from vertex iii to vertex jjj.

- **Space Complexity**: O(V2)O(V^2)O(V2), where VVV is the number of vertices.

Example in C:

```
#include <stdio.h>

#define V 4

void printMatrix(int graph[V][V]) {
    for (int i = 0; i < V; i++) {
        for (int j = 0; j < V; j++) {
            printf("%d ", graph[i][j]);
```

```
        }
        printf("\n");
    }
}

int main() {
    int graph[V][V] = {
        {0, 1, 0, 1},
        {1, 0, 1, 0},
        {0, 1, 0, 1},
        {1, 0, 1, 0}
    };
    printMatrix(graph);
    return 0;
}
```

OUTPUT

```
0 1 0 1
1 0 1 0
0 1 0 1
1 0 1 0
```

Code Explanation:

This C code represents an undirected graph using an adjacency matrix and prints the matrix representation of the graph. Let's break it down step by step:

1. Preprocessor Directive and Macro Definition:

```
#define V 4
```

- This line defines a constant V with the value 4. V represents the number of vertices in the graph. The graph in this case is a 4x4 adjacency matrix, meaning the graph has 4 vertices. You can change V to any other number to represent a graph with a different number of vertices.

2. Function Definition: printMatrix

```
void printMatrix(int graph[V][V]) {
    for (int i = 0; i < V; i++) {
        for (int j = 0; j < V; j++) {
            printf("%d ", graph[i][j]);
        }
        printf("\n");
    }
}
```

- printMatrix is a function that takes a 2D array graph of size VxV (in this case, 4x4) as an argument and prints the matrix.
- The function uses two nested for loops to traverse through the 2D array (graph):
    - The outer loop iterates through each row of the matrix (i from 0 to V-1).
    - The inner loop iterates through each column of the current row (j from 0 to V-1).
- For each element graph[i][j], it prints the value followed by a space (printf("%d ", graph[i][j])).
- After printing the elements of one row, printf("\n") is used to move to the next line to print the next row.

3. Main Function

```
int main() {
    int graph[V][V] = {
        {0, 1, 0, 1},
        {1, 0, 1, 0},
        {0, 1, 0, 1},
        {1, 0, 1, 0}
    };
    printMatrix(graph);
    return 0;
}
```

- The main function is the entry point of the program. It creates and initializes a 4x4 adjacency matrix graph representing an undirected graph.
    - **Matrix Representation:**

The matrix graph[V][V] is a 2D array with 4 rows and 4 columns, initialized as:

```
{0, 1, 0, 1},
{1, 0, 1, 0},
{0, 1, 0, 1},
{1, 0, 1, 0}
```

- Each element graph[i][j] indicates whether there is an edge between vertex i and vertex j.
- If graph[i][j] = 1, there is an edge between vertex i and vertex j.
- If graph[i][j] = 0, there is no edge between vertex i and vertex j.
- This matrix represents an **undirected graph**, so graph[i][j] equals graph[j][i]. For example, graph[0][1] = 1 and graph[1][0] = 1.

The graph's adjacency matrix can be interpreted as:

```
Vertex 0: connected to 1 and 3
Vertex 1: connected to 0 and 2
Vertex 2: connected to 1 and 3
Vertex 3: connected to 0 and 2
```

- The function printMatrix(graph) is called to print the graph's adjacency matrix.
- The program ends with return 0; indicating that the program executed successfully.

2. Adjacency List

In an adjacency list, each vertex stores a list of adjacent vertices. This representation is efficient in terms of space for sparse graphs.

- **Space Complexity**: O(V+E), where E is the number of edges.

Example in C:

```
#include <stdio.h>
#include <stdlib.h>

struct Node {
    int dest;
    struct Node* next;
};

struct Graph {
    int V;
    struct Node** adjList;
};

struct Graph* createGraph(int V) {
    struct Graph* graph = (struct
Graph*)malloc(sizeof(struct Graph));
    graph->V = V;
    graph->adjList = (struct Node**)malloc(V * sizeof(struct
Node*));
    for (int i = 0; i < V; i++)
        graph->adjList[i] = NULL;
    return graph;
}

void addEdge(struct Graph* graph, int src, int dest) {
    struct Node* newNode = (struct
Node*)malloc(sizeof(struct Node));
    newNode->dest = dest;
```

```
    newNode->next = graph->adjList[src];
    graph->adjList[src] = newNode;

    newNode = (struct Node*)malloc(sizeof(struct Node));
    newNode->dest = src;
    newNode->next = graph->adjList[dest];
    graph->adjList[dest] = newNode;
}

void printGraph(struct Graph* graph) {
    for (int v = 0; v < graph->V; v++) {
        struct Node* temp = graph->adjList[v];
        printf("Vertex %d: ", v);
        while (temp) {
            printf(" -> %d", temp->dest);
            temp = temp->next;
        }
        printf("\n");
    }
}

int main() {
    int V = 4;
    struct Graph* graph = createGraph(V);
    addEdge(graph, 0, 1);
    addEdge(graph, 0, 2);
    addEdge(graph, 1, 2);
    addEdge(graph, 1, 3);
    printGraph(graph);
    return 0;
}
```

OUTPUT

```
Vertex 0:  -> 2 -> 1
Vertex 1:  -> 3 -> 2 -> 0
Vertex 2:  -> 1 -> 0
```

```
Vertex 3: -> 1
```

Code Explanation:

This code represents a simple undirected graph using adjacency lists and demonstrates how to create and print the graph. Here's a step-by-step breakdown:

1. Struct Definitions

```
struct Node {
    int dest;
    struct Node* next;
};
```

- **Node Struct**: This defines a node in the adjacency list. Each node represents an edge from a vertex to another vertex (dest). It also contains a pointer to the next node (next), allowing the list to chain nodes together.

```
struct Graph {
    int V;
    struct Node** adjList;
};
```

- **Graph Struct**: This defines the graph. It contains:
    - V: The number of vertices in the graph.
    - adjList: A pointer to an array of pointers, where each element of the array is the head of a linked list representing adjacent vertices (edges) for a given vertex.

2. createGraph Function

```
struct Graph* createGraph(int V) {
    struct Graph* graph = (struct
Graph*)malloc(sizeof(struct Graph));
    graph->V = V;
```

```
    graph->adjList = (struct Node**)malloc(V * sizeof(struct
Node*));
    for (int i = 0; i < V; i++)
        graph->adjList[i] = NULL;
    return graph;
}
```

- This function creates and initializes a graph:
    1. Allocates memory for the Graph struct using malloc.
    2. Sets the number of vertices V in the graph.
    3. Allocates memory for the adjacency list array, with one pointer for each vertex.
    4. Initializes each vertex's adjacency list as NULL (meaning no edges yet).
    5. Returns the created graph.

3. addEdge Function

```
void addEdge(struct Graph* graph, int src, int dest) {
    struct Node* newNode = (struct
Node*)malloc(sizeof(struct Node));
    newNode->dest = dest;
    newNode->next = graph->adjList[src];
    graph->adjList[src] = newNode;

    newNode = (struct Node*)malloc(sizeof(struct Node));
    newNode->dest = src;
    newNode->next = graph->adjList[dest];
    graph->adjList[dest] = newNode;
}
```

- This function adds an edge to the graph:
    1. It first adds an edge from src to dest. A new node is created, with dest as its destination. This node is inserted at the head of the adjacency list of src.

2. It then adds an edge from dest to src (because the graph is undirected). A new node is created with src as its destination, and it is added to the adjacency list of dest.

4. printGraph Function

```
void printGraph(struct Graph* graph) {
    for (int v = 0; v < graph->V; v++) {
        struct Node* temp = graph->adjList[v];
        printf("Vertex %d: ", v);
        while (temp) {
            printf(" -> %d", temp->dest);
            temp = temp->next;
        }
        printf("\n");
    }
}
```

- This function prints the graph:
    1. It loops through each vertex (v).
    2. For each vertex, it prints the vertex label.
    3. It then traverses the adjacency list of that vertex and prints the destination of each edge, i.e., the connected vertices.

5. main Function

```
int main() {
    int V = 4;
    struct Graph* graph = createGraph(V);
    addEdge(graph, 0, 1);
    addEdge(graph, 0, 2);
    addEdge(graph, 1, 2);
    addEdge(graph, 1, 3);
    printGraph(graph);
    return 0;
}
```

- This is the main program where the graph is created and edges are added:
    1. A graph with 4 vertices is created by calling createGraph(V).
    2. Four edges are added using addEdge:
        - 0 -> 1
        - 0 -> 2
        - 1 -> 2
        - 1 -> 3
    3. Finally, the printGraph function is called to display the adjacency lists.

Depth-First Search (DFS) is an algorithm for traversing or searching tree or graph data structures. It explores as far as possible along each branch before backtracking, making it useful for tasks that require searching deep into a structure, such as puzzle-solving or pathfinding.

Key Concepts:

1. **Recursive or Iterative**: DFS can be implemented either recursively or iteratively (using a stack).
2. **Stack-Based**: DFS uses a stack data structure to keep track of nodes to be explored. In the recursive version, the call stack serves this purpose.
3. **Backtracking**: DFS goes as deep as possible along each branch and, when it cannot go further, it backtracks to the previous node to explore other paths.
4. **Applications**: DFS is used in applications such as:
    - Finding connected components in a graph.
    - Solving mazes and puzzles.
    - Detecting cycles in graphs.
    - Topological sorting.

How DFS Works:

1. Start at a given node, marking it as visited.
2. Explore each adjacent node one by one:
    - If an adjacent node hasn't been visited, move to that node and continue the process.
    - If all adjacent nodes are visited, backtrack to the previous node.
3. Repeat until all nodes are visited or a specified goal is reached.

DFS in C (using Adjacency List Representation)

```
#include <stdio.h>
#include <stdlib.h>

#define MAX 100

struct Node {
    int vertex;
    struct Node* next;
};

struct Graph {
    int numVertices;
    struct Node** adjLists;
    int* visited;
};

// Function to create a node
struct Node* createNode(int v) {
    struct Node* newNode = malloc(sizeof(struct Node));
    newNode->vertex = v;
    newNode->next = NULL;
    return newNode;
}

// Function to create a graph
struct Graph* createGraph(int vertices) {
    struct Graph* graph = malloc(sizeof(struct Graph));
    graph->numVertices = vertices;
```

```
    graph->adjLists = malloc(vertices * sizeof(struct
Node*));
    graph->visited = malloc(vertices * sizeof(int));

    for (int i = 0; i < vertices; i++) {
        graph->adjLists[i] = NULL;
        graph->visited[i] = 0;
    }
    return graph;
}

// Add edge to graph
void addEdge(struct Graph* graph, int src, int dest) {
    // Add edge from src to dest
    struct Node* newNode = createNode(dest);
    newNode->next = graph->adjLists[src];
    graph->adjLists[src] = newNode;

    // Since graph is undirected, add edge from dest to src
    newNode = createNode(src);
    newNode->next = graph->adjLists[dest];
    graph->adjLists[dest] = newNode;
}

// DFS algorithm
void DFS(struct Graph* graph, int vertex) {
    struct Node* adjList = graph->adjLists[vertex];
    struct Node* temp = adjList;

    graph->visited[vertex] = 1;
    printf("%d ", vertex);

    while (temp != NULL) {
        int connectedVertex = temp->vertex;

        if (graph->visited[connectedVertex] == 0) {
            DFS(graph, connectedVertex);
```

```
        }
        temp = temp->next;
    }
}

// Main function
int main() {
    int vertices = 6;
    struct Graph* graph = createGraph(vertices);
    addEdge(graph, 0, 1);
    addEdge(graph, 0, 2);
    addEdge(graph, 1, 2);
    addEdge(graph, 1, 3);
    addEdge(graph, 2, 4);
    addEdge(graph, 3, 4);
    addEdge(graph, 3, 5);

    printf("Depth First Traversal starting from vertex
0:\n");
    DFS(graph, 0);

    return 0;
}
```

OUTPUT

```
Depth First Traversal starting from vertex 0:
0 2 4 3 5 1
```

Explanation

1. **Graph Representation**: The graph is represented using an adjacency list, where each vertex has a linked list of adjacent vertices.
2. **DFS Function**: The DFS function recursively visits each vertex, marking it as visited and then calling DFS on each of its unvisited adjacent vertices.
3. **Traversal Output**: When DFS is called, it prints

the vertices in depth-first order starting from the specified source vertex.

1. Header files

```
#include <stdio.h>
#include <stdlib.h>
```

- **stdio.h**: This header is used for input/output functions such as printf for printing output.
- **stdlib.h**: This header is used for memory allocation functions like malloc to allocate memory dynamically.

2. Define constant MAX

```
#define MAX 100
```

This defines a constant MAX with a value of 100. However, it is not used anywhere in the code.

3. Define Node structure

```
struct Node {
    int vertex;
    struct Node* next;
};
```

- **struct Node** represents a **node** in the adjacency list. It contains:
    - vertex: This holds the vertex (node) number.
    - next: This is a pointer to the next node in the linked list.

4. Define Graph structure

```
struct Graph {
    int numVertices;
    struct Node** adjLists;
    int* visited;
};
```

- **struct Graph** represents the graph.
  - numVertices: This stores the number of vertices in the graph.
  - adjLists: An array of pointers to Node structures (adjacency list) where each list represents a vertex and its connected neighbors.
  - visited: An array that tracks whether a vertex has been visited during the DFS traversal.

5. Function to create a new node

```
struct Node* createNode(int v) {
    struct Node* newNode = malloc(sizeof(struct Node));
    newNode->vertex = v;
    newNode->next = NULL;
    return newNode;
}
```

- **createNode(int v)**: This function creates a new node with a given vertex v. It:
  - Allocates memory for a new Node.
  - Sets the vertex field to v.
  - Initializes the next pointer to NULL (indicating the end of the linked list).

6. Function to create a graph

```
struct Graph* createGraph(int vertices) {
    struct Graph* graph = malloc(sizeof(struct Graph));
    graph->numVertices = vertices;

    graph->adjLists = malloc(vertices * sizeof(struct
Node*));
    graph->visited = malloc(vertices * sizeof(int));

    for (int i = 0; i < vertices; i++) {
        graph->adjLists[i] = NULL;
```

```
        graph->visited[i] = 0;
    }
    return graph;
}
```

- **createGraph(int vertices)**: This function creates a graph with the given number of vertices vertices. It:
    - Allocates memory for the graph itself.
    - Initializes the numVertices field to vertices.
    - Allocates memory for the adjLists array to store adjacency lists for each vertex.
    - Allocates memory for the visited array to keep track of which vertices have been visited.
    - Initializes each adjacency list pointer to NULL and marks each vertex as not visited (initial value 0).

7. Function to add an edge

```
void addEdge(struct Graph* graph, int src, int dest) {
    struct Node* newNode = createNode(dest);
    newNode->next = graph->adjLists[src];
    graph->adjLists[src] = newNode;

    newNode = createNode(src);
    newNode->next = graph->adjLists[dest];
    graph->adjLists[dest] = newNode;
}
```

- **addEdge(struct Graph* graph, int src, int dest)**: This function adds an undirected edge between two vertices src and dest. It:
    - Creates a new node for the destination vertex (dest) and adds it to the adjacency list of the source vertex (src).
    - Creates another node for the source vertex

(src) and adds it to the adjacency list of the destination vertex (dest), making the graph undirected.

8. Depth-First Search (DFS) function

```
void DFS(struct Graph* graph, int vertex) {
    struct Node* adjList = graph->adjLists[vertex];
    struct Node* temp = adjList;

    graph->visited[vertex] = 1;
    printf("%d ", vertex);

    while (temp != NULL) {
        int connectedVertex = temp->vertex;

        if (graph->visited[connectedVertex] == 0) {
            DFS(graph, connectedVertex);
        }
        temp = temp->next;
    }
}
```

- **DFS(struct Graph* graph, int vertex)**: This function performs a Depth-First Search starting from the given vertex vertex. It:
    - Marks the current vertex as visited (graph->visited[vertex] = 1).
    - Prints the current vertex (printf("%d ", vertex)).
    - Iterates through the adjacency list of the current vertex and recursively calls DFS for any connected vertex that has not been visited yet.

9. Main function

```
int main() {
    int vertices = 6;
    struct Graph* graph = createGraph(vertices);
```

```
    addEdge(graph, 0, 1);
    addEdge(graph, 0, 2);
    addEdge(graph, 1, 2);
    addEdge(graph, 1, 3);
    addEdge(graph, 2, 4);
    addEdge(graph, 3, 4);
    addEdge(graph, 3, 5);

    printf("Depth First Traversal starting from vertex
0:\n");
    DFS(graph, 0);

    return 0;
}
```

- **int main()**: This is the main function where the graph is created and DFS is executed.
    - It creates a graph with 6 vertices.
    - It adds edges between various vertices using the addEdge function.
    - It calls the DFS function starting from vertex 0 to traverse the graph using Depth-First Search.
    - Finally, it prints the Depth-First Traversal of the graph starting from vertex 0.

This approach effectively covers the DFS traversal for an undirected graph.

To implement DFS for a directed graph, the main change involves how edges are added. In a directed graph, an edge from vertex AAA to vertex BBB only means A→BA \rightarrow BA→B, not B→AB \rightarrow AB→A. This only requires modifying the addEdge function so that it only creates one directed link between nodes.

Here's the modified code:

DFS in C (Directed Graph)

```
#include <stdio.h>
#include <stdlib.h>

#define MAX 100

struct Node {
    int vertex;
    struct Node* next;
};

struct Graph {
    int numVertices;
    struct Node** adjLists;
    int* visited;
};

// Function to create a node
struct Node* createNode(int v) {
    struct Node* newNode = malloc(sizeof(struct Node));
    newNode->vertex = v;
    newNode->next = NULL;
    return newNode;
}

// Function to create a graph
struct Graph* createGraph(int vertices) {
    struct Graph* graph = malloc(sizeof(struct Graph));
    graph->numVertices = vertices;

    graph->adjLists = malloc(vertices * sizeof(struct
Node*));
    graph->visited = malloc(vertices * sizeof(int));

    for (int i = 0; i < vertices; i++) {
        graph->adjLists[i] = NULL;
        graph->visited[i] = 0;
    }
    return graph;
```

```
}

// Add edge to graph (directed)
void addEdge(struct Graph* graph, int src, int dest) {
    // Add edge from src to dest
    struct Node* newNode = createNode(dest);
    newNode->next = graph->adjLists[src];
    graph->adjLists[src] = newNode;
}

// DFS algorithm
void DFS(struct Graph* graph, int vertex) {
    struct Node* adjList = graph->adjLists[vertex];
    struct Node* temp = adjList;

    graph->visited[vertex] = 1;
    printf("%d ", vertex);

    while (temp != NULL) {
        int connectedVertex = temp->vertex;

        if (graph->visited[connectedVertex] == 0) {
            DFS(graph, connectedVertex);
        }
        temp = temp->next;
    }
}

// Main function
int main() {
    int vertices = 6;
    struct Graph* graph = createGraph(vertices);
    addEdge(graph, 0, 1);
    addEdge(graph, 0, 2);
    addEdge(graph, 1, 3);
    addEdge(graph, 2, 4);
    addEdge(graph, 3, 5);
```

```
    addEdge(graph, 4, 5);

    printf("Depth First Traversal starting from vertex
0:\n");
    DFS(graph, 0);

    return 0;
}
```

OUTPUT

```
Depth First Traversal starting from vertex 0:
0 2 4 5 1 3
```

Code Explanation

1. **Directed Edge Addition**: In the addEdge function, only a single edge from src to dest is added, as required for a directed graph.
2. **DFS Traversal**: The DFS function works the same way as for an undirected graph; it simply explores all nodes it can reach in a depth-first manner from the starting vertex.

This C program implements a **Depth First Search (DFS)** algorithm on a **directed graph** using an adjacency list. Below is a step-by-step explanation of each section of the code:

1. Including Headers

```
#include <stdio.h>
#include <stdlib.h>
```

- stdio.h is included for input/output operations (like printf).
- stdlib.h is included for memory allocation (malloc).

2. Defining Constants and Structures

```
#define MAX 100
```

- MAX is defined as 100, but it's not used in this code. It's a typical way to define a maximum size for arrays in some programs.

```
struct Node {
    int vertex;
    struct Node* next;
};
```

- A **Node** structure is defined to represent a vertex in the graph. It contains:
    - vertex: The actual vertex number.
    - next: A pointer to the next node (this is used to form the linked list for each adjacency list).

```
struct Graph {
    int numVertices;
    struct Node** adjLists;
    int* visited;
};
```

- A **Graph** structure is defined to represent the entire graph. It contains:
    - numVertices: The total number of vertices in the graph.
    - adjLists: An array of pointers to Node, representing the adjacency list of each vertex.
    - visited: An array to track whether a vertex has been visited in the DFS traversal.

3. Function to Create a Node

```
struct Node* createNode(int v) {
    struct Node* newNode = malloc(sizeof(struct Node));
    newNode->vertex = v;
```

```
    newNode->next = NULL;
    return newNode;
}
```

- **createNode** function creates a new node for a given vertex (v).
    - It allocates memory for a new Node structure.
    - Sets the vertex field to the given value (v).
    - Sets the next pointer to NULL, as it's the last node in the adjacency list initially.
    - It returns the pointer to the new node.

4. Function to Create a Graph

```
struct Graph* createGraph(int vertices) {
    struct Graph* graph = malloc(sizeof(struct Graph));
    graph->numVertices = vertices;
    graph->adjLists = malloc(vertices * sizeof(struct
Node*));
    graph->visited = malloc(vertices * sizeof(int));

    for (int i = 0; i < vertices; i++) {
        graph->adjLists[i] = NULL;
        graph->visited[i] = 0;
    }
    return graph;
}
```

- **createGraph** function creates a graph with the given number of vertices (vertices).
    - It allocates memory for the Graph structure.
    - It initializes the adjacency list array (adjLists) for each vertex, setting all elements to NULL.
    - It initializes the visited array to track whether each vertex has been visited, setting all values to 0 (not visited).

- Finally, it returns the pointer to the created graph.

5. Function to Add an Edge to the Graph

```
void addEdge(struct Graph* graph, int src, int dest) {
    struct Node* newNode = createNode(dest);
    newNode->next = graph->adjLists[src];
    graph->adjLists[src] = newNode;
}
```

- **addEdge** function adds a directed edge from vertex src to vertex dest:
    - It creates a new node for the destination vertex (dest).
    - The new node's next pointer is set to the current adjacency list for src.
    - The adjacency list for src is updated to point to the new node, effectively adding the edge.

6. Depth First Search (DFS) Algorithm

```
void DFS(struct Graph* graph, int vertex) {
    struct Node* adjList = graph->adjLists[vertex];
    struct Node* temp = adjList;

    graph->visited[vertex] = 1;
    printf("%d ", vertex);

    while (temp != NULL) {
        int connectedVertex = temp->vertex;

        if (graph->visited[connectedVertex] == 0) {
            DFS(graph, connectedVertex);
        }
        temp = temp->next;
    }
}
```

- **DFS** function performs Depth First Search starting from a given vertex (vertex):
  - It first marks the current vertex as visited (visited[vertex] = 1).
  - It then prints the vertex (printf("%d ", vertex)).
  - It traverses the adjacency list of the current vertex (adjList), visiting all its connected vertices.
  - For each unvisited connected vertex, it recursively calls DFS to visit that vertex.
  - This continues until all reachable vertices from the starting vertex are visited.

7. Main Function

```
int main() {
    int vertices = 6;
    struct Graph* graph = createGraph(vertices);
    addEdge(graph, 0, 1);
    addEdge(graph, 0, 2);
    addEdge(graph, 1, 3);
    addEdge(graph, 2, 4);
    addEdge(graph, 3, 5);
    addEdge(graph, 4, 5);

    printf("Depth First Traversal starting from vertex 
0:\n");
    DFS(graph, 0);

    return 0;
}
```

- **main** function creates a graph with 6 vertices:
  - The graph is created with 6 vertices.
  - Several edges are added to the graph using addEdge, making it a directed graph with

connections like 0 -> 1, 0 -> 2, 1 -> 3, etc.

- After setting up the graph, it prints a message indicating the start of the DFS traversal.
- It calls the DFS function starting from vertex 0, which performs the Depth First Search and prints the order of vertices visited during the traversal.

Breadth-First Search (BFS) Explanation

Breadth-First Search (BFS) is an algorithm used to traverse or search through a graph (or tree). It starts at the root (or an arbitrary node in the case of a graph) and explores all the neighboring nodes at the present depth level before moving on to nodes at the next depth level. BFS is particularly useful for finding the shortest path in an unweighted graph.

BFS Characteristics:

1. **Level-order traversal**: BFS explores nodes level by level.
2. **Queue-based**: BFS uses a queue data structure to keep track of nodes to explore.
3. **Time Complexity**: The time complexity of BFS is O(V + E), where V is the number of vertices and E is the number of edges.

BFS Steps:

1. Start at the root node (or any arbitrary node in the graph).
2. Visit the node and enqueue all its adjacent nodes that have not been visited.
3. Dequeue a node from the front of the queue and repeat step 2 until all nodes are visited or the queue is empty.

BFS C Code Example

Below is a C implementation of BFS for a graph represented by an adjacency list:

```
#include <stdio.h>
#include <stdlib.h>

// Structure to represent a graph node
struct Node {
    int data;
    struct Node* next;
};

// Structure to represent a graph
struct Graph {
    int V;  // Number of vertices
    struct Node** adjList;  // Array of adjacency lists
};

// Queue structure for BFS
struct Queue {
    int* arr;
    int front;
    int rear;
    int size;
};

// Function to create a graph
struct Graph* createGraph(int V) {
    struct Graph* graph = (struct
Graph*)malloc(sizeof(struct Graph));
    graph->V = V;
    graph->adjList = (struct Node**)malloc(V * sizeof(struct
Node*));

    for (int i = 0; i < V; i++) {
        graph->adjList[i] = NULL;
    }

    return graph;
}
```

```
// Function to add an edge to the graph
void addEdge(struct Graph* graph, int src, int dest) {
    // Add edge from src to dest
    struct Node* newNode = (struct
Node*)malloc(sizeof(struct Node));
    newNode->data = dest;
    newNode->next = graph->adjList[src];
    graph->adjList[src] = newNode;

    // Add edge from dest to src (for undirected graph)
    newNode = (struct Node*)malloc(sizeof(struct Node));
    newNode->data = src;
    newNode->next = graph->adjList[dest];
    graph->adjList[dest] = newNode;
}

// Function to initialize a queue
struct Queue* createQueue(int size) {
    struct Queue* queue = (struct
Queue*)malloc(sizeof(struct Queue));
    queue->size = size;
    queue->arr = (int*)malloc(size * sizeof(int));
    queue->front = -1;
    queue->rear = -1;
    return queue;
}

// Function to check if the queue is empty
int isEmpty(struct Queue* queue) {
    return queue->front == -1;
}

// Function to enqueue an element
void enqueue(struct Queue* queue, int value) {
    if (queue->rear == queue->size - 1) {
        printf("Queue overflow\n");
```

```
        return;
    }
    if (queue->front == -1) {
        queue->front = 0;
    }
    queue->arr[++queue->rear] = value;
}

// Function to dequeue an element
int dequeue(struct Queue* queue) {
    if (isEmpty(queue)) {
        printf("Queue underflow\n");
        return -1;
    }
    int value = queue->arr[queue->front];
    if (queue->front == queue->rear) {
        queue->front = queue->rear = -1;
    } else {
        queue->front++;
    }
    return value;
}

// BFS algorithm
void BFS(struct Graph* graph, int startVertex) {
    // Create a visited array and initialize all vertices as
unvisited
    int* visited = (int*)malloc(graph->V * sizeof(int));
    for (int i = 0; i < graph->V; i++) {
        visited[i] = 0;  // 0 means unvisited
    }

    // Create a queue for BFS
    struct Queue* queue = createQueue(graph->V);

    // Mark the start vertex as visited and enqueue it
    visited[startVertex] = 1;
```

```
    enqueue(queue, startVertex);

    while (!isEmpty(queue)) {
        // Dequeue a vertex from the queue and print it
        int currentVertex = dequeue(queue);
        printf("%d ", currentVertex);

        // Get all the adjacent vertices of the dequeued
vertex
        struct Node* temp = graph->adjList[currentVertex];
        while (temp != NULL) {
            int adjVertex = temp->data;

            // If the adjacent vertex is unvisited, mark it
visited and enqueue it
            if (!visited[adjVertex]) {
                visited[adjVertex] = 1;
                enqueue(queue, adjVertex);
            }
            temp = temp->next;
        }
    }

    free(visited);
    free(queue->arr);
    free(queue);
}

// Main function to test the BFS implementation
int main() {
    struct Graph* graph = createGraph(6);  // Create a graph
with 6 vertices

    addEdge(graph, 0, 1);
    addEdge(graph, 0, 2);
    addEdge(graph, 1, 3);
    addEdge(graph, 1, 4);
```

```
    addEdge(graph, 2, 5);

    printf("Breadth-First Search starting from vertex 0:\n");
    BFS(graph, 0); // Perform BFS starting from vertex 0

    // Free the graph memory
    for (int i = 0; i < graph->V; i++) {
        struct Node* temp = graph->adjList[i];
        while (temp != NULL) {
            struct Node* toDelete = temp;
            temp = temp->next;
            free(toDelete);
        }
    }
    free(graph->adjList);
    free(graph);

    return 0;
}
```

OUTPUT

```
Breadth-First Search starting from vertex 0:
0 2 1 5 4 3
```

Code Explanation:

1. **Graph Representation**:
    - The graph is represented using an adjacency list, where each vertex points to a linked list of its neighbors.
2. **Queue Implementation**:
    - A queue is implemented using an array to store vertices during BFS traversal.
3. **BFS Algorithm**:
    - The BFS function starts by marking the start vertex as visited and then explores all its neighbors.
    - Nodes are added to the queue when they

are discovered, and they are processed in the order they are dequeued.

4. **Add Edge Function**:
    - The addEdge function adds an undirected edge between two vertices by adding nodes to both vertex's adjacency lists.

1. Header Files

```
#include <stdio.h>
#include <stdlib.h>
```

- stdio.h: Includes functions for input and output (e.g., printf).
- stdlib.h: Includes functions for memory allocation (e.g., malloc), which is used to dynamically allocate memory.

2. Structure Definitions

```
// Structure to represent a graph node
struct Node {
    int data;
    struct Node* next;
};
```

- Node: This structure represents a node in the adjacency list of a graph. Each node stores:
    - data: The vertex (or node) it points to.
    - next: A pointer to the next node (in case of multiple edges to other vertices).

```
// Structure to represent a graph
struct Graph {
    int V; // Number of vertices
    struct Node** adjList; // Array of adjacency lists
};
```

- Graph: This structure represents a graph, which

consists of:
  - V: The number of vertices in the graph.
  - adjList: A pointer to an array of pointers (Node**), where each element points to the head of a linked list representing an adjacency list of a vertex.

```
// Queue structure for BFS
struct Queue {
    int* arr;
    int front;
    int rear;
    int size;
};
```

- Queue: This structure is used to implement a queue, necessary for performing Breadth-First Search (BFS). The queue is used to explore the graph level by level.
  - arr: An array to hold the elements of the queue.
  - front: The front index of the queue.
  - rear: The rear index of the queue.
  - size: The maximum size of the queue.

3. Graph Creation Function

```
struct Graph* createGraph(int V) {
    struct Graph* graph = (struct
Graph*)malloc(sizeof(struct Graph));
    graph->V = V;
    graph->adjList = (struct Node**)malloc(V * sizeof(struct
Node*));

    for (int i = 0; i < V; i++) {
        graph->adjList[i] = NULL;
    }

    return graph;
```

```
}
```

- This function creates a new graph with V vertices.
    - Allocates memory for the graph and initializes the adjacency list for each vertex to NULL (no edges initially).

4. Add Edge Function

```
void addEdge(struct Graph* graph, int src, int dest) {
    // Add edge from src to dest
    struct Node* newNode = (struct
Node*)malloc(sizeof(struct Node));
    newNode->data = dest;
    newNode->next = graph->adjList[src];
    graph->adjList[src] = newNode;

    // Add edge from dest to src (for undirected graph)
    newNode = (struct Node*)malloc(sizeof(struct Node));
    newNode->data = src;
    newNode->next = graph->adjList[dest];
    graph->adjList[dest] = newNode;
}
```

- This function adds an undirected edge between two vertices src and dest.
    - A new node is created and added to the adjacency list of src, pointing to dest.
    - Another new node is created and added to the adjacency list of dest, pointing back to src (undirected graph).

5. Queue Initialization Function

```
struct Queue* createQueue(int size) {
    struct Queue* queue = (struct
Queue*)malloc(sizeof(struct Queue));
    queue->size = size;
    queue->arr = (int*)malloc(size * sizeof(int));
```

```
    queue->front = -1;
    queue->rear = -1;
    return queue;
}
```

- This function initializes a queue of a given size.
  - arr: An array to hold the elements in the queue.
  - front and rear: Both initialized to -1 (indicating the queue is empty).

6. Queue Operations

```
int isEmpty(struct Queue* queue) {
    return queue->front == -1;
}
```

- Checks if the queue is empty by verifying if the front index is -1.

```
void enqueue(struct Queue* queue, int value) {
    if (queue->rear == queue->size - 1) {
        printf("Queue overflow\n");
        return;
    }
    if (queue->front == -1) {
        queue->front = 0;
    }
    queue->arr[++queue->rear] = value;
}
```

- Adds an element to the rear of the queue. If the queue is full, it prints an overflow message.
- If the queue was empty, the front index is set to 0.

```
int dequeue(struct Queue* queue) {
    if (isEmpty(queue)) {
```

```
        printf("Queue underflow\n");
        return -1;
    }
    int value = queue->arr[queue->front];
    if (queue->front == queue->rear) {
        queue->front = queue->rear = -1;
    } else {
        queue->front++;
    }
    return value;
}
```

- Removes and returns the element from the front of the queue. If the queue is empty, it prints an underflow message.

7. BFS Algorithm

```
void BFS(struct Graph* graph, int startVertex) {
    int* visited = (int*)malloc(graph->V * sizeof(int));
    for (int i = 0; i < graph->V; i++) {
        visited[i] = 0; // 0 means unvisited
    }

    struct Queue* queue = createQueue(graph->V);

    visited[startVertex] = 1;
    enqueue(queue, startVertex);

    while (!isEmpty(queue)) {
        int currentVertex = dequeue(queue);
        printf("%d ", currentVertex);

        struct Node* temp = graph->adjList[currentVertex];
        while (temp != NULL) {
            int adjVertex = temp->data;

            if (!visited[adjVertex]) {
```

```
                visited[adjVertex] = 1;
                enqueue(queue, adjVertex);
            }
            temp = temp->next;
        }
    }

    free(visited);
    free(queue->arr);
    free(queue);
}
```

- This function implements the BFS algorithm:
    - A visited array is used to track which vertices have been visited.
    - A queue is initialized to hold vertices that need to be processed.
    - The start vertex is marked as visited and added to the queue.
    - While the queue is not empty, a vertex is dequeued, printed, and all its unvisited neighbors are enqueued.

8. Main Function

```
int main() {
    struct Graph* graph = createGraph(6);  // Create a graph
with 6 vertices

    addEdge(graph, 0, 1);
    addEdge(graph, 0, 2);
    addEdge(graph, 1, 3);
    addEdge(graph, 1, 4);
    addEdge(graph, 2, 5);

    printf("Breadth-First Search starting from vertex 0:\n");
    BFS(graph, 0);  // Perform BFS starting from vertex 0
```

```
    for (int i = 0; i < graph->V; i++) {
        struct Node* temp = graph->adjList[i];
        while (temp != NULL) {
            struct Node* toDelete = temp;
            temp = temp->next;
            free(toDelete);
        }
    }
    free(graph->adjList);
    free(graph);

    return 0;
}
```

- A graph with 6 vertices is created.
- Edges are added between various pairs of vertices.
- BFS is performed starting from vertex 0, and the result is printed.
- Memory is freed after the BFS operation to avoid memory leaks.

Dijkstra's Algorithm

Dijkstra's Algorithm is used to find the shortest path between two nodes in a graph. It works by iteratively selecting the node with the smallest tentative distance, visiting its neighbors, and updating their tentative distances. The algorithm uses a priority queue (or min-heap) to efficiently select the next node to visit.

- **Objective**: Find the shortest path from a single source vertex to all other vertices in a weighted graph.
- **Time Complexity**: O(V^2) or O((V+E)logV) (with a min-priority queue).
- **Use Cases**: Shortest path in road networks, routing

algorithms.

Here's an implementation of Dijkstra's Algorithm in C:

Dijkstra's Algorithm in C

```
#include <stdio.h>
#include <stdlib.h>
#include <limits.h>

#define V 9 // Number of vertices

// Function to find the vertex with the minimum distance
value that hasn't been visited yet

int minDistance(int dist[], int sptSet[]) {
    int min = INT_MAX, min_index;

    for (int v = 0; v < V; v++) {
        if (sptSet[v] == 0 && dist[v] <= min) {
            min = dist[v];
            min_index = v;
        }
    }

    return min_index;
}

// Function to implement Dijkstra's algorithm for a graph
represented by an adjacency matrix

void dijkstra(int graph[V][V], int src) {
    int dist[V];  // The output array that holds the shortest
distance from src to each vertex
    int sptSet[V]; // sptSet[i] will be true if vertex i is
included in the shortest path tree

    // Initialize all distances as INFINITE and sptSet[] as
false
    for (int i = 0; i < V; i++) {
```

```
        dist[i] = INT_MAX;
        sptSet[i] = 0;
    }

    // Distance from source to itself is always 0

    dist[src] = 0;

    // Find the shortest path for all vertices

    for (int count = 0; count < V - 1; count++) {

        // Pick the minimum distance vertex from the set of
vertices not yet processed

        int u = minDistance(dist, sptSet);

        // Mark the picked vertex as processed
        sptSet[u] = 1;

        // Update the distance value of the adjacent vertices
of the picked vertex

        for (int v = 0; v < V; v++) {

            // Update dist[v] if and only if the current vertex is
not in sptSet,
            // there is an edge from u to v, and the distance to
v through u is smaller

            if (!sptSet[v] && graph[u][v] != 0 && dist[u] !=
INT_MAX && dist[u] + graph[u][v] < dist[v]) {
                dist[v] = dist[u] + graph[u][v];
            }
        }
    }

    // Print the constructed distance array

    printf("Vertex \t Distance from Source\n");
```

```
    for (int i = 0; i < V; i++) {
        printf("%d \t %d\n", i, dist[i]);
    }
}

int main() {

    // Adjacency matrix representation of the graph

    int graph[V][V] = {
        {0, 4, 0, 0, 0, 0, 0, 8, 0},
        {4, 0, 8, 0, 0, 0, 0, 0, 0},
        {0, 8, 0, 7, 0, 4, 0, 0, 2},
        {0, 0, 7, 0, 9, 14, 0, 0, 0},
        {0, 0, 0, 9, 0, 10, 0, 0, 0},
        {0, 0, 4, 14, 10, 0, 2, 0, 0},
        {0, 0, 0, 0, 0, 2, 0, 1, 6},
        {8, 0, 0, 0, 0, 0, 1, 0, 7},
        {0, 0, 2, 0, 0, 0, 6, 7, 0}
    };

    int source = 0; // Start node
    dijkstra(graph, source);

    return 0;
}
```

OUTPUT

```
Vertex      Distance from Source
0            0
1            4
2           12
3           19
4           21
5           11
6            9
7            8
```

8	14

Explanation of the Code:

1. **Graph Representation**: The graph is represented as an adjacency matrix, where graph[i][j] contains the weight of the edge between vertex i and vertex j. A value of 0 means there is no direct edge between those vertices.
2. **minDistance()**: This function returns the vertex with the smallest tentative distance that has not yet been included in the shortest path tree.
3. **dijkstra()**: This is the main function where the algorithm is implemented:
   - dist[] array stores the shortest distance from the source to each vertex.
   - sptSet[] array keeps track of vertices that are already processed.
   - The algorithm selects the vertex with the minimum distance and updates the distances of its neighbors.

1. Header Files and Constants

```
#include <stdio.h>
#include <stdlib.h>
#include <limits.h>

#define V 9 // Number of vertices
```

- stdio.h: For standard input and output functions like printf.
- stdlib.h: For functions like malloc, free, and other utilities.
- limits.h: For the constant INT_MAX which represents infinity.
- V: Defines the number of vertices in the graph (9 vertices in this case).

2. Function: minDistance

```
int minDistance(int dist[], int sptSet[]) {
    int min = INT_MAX, min_index;

    for (int v = 0; v < V; v++) {
        if (sptSet[v] == 0 && dist[v] <= min) {
            min = dist[v];
            min_index = v;
        }
    }

    return min_index;
}
```

This function finds the vertex with the minimum distance that hasn't been included in the shortest path tree (sptSet).

- **Input:**
    - dist[]: Array of shortest distances from the source to each vertex.
    - sptSet[]: Array of flags to indicate whether a vertex has been processed or not.
- **Working:**
    - It iterates through all vertices (v), checking if the vertex is not yet processed (sptSet[v] == 0) and if its distance (dist[v]) is smaller than the current minimum.
    - It updates the min and min_index accordingly to return the vertex with the smallest distance.
- **Output:** The index of the vertex with the minimum distance.

3. Function: dijkstra

```
void dijkstra(int graph[V][V], int src) {
    int dist[V]; // The output array that holds the shortest
distance from src to each vertex
```

```
    int sptSet[V]; // sptSet[i] will be true if vertex i is
included in the shortest path tree

    // Initialize all distances as INFINITE and sptSet[] as
false
    for (int i = 0; i < V; i++) {
        dist[i] = INT_MAX;
        sptSet[i] = 0;
    }

    // Distance from source to itself is always 0
    dist[src] = 0;
```

- **Input:**
  - graph[V][V]: The adjacency matrix representing the graph. graph[i][j] holds the weight of the edge between vertex i and vertex j.
  - src: The starting vertex for the shortest path calculation.
- **Working:**
  - dist[] is initialized to INT_MAX to signify that all vertices are initially at an infinite distance.
  - sptSet[] is initialized to 0, meaning no vertices are processed initially.
  - The distance from the source to itself is set to 0.

4. Main Dijkstra's Loop

```
// Find the shortest path for all vertices
    for (int count = 0; count < V - 1; count++) {
        // Pick the minimum distance vertex from the set of
vertices not yet processed
        int u = minDistance(dist, sptSet);

        // Mark the picked vertex as processed
```

```
        sptSet[u] = 1;
```

Working:

- The main loop runs for V-1 iterations because in a graph with V vertices, we need V-1 steps to process all vertices.
- In each iteration, the minDistance function is called to find the vertex u with the smallest distance that hasn't been processed yet.
- sptSet[u] = 1 marks vertex u as processed.

5. Update the Distance of Adjacent Vertices

```
        // Update the distance value of the adjacent vertices
of the picked vertex
        for (int v = 0; v < V; v++) {
            // Update dist[v] if and only if the current vertex is
not in sptSet,
            // there is an edge from u to v, and the distance to
v through u is smaller
            if (!sptSet[v] && graph[u][v] != 0 && dist[u] !=
INT_MAX && dist[u] + graph[u][v] < dist[v]) {
                dist[v] = dist[u] + graph[u][v];
            }
        }
    }
```

- **Working:**
    - After picking the vertex u, we loop through all vertices v to check if there is an edge from u to v (i.e., graph[u][v] != 0).
    - If vertex v is not yet processed (sptSet[v] == 0), and the new calculated distance (dist[u] + graph[u][v]) is smaller than the current distance (dist[v]), we update dist[v].

6. Print the Final Distances

```
    // Print the constructed distance array
    printf("Vertex \t Distance from Source\n");
    for (int i = 0; i < V; i++) {
        printf("%d \t %d\n", i, dist[i]);
    }
}
```

- After all the vertices are processed, the function prints the shortest distances from the source vertex to all other vertices.

7. Main Function

```
int main() {
    // Adjacency matrix representation of the graph
    int graph[V][V] = {
        {0, 4, 0, 0, 0, 0, 0, 8, 0},
        {4, 0, 8, 0, 0, 0, 0, 0, 0},
        {0, 8, 0, 7, 0, 4, 0, 0, 2},
        {0, 0, 7, 0, 9, 14, 0, 0, 0},
        {0, 0, 0, 9, 0, 10, 0, 0, 0},
        {0, 0, 4, 14, 10, 0, 2, 0, 0},
        {0, 0, 0, 0, 0, 2, 0, 1, 6},
        {8, 0, 0, 0, 0, 0, 1, 0, 7},
        {0, 0, 2, 0, 0, 0, 6, 7, 0}
    };

    int source = 0; // Start node
    dijkstra(graph, source);

    return 0;
}
```

- The main function defines an adjacency matrix graph[V][V] representing the graph and calls the dijkstra function, passing the source vertex 0.

Explanation of the Graph

The graph is represented by an adjacency matrix where each element graph[i][j] represents the weight of the edge between vertices i and j. A value of 0 means there is no direct edge between i and j.

Prim's and Kruskal's algorithms are both used to find the **Minimum Spanning Tree (MST)** of a graph, which is a subset of the edges that connect all the vertices in the graph with the minimum possible total edge weight. Here's an in-depth explanation of each algorithm along with code examples in C.

1. Prim's Algorithm

Prim's Algorithm starts with a single vertex and grows the MST one vertex at a time by adding the shortest edge that connects the tree to a vertex not yet in the tree.

Steps:

1. Initialize a set of MST vertices (starts with one vertex).
2. Select the edge with the minimum weight connecting a vertex in the MST to a vertex outside it.
3. Add the selected vertex to the MST set.
4. Repeat steps 2-3 until all vertices are in the MST.

C Code Example for Prim's Algorithm:

```
#include <stdio.h>
#include <limits.h>
#include <stdbool.h>  // Include this header for 'bool'

// Number of vertices in the graph
#define V 5

// Function to find the vertex with the minimum key
value
int minKey(int key[], bool mstSet[]) {
    int min = INT_MAX, minIndex;

    for (int v = 0; v < V; v++) {
        if (!mstSet[v] && key[v] < min) {
```

```
            min = key[v];
            minIndex = v;
        }
    }
    return minIndex;
}

// Function to print the constructed MST
void printMST(int parent[], int graph[V][V]) {
    printf("Edge \tWeight\n");
    for (int i = 1; i < V; i++) {
        printf("%d - %d \t%d\n", parent[i], i, graph[i]
[parent[i]]);
    }
}

// Function to implement Prim's algorithm
void primMST(int graph[V][V]) {
    int parent[V]; // Array to store the MST
    int key[V];   // Key values used to pick the minimum
weight edge
    bool mstSet[V]; // To represent vertices included in the
MST

    // Initialize all keys as INFINITE and mstSet as false
    for (int i = 0; i < V; i++) {
        key[i] = INT_MAX;
        mstSet[i] = false;
    }

    // Always include the first vertex in the MST
    key[0] = 0;
    parent[0] = -1; // First node is the root of the MST

    // The MST will have V vertices
    for (int count = 0; count < V - 1; count++) {
        // Pick the minimum key vertex from the set of
```

```
vertices not yet included in MST
        int u = minKey(key, mstSet);
        mstSet[u] = true; // Include the picked vertex in the
MST

        // Update the key and parent values of the adjacent
vertices of the picked vertex
        for (int v = 0; v < V; v++) {
            if (graph[u][v] && !mstSet[v] && graph[u][v] <
key[v]) {
                key[v] = graph[u][v];
                parent[v] = u;
            }
        }
    }

    // Print the constructed MST
    printMST(parent, graph);
}

int main() {
    // Example graph (adjacency matrix)
    int graph[V][V] = {
        {0, 2, 0, 6, 0},
        {2, 0, 3, 8, 5},
        {0, 3, 0, 0, 7},
        {6, 8, 0, 0, 9},
        {0, 5, 7, 9, 0}
    };

    // Call the function to construct the MST
    primMST(graph);

    return 0;
}
```

OUTPUT

```
Edge  Weight
0 - 1  2
1 - 2  3
0 - 3  6
1 - 4  5
```

Code Explanation step by step:

- The graph is represented using an adjacency matrix.
- The function minKey() is used to select the vertex with the minimum key that is not yet included in the MST.
- The algorithm continues to select the minimum-weight edge connecting the MST to the remaining vertices.

1. Includes and Definitions:

```
#include <stdio.h>
#include <limits.h>
#include <stdbool.h>  // Include this header for 'bool'

// Number of vertices in the graph
#define V 5
```

- **stdio.h**: Includes the standard input/output library for using printf to print the results.
- **limits.h**: Used for the constant INT_MAX, which represents the largest possible integer, used to initialize key values to an "infinite" value.
- **stdbool.h**: This header provides the bool data type in C, which can be used for logical operations (true/ false).
- **#define V 5**: Defines the number of vertices in the graph (V = 5), which is used in the adjacency matrix

and various arrays.

2. minKey Function:

```
int minKey(int key[], bool mstSet[]) {
    int min = INT_MAX, minIndex;

    for (int v = 0; v < V; v++) {
        if (!mstSet[v] && key[v] < min) {
            min = key[v];
            minIndex = v;
        }
    }
    return minIndex;
}
```

- This function finds the vertex that has the minimum key value, but has not yet been included in the MST (mstSet).
- **Parameters**:
    - key[]: An array of key values, where each element represents the weight of the edge connecting a vertex to the MST.
    - mstSet[]: A boolean array where true means the vertex is included in the MST, and false means it's not.
- **Steps**:
    - Initialize min as INT_MAX (to represent an infinite weight) and minIndex for storing the vertex index with the smallest key value.
    - Loop over all vertices, check if they are not in mstSet and if their key value is smaller than the current min.
    - Update min and minIndex accordingly.
    - Return the index of the vertex with the minimum key.

3. printMST Function:

```
void printMST(int parent[], int graph[V][V]) {
    printf("Edge \tWeight\n");
    for (int i = 1; i < V; i++) {
        printf("%d - %d \t%d\n", parent[i], i, graph[i]
[parent[i]]);
    }
}
```

- This function prints the constructed **Minimum Spanning Tree (MST).**
- **Parameters**:
    - parent[]: An array that stores the parent vertex of each vertex in the MST.
    - graph[][]: The adjacency matrix representing the graph, where graph[i][j] is the weight of the edge between vertex i and vertex j.
- **Steps**:
    - Print the header "Edge Weight".
    - Loop through each vertex i starting from 1 (since vertex 0 is the root of the MST and has no parent).
    - For each vertex, print the edge connecting parent[i] to i and its weight graph[i][parent[i]].

4. primMST Function (Core of the Algorithm):

```
void primMST(int graph[V][V]) {
    int parent[V]; // Array to store the MST
    int key[V];    // Key values used to pick the minimum
weight edge
    bool mstSet[V]; // To represent vertices included in the
MST

    // Initialize all keys as INFINITE and mstSet as false
    for (int i = 0; i < V; i++) {
        key[i] = INT_MAX;
```

```
        mstSet[i] = false;
    }

    // Always include the first vertex in the MST
    key[0] = 0;
    parent[0] = -1; // First node is the root of the MST

    // The MST will have V vertices
    for (int count = 0; count < V - 1; count++) {
        // Pick the minimum key vertex from the set of
vertices not yet included in MST
        int u = minKey(key, mstSet);
        mstSet[u] = true; // Include the picked vertex in the
MST

        // Update the key and parent values of the adjacent
vertices of the picked vertex
        for (int v = 0; v < V; v++) {
            if (graph[u][v] && !mstSet[v] && graph[u][v] <
key[v]) {
                key[v] = graph[u][v];
                parent[v] = u;
            }
        }
    }

    // Print the constructed MST
    printMST(parent, graph);
}
```

This function implements **Prim's Algorithm** to find the MST.

- **Parameters**:
    - graph[][]: The adjacency matrix representing the graph.
- **Steps**:
    1. **Initialization**:
        - parent[]: To store the parent

vertex of each vertex in the MST.

- key[]: To store the minimum weight edge that connects each vertex to the MST.
- mstSet[]: To mark vertices that are included in the MST.
- Initialize all keys to INT_MAX (infinity), mstSet[] to false, and the first vertex's key (key[0]) to 0, marking it as the root of the MST.

2. **Main Loop**:
   - The algorithm iterates V - 1 times (since there are V - 1 edges in the MST).
   - **Find the vertex u with the minimum key value**: This is done by calling minKey().
   - **Mark the vertex as part of the MST**: Set mstSet[u] = true.
   - **Update adjacent vertices**: For each adjacent vertex v to u, if v is not in the MST and the edge weight from u to v is smaller than key[v], update key[v] and set parent[v] to u. This ensures that v will be connected to the MST with the minimum weight edge.

3. **Print the MST**: After the loop ends, all vertices are included in the MST, and the printMST() function is called to print the edges and their weights.

5. main Function:

```
int main() {
    // Example graph (adjacency matrix)
    int graph[V][V] = {
        {0, 2, 0, 6, 0},
        {2, 0, 3, 8, 5},
```

```
        {0, 3, 0, 0, 7},
        {6, 8, 0, 0, 9},
        {0, 5, 7, 9, 0}
    };

    // Call the function to construct the MST
    primMST(graph);

    return 0;
}
```

- **Graph Representation**: The graph is represented as an **adjacency matrix**, where graph[i][j] holds the weight of the edge between vertex i and vertex j. A 0 means there is no edge between those vertices.
- **Call primMST()**: The graph is passed to the primMST() function to find and print the MST.

Graph:

The adjacency matrix represents the following graph:

```
   2   3
(0)---(1)---(2)
 |\   |   |
 6 5  8   7
 |  \|  /
(3)---(4)
```

2. Kruskal's Algorithm

Kruskal's Algorithm works by sorting all the edges in non-decreasing order of their weights. It then picks edges one by one, and includes them in the MST if they don't form a cycle (using a union-find data structure to detect cycles).

- **Objective**: Find the Minimum Spanning Tree (MST) of a connected, undirected graph.

- **Time Complexity**: O(E logE)
- **Use Cases**: Network design, cluster analysis, approximation algorithms.

Steps:

1. Sort all the edges in the graph by their weights.
2. Initialize a disjoint set (union-find) to keep track of connected components.
3. Pick the smallest edge. If including it doesn't form a cycle, add it to the MST.
4. Repeat until there are V−1V-1V−1 edges in the MST.

C Code Example for Kruskal's Algorithm:

```
#include <stdio.h>
#include <stdlib.h>

#define V 5 // Number of vertices in the graph

// Structure to represent an edge
struct Edge {
    int src, dest, weight;
};

// Structure to represent a subset for union-find
struct Subset {
    int parent;
    int rank;
};

// Function to compare two edges (for sorting)
int compareEdges(const void *a, const void *b) {
    return ((struct Edge *)a)->weight - ((struct Edge *)b)-
>weight;
}

// Find function for union-find
int find(struct Subset subsets[], int i) {
    if (subsets[i].parent != i)
```

```
        subsets[i].parent = find(subsets, subsets[i].parent); //
Path compression
    return subsets[i].parent;
}

// Union function for union-find
void Union(struct Subset subsets[], int x, int y) {
    int rootX = find(subsets, x);
    int rootY = find(subsets, y);

    if (subsets[rootX].rank < subsets[rootY].rank)
        subsets[rootX].parent = rootY;
    else if (subsets[rootX].rank > subsets[rootY].rank)
        subsets[rootY].parent = rootX;
    else {
        subsets[rootY].parent = rootX;
        subsets[rootX].rank++;
    }
}

// Function to implement Kruskal's algorithm
void kruskalMST(struct Edge edges[], int E) {
    struct Edge result[V - 1];  // To store the MST
    int e = 0;  // Index to store the next edge
    int i = 0;  // Index for sorted edges

    // Step 1: Sort all the edges in non-decreasing order of
their weight
    qsort(edges, E, sizeof(edges[0]), compareEdges);

    // Create V subsets with single elements
    struct Subset subsets[V];
    for (int v = 0; v < V; v++) {
        subsets[v].parent = v;
        subsets[v].rank = 0;
    }
```

```
    // Step 2: Pick the smallest edge and check if it forms a
cycle
    while (e < V - 1 && i < E) {
        struct Edge next_edge = edges[i++];

        int x = find(subsets, next_edge.src);
        int y = find(subsets, next_edge.dest);

        // If including this edge does not form a cycle,
include it in the result
        if (x != y) {
            result[e++] = next_edge;
            Union(subsets, x, y);
        }
    }

    // Print the constructed MST
    printf("Edge \tWeight\n");
    for (i = 0; i < e; i++) {
        printf("%d - %d \t%d\n", result[i].src, result[i].dest,
result[i].weight);
    }
}

int main() {
    // Example graph with edges {src, dest, weight}
    struct Edge edges[] = {
        {0, 1, 2},
        {0, 3, 6},
        {1, 2, 3},
        {1, 3, 8},
        {1, 4, 5},
        {2, 4, 7},
        {3, 4, 9}
    };
    int E = sizeof(edges) / sizeof(edges[0]);
```

```
    // Call the function to construct the MST
    kruskalMST(edges, E);

    return 0;
}
```

OUTPUT:

```
Edge  Weight
0 - 1  2
1 - 2  3
1 - 4  5
0 - 3  6
```

Explanation:

- The graph is represented by a list of edges, each containing the source, destination, and weight.
- The edges are sorted by weight using the qsort() function.
- The union-find structure is used to manage disjoint sets of vertices to ensure no cycles are formed in the MST.
- The algorithm continues until the MST contains V −1V-1V−1 edges.

This C program implements **Kruskal's Algorithm** for finding the **Minimum Spanning Tree (MST)** of a connected, undirected graph. Let's break it down step by step:

Step 1: Include Header Files

```
#include <stdio.h>
#include <stdlib.h>
```

- stdio.h is included for input and output operations (like printf).

- stdlib.h is included for dynamic memory allocation (qsort in this case).

Step 2: Define Constants and Structures

```
#define V 5 // Number of vertices in the graph
```

- V is the number of vertices in the graph. Here, it's defined as 5.

```
struct Edge {
    int src, dest, weight;
};
```

- Edge structure represents an edge in the graph. Each edge has:
  - src: Source vertex
  - dest: Destination vertex
  - weight: Weight of the edge.

```
struct Subset {
    int parent;
    int rank;
};
```

- Subset structure is used for the **Union-Find** data structure:
  - parent: Represents the parent of the set.
  - rank: Helps in optimizing the union operation by keeping the tree flat.

Step 3: Sorting Function for Edges

```
int compareEdges(const void *a, const void *b) {
    return ((struct Edge *)a)->weight - ((struct Edge *)b)-
>weight;
}
```

- compareEdges is a comparison function used by

qsort to sort the edges based on their weight in non-decreasing order.

Step 4: Union-Find Operations

- **Find Operation (Path Compression)**

```
int find(struct Subset subsets[], int i) {
    if (subsets[i].parent != i)
        subsets[i].parent = find(subsets, subsets[i].parent); //
Path compression
    return subsets[i].parent;
}
```

- The find function is used to find the parent of a vertex. It uses **path compression**, which flattens the tree for faster future lookups by making each node in the tree point directly to the root.

- **Union Operation**

```
void Union(struct Subset subsets[], int x, int y) {
    int rootX = find(subsets, x);
    int rootY = find(subsets, y);

    if (subsets[rootX].rank < subsets[rootY].rank)
        subsets[rootX].parent = rootY;
    else if (subsets[rootX].rank > subsets[rootY].rank)
        subsets[rootY].parent = rootX;
    else {
        subsets[rootY].parent = rootX;
        subsets[rootX].rank++;
    }
}
```

- The Union function merges two sets. It uses **union by rank** to keep the tree balanced. The root of the tree with a higher rank becomes the parent, and if the ranks are equal, one tree becomes the root and its rank is increased.

Step 5: Kruskal's Algorithm to Find the MST

```
void kruskalMST(struct Edge edges[], int E) {
    struct Edge result[V - 1]; // To store the MST
    int e = 0; // Index to store the next edge
    int i = 0; // Index for sorted edges
```

- result stores the MST edges.
- e keeps track of the number of edges included in the MST (should be V-1).
- i iterates through the sorted edges.

```
    qsort(edges, E, sizeof(edges[0]), compareEdges);
```

- qsort sorts the edges based on their weights using the compareEdges function.

```
    struct Subset subsets[V];
    for (int v = 0; v < V; v++) {
        subsets[v].parent = v;
        subsets[v].rank = 0;
    }
```

- Each vertex is initialized as its own parent (each vertex is its own set), and the rank is set to 0.

```
while (e < V - 1 && i < E) {
        struct Edge next_edge = edges[i++];
        int x = find(subsets, next_edge.src);
        int y = find(subsets, next_edge.dest);

        if (x != y) {
            result[e++] = next_edge;
            Union(subsets, x, y);
        }
    }
```

This loop processes each edge in the sorted list:

- For the current edge, find the roots of the source (x) and destination (y) vertices.
- If they are in different sets (x != y), the edge is added to the MST, and the two sets are merged using Union.

Step 6: Print the MST

```
    printf("Edge \tWeight\n");
    for (i = 0; i < e; i++) {
        printf("%d - %d \t%d\n", result[i].src, result[i].dest,
result[i].weight);
    }
}
```

- This loop prints the edges that are included in the MST along with their weights.

Step 7: Main Function

```
int main() {
    struct Edge edges[] = {
        {0, 1, 2},
        {0, 3, 6},
        {1, 2, 3},
        {1, 3, 8},
        {1, 4, 5},
        {2, 4, 7},
        {3, 4, 9}
    };
    int E = sizeof(edges) / sizeof(edges[0]);

    kruskalMST(edges, E);

    return 0;
}
```

- The main function defines the edges of the graph with the format {src, dest, weight}. It calculates the number of edges E and calls kruskalMST to compute the MST.

Conclusion

Sorting, hashing, and graph algorithms form the backbone of many data-intensive applications, each playing a vital role in optimizing data handling and decision-making processes.

- **Sorting algorithms** allow data to be organized systematically, enabling faster search and retrieval, which is essential in applications like databases, data analysis, and user interfaces. Proper sorting can improve performance and usability by reducing the time it takes to find information.
- **Hashing** is crucial for efficient data retrieval in constant or near-constant time. Its application spans from implementing hash tables in databases to managing cache memory in systems, making it indispensable for efficient memory management, fast data access, and security measures like data encryption.
- **Graph algorithms** model and solve relational problems, representing connections in networks such as social media, transportation, or the internet. They provide tools to solve complex problems related to routing, scheduling, and connectivity, which are pivotal in network analysis, recommendation systems, and logistics.

Key Considerations in Algorithm Selection

When selecting algorithms, the choice often depends on the data structure and the application requirements:

1. **Time and Space Complexity:** Prioritize algorithms that offer a balanced trade-off between execution

time and memory usage, based on the problem's constraints and expected data size.

2. **Data Characteristics:** Consider whether the data is static or dynamic. Some algorithms are better suited to static datasets, while others handle dynamic data more effectively.
3. **Application Requirements:** For example, real-time applications may need highly optimized, low-latency algorithms, whereas batch processing tasks can tolerate higher complexity.
4. **Scalability:** For large-scale applications, select algorithms that maintain performance as data volume grows.

In conclusion, mastering sorting, hashing, and graph algorithms, and understanding the nuances of when to apply each, is essential for creating efficient, scalable solutions tailored to specific problem domains.

C Preprocessor: Macros, #include, #define, #ifdef, etc.

The **C Preprocessor** is a tool that processes the code before it is passed to the compiler. It handles directives that are used to perform text substitution, include other files, and conditionally include or exclude parts of the code. It is not technically a part of the C language itself, but it plays a significant role in code compilation.

Macros

A **macro** is a fragment of code which is given a name. Whenever the name is used, the preprocessor replaces it with the associated code. Macros are defined using the #define directive.

Syntax:

```
#define MACRO_NAME replacement_text
```

For example:

```
#define PI 3.14
```

Every occurrence of PI in the program will be replaced with 3.14 before the compilation begins.

Macros can also accept arguments:

```
#define SQUARE(x) ((x) * (x))
```

This creates a macro that computes the square of a number.

#include

The #include directive is used to include header files in a C program. These headers provide definitions for functions, macros, and other resources that the program can use. There are two forms of #include:

1. **Standard Library Include:**

```
#include <stdio.h>
```

This tells the preprocessor to look for the stdio.h file in standard system directories.

2. **User-defined Include:**

```
#include "myheader.h"
```

This tells the preprocessor to search for the file myheader.h in the current directory first, and then in the system directories if it is not found.

#define

The #define directive can be used not just for macros but also to define constants.

For example:

```
#define MAX_SIZE 100
```

This replaces MAX_SIZE with 100 wherever it is used in the code.

You can also define conditional macros to allow conditional

compilation in different environments:

```
#define DEBUG
```

Later in the code, you can use the #ifdef directive to conditionally include parts of code.

#ifdef and #endif

#ifdef is used to check if a macro is defined. If it is, the code between #ifdef and #endif will be included during compilation. It is often used in header files to prevent multiple inclusions.

Syntax:

```
#ifdef MACRO_NAME
  // Code here
#endif
```

For example:

```
#ifdef DEBUG
    printf("Debugging info...\n");
#endif
```

If the DEBUG macro is defined, the code inside the #ifdef block will be included. If it is not defined, the block is ignored.

ERROR HANDLING AND DEBUGGING IN C

Error handling and debugging are crucial aspects of software development. In C, error handling is typically done through the use of **return codes** and **errno** for system-level errors. For debugging, there are tools and techniques that help locate issues in the code.

Error Handling in C

1. **Return Codes**: Many C functions return an integer value that indicates success or failure. A return code of 0 generally indicates success, and non-zero values indicate errors.

Example:

```
int func() {
    if (some_error_condition) {
        return -1; // Error code
    }
    return 0; // Success
}
```

2. **errno**: The errno variable is set to indicate the specific error that occurred during the execution of a system call. It is defined in errno.h.

Example:

```
#include <stdio.h>
#include <errno.h>
#include <string.h>
```

```
FILE *f = fopen("nonexistent.txt", "r");
if (f == NULL) {
    printf("Error: %s\n", strerror(errno));
}
```

This will print the error message corresponding to the failure of fopen.

3. **Assertions**: The assert() function is often used during development to check that certain conditions hold true. If the condition is false, the program will terminate.

Example:

```
#include <assert.h>

int divide(int a, int b) {
    assert(b != 0);  // Check for division by zero
    return a / b;
}
```

The program will terminate with an assertion failure message if b is 0.

Debugging Tools

1. **GDB (GNU Debugger)**: One of the most widely used debugging tools for C. It allows you to run the program step by step, examine variables, set breakpoints, and much more.

Example of using GDB:

```
gdb ./my_program
(gdb) break main
(gdb) run
(gdb) print variable_name
```

2. **Valgrind**: A tool used to detect memory leaks, memory access errors, and undefined memory usage. It helps in identifying issues like buffer overflows or

invalid memory accesses.

Example of using Valgrind:

```
valgrind ./my_program
```

3. **Logging**: For more complex programs, logging is used to track the behavior of the program at runtime. This can be done using libraries like syslog or simple print statements.

CONCLUSION

Learning C programming is a foundational step for anyone interested in software development, systems programming, and understanding how computers work at a deeper level. Throughout the journey, you've explored a variety of key concepts that will serve as the backbone of your programming knowledge.

Key Concepts in C:

1. **Data Types and Variables**: Understanding the basic data types such as int, float, char, and others is essential for handling and storing data.
2. **Control Structures**: Concepts like if-else, loops (for, while, do-while), and switch statements allow you to control the flow of the program.
3. **Functions**: Functions enable modular programming by breaking down code into smaller, reusable blocks.
4. **Arrays and Strings**: These structures help manage collections of data, enabling efficient manipulation and storage.
5. **Pointers**: Pointers are fundamental in C, allowing direct access to memory and facilitating dynamic memory management.
6. **Memory Management**: Understanding dynamic memory allocation with malloc, calloc, and free is crucial in working with resources efficiently.
7. **Structures and Unions**: These data types allow you to group related data together, useful for creating complex data models.
8. **File Handling**: File input/output operations enable you to read and write data to files, a key aspect of many applications.

9. **Preprocessor Directives**: Includes macros, conditional compilation, and file inclusion to customize and streamline code compilation.

How to Continue Learning and Advancing in C:

1. **Practice Regularly**: C programming requires practice. The more you code, the more comfortable you'll become with its syntax and nuances. Start by solving small problems and progressively move to complex ones.
2. **Build Projects**: Apply what you've learned by developing simple projects such as text editors, basic games, or file management systems. This helps solidify concepts and demonstrates real-world applications.
3. **Learn Data Structures and Algorithms**: A strong grasp of data structures (like linked lists, stacks, and trees) and algorithms (such as sorting and searching) is essential for becoming a proficient C programmer.
4. **Explore Advanced Topics**: Learn about advanced topics like multi-threading, networking, and system-level programming, which will help you work on more complex applications.
5. **Contribute to Open Source**: Contributing to open-source projects is an excellent way to learn from experienced developers and improve your skills.

www.ingramcontent.com/pod-product-compliance
Lightning Source LLC
Chambersburg PA
CBHW051351220526
45469CB00001B/206

9798302493507